Life after Suicide

A Ray of Hope
for Those Left Behind

Life after Suicide

A Ray of Hope for Those Left Behind

E. BETSY ROSS

Foreword by
JOSEPH RICHMAN, Ph.D.

 INSIGHT BOOKS

PLENUM PRESS • NEW YORK AND LONDON

Library of Congress Cataloging-in-Publication Data

On file

Parts of this book first appeared in 1980 as a 24-page booklet, "After Suicide: A Unique Grief Process." In 1986 it was expanded into a manual entitled *After Suicide: A Ray of Hope*. An expanded self-published paperback (1990) preceded the present revised volume.

ISBN 0-306-45630-3

© 1997 E. Betsy Ross
Insight Books is a Division of Plenum Publishing Corporation
233 Spring Street, New York, N.Y. 10013-1578
http://www.plenum.com

An Insight Book

10 9 8 7 6 5 4 3 2 1

To all Ray of Hope chapter members everywhere
and
In memory of William W. Ross

Hope is a thing with feathers

That perches in the soul

And sings the tune without the words

And never stops at all.

Emily Dickinson

Foreword

Joseph Richman, Ph.D.

It is a welcome task to introduce the public to this new version of *Life after Suicide: A Ray of Hope for Those Left Behind*. The first version was a pioneering work; Betsy Ross was one of the first to recognize and confront the widespread phenomenon of being a survivor of suicide. It was a role with no guidelines when she became a survivor and eventually a healer of other survivors of suicide. Her work was, and still is, the best book on the topic.

Life after Suicide: A Ray of Hope for Those Left Behind should be in the hands of the family and friends of all those who have suffered a loss. The book outlines the dilemmas faced by survivors, including the feelings of guilt and shame, the sense of stigma, the turmoil of conflicting emotions, and the tendency to withdraw and lick their wounds while dwelling on the trauma. Many readers will be all too familiar with these experiences.

Betsy Ross's description of the steps necessary for eventual recovery is especially valuable. Her honest self-revelations in dealing with the suffering and loss of suicide and its aftermath, and her ability to provide others with means for psychic survival, have helped countless survivors who felt trapped and thought there was nowhere to turn. Betsy offers guidance and hope, and explains why and how the bereaved must come to terms with the death so that the loss will not have been in vain.

Betsy makes the process of recovery come alive through gripping personal stories of herself and other survivors. She spells out how to achieve a state of consolation, an ability to remember the deceased loved one without pain, and a return to normal living. The further result is an increase in compassion and the love of life. That is why this book is so fittingly subtitled *A Ray of Hope for Those Left Behind*.

Betsy Ross has earned the right to be a model. She is wise beyond her years and has much to offer professionals, as well as survivors. She has helped many more people than she herself realizes, including this writer. While rereading her book, I gained an additional understanding of her perceptiveness and wisdom. I would say that the ultimate test for acceptance and recovery after a suicide is the ability to develop a constructive approach. Betsy Ross tackles this difficult task and its various solutions with such skill that it alone is worth the purchase of the book.

Her message is universal, as I learned from personal experience. I had recently lost a beloved niece, and our entire family was thrown unexpectedly and without an opportunity for preparation into deep mourning. Betsy, who had recently lost her own mother, sent us a letter with such inspiring words about the immortality of close and loving relationships that it moved and consoled all of us. That caring spirit pervades this book.

Survivors of suicide are not the only ones who are bereaved. The slogan "Turn Your Grief Process into a Growth Experience" can be adopted by all of us who are concerned with helping others deal with grief. We are all survivors, and that is why this book deserves and, I predict, will attract a wide audience. She is destined to help many more survivors for generations to come.

*   *   *   *   *

Dr. Richman is Professor Emeritus at the Albert Einstein College of Medicine in New York City, a senior psychologist at the Bronx Municipal Hospital Center, and a faculty member of the New York Center for Psychoanalytic Training. He has a private practice and conducts workshops and seminars. He has published the book Family Therapy for Suicidal People, *as well as more than sixty articles and book chapters.*

Preface

I could believe that my husband was dead, but I could not believe that he had chosen to die. I knew I would eventually accept his death, because it is natural to die sometime. However, I was not sure I could ever accept his death by suicide. That was *not* natural, in spite of the fact that Bill had talked about it at great length. Other people, it seemed to me, were overly curious and fascinated about Bill's self-inflicted death.

People often asked if guilt bothered me the most. I thought so at times; but so did the anger, the loneliness, the rejection, accusations, and the constant searching for answers. I found myself explaining and justifying Bill's actions, my own actions, and our relationship—as if I were deficient because my husband had committed suicide; inept and simple-minded because I was grieving. He lost his life; I lost my validity and credibility.

I believe what actually did bother me most was simply the inability to find a sustained balance of conflicting emotions and messages. I was so confused and so busy trying to explore something I could not yet accept or understand that I lost my freedom to grieve.

For nearly four years after Bill's death, I thought a part of myself had also died. The tiny bit that remained had retreated deep inside my heart, protecting itself while my mind searched for reason and order. That casing was necessary; it housed the fragile, vulnerable bit of spirit called hope that saved my life, helped me heal, and turned me toward the future.

It is a terrible thing—not to be able to claim your own future.

It leads to helplessness and hopelessness. We cannot exist without that spark of hope which lies deep in the very core of ourselves. When it goes, the will to live goes, leaving in its place a terrible void inhabited by primal fears.

Bill encountered those fears and took control of the situation by ending his life. I took control of my destiny by turning my life around. I waded through painful childhood memories, the dynamics of a dysfunctional family heritage, the residue of two marriages (both severely affected by alcoholism), the trauma of Bill's suicide, and the challenge of a college education to do it, but it was worth every minute. I put an end to involvement with abusive relationships, overcame feelings of rejection and worthlessness, and claimed a new future.

I returned to the University of Iowa (at age forty-something) just two weeks after Bill's death to study for a Bachelor of General Studies (BGS) in psychology, religion, and journalism. But feeling isolated and uneasy with other widows, I needed to meet others who had lost a loved one to suicide. With help from the Campus Ministries Office and local media, a meeting for suicide survivors was announced and held—with an overwhelming response. After only one meeting, we knew we wanted to continue the group.

This happened early in 1977, before the support group movement had expanded much beyond Alcoholics Anonymous, Al-Anon, Make Today Count, and Compassionate Friends, so the concept of a group just for suicide survivors was news. By the end of the year, we had been written about and interviewed extensively, had become an official charitable organization, and were giving workshops in answer to requests for information and help.

In 1979, our group appeared as guests on *Donahue* and a flood of mail followed. In 1980, with sponsorship from the University of Iowa College of Medicine, Ray of Hope held the first national conference to deal specifically with suicide postvention. Even then, requests for information increased until the only way to answer them all and reach as many people as possible was through a book, so I wrote the first version of *After Suicide: A Ray of Hope* in 1986, and the first revision in 1990.

Bill's suicide turned my life completely around. When I finally stopped spinning, I discovered his death was not meaningless, and my grief was not a waste of time. The experience had provided me with a key to get in touch with myself, with God, and with others in a new and exciting way. As I look back over those years, I am aware that among the greatest moments of my life have been those of experiencing the depths and the heights, layer by layer.

I invested a great deal of time and energy examining my life and my past from many perspectives—looking for what went wrong and affirming what was right. Even though much of that meant focusing on the troubled side of things, it helped me deal with the present and finally decide that, unlike the lightning bug who bumbles through life with its headlight on its behind, I could no longer spend all of my time looking at where I'd been. I could again look ahead.

My answer to the philosophical question "Is life worth living?" is, at least for me, a resounding "yes." I say that because I did not create myself; I did not give myself life. It was given *to* me, and it's my privilege to care for this life—and the body I am carrying it around in—as best I can. That way, I can stay around as long as possible, if only to see what's going to happen next.

Although the passage of time, support from others, education, and information aided my recovery, the single most important and influential factor at all times was my deep unshakable belief in God. Without that faith, I would never have found the strength to develop Ray of Hope and carry out its mission. Ray of Hope's ministry has been a gift of healing for myself and countless others, so I give tribute and recognition to the giver. I realize, however, that not all people share this view—nor is this ministry only for those who share my view. Take what you can from the message and blend it with your own beliefs, so you can heal as is best for you.

Sometimes, when I explain ROH's policy and function to people, they grimace and say, "Oh my, isn't it terribly depressing to be working with all that suicide stuff?" Often, they never heard the word *ministry* and completely miss the point. My answer is no, it is not depressing; it *is* uplifting and inspiring because I proudly deal with people who are discovering that they are made of extraordinary *stuff*. They know what life means; they know what priorities are valuable; they are very brave and special people who have greatly enriched my life.

Every time I share Bill's story, or lead a support-group meeting, or counsel with a grieving family, I believe that a little something of Bill lives on in each person who is helped. (Bill would approve—he loved attention.) Our ministry is not about sorrow; it is about spiritual strength.

This book is my way of taking you by the hand and saying, "Look, what has happened to you is fact, not fantasy. You hurt. Your spirit hurts. You're in such pain that the ends of your hair hurt. And you want to quit hurting." Before that can happen, it may help to know what you can expect to experience or feel, and what you can do about it. This book offers you hope and help in getting through this dark, murky period in your life without falling in. The journey, though tiring and tormenting at times, can be interesting. If you want to, you can come through this as more than just another suicide survivor–victim.

This journey it not a preoccupation with death; it is a celebration of life. You can turn your grief process into a growth experience. That is the other reason for this book.

ELEANORA "BETSY" ROSS

Acknowledgments

Far more people than I can mention have helped and supported me in the writing of this book, and I am deeply grateful to them all. But some very special thank yous go to all the Ray of Hope group members who opened their hearts to contribute such very personal beliefs and stories; especially Verabeth Bricker, Rhonnie DeStefano, Wendy Workman, Larry Kaplan, Carole Buhl, and Ruby Bollinger; to the many people who have believed in me through the ups and downs of either the first version of this book, or the current version, and in-between; they are Joyce Strabala, Hannelore Bozeman, Matt Gaumer, Jan Ashman, Ardath Jagnow, Joan Liffering-Zug, Matthew Johnson, Barbara Fox, Faye Teeple, and my sons, Daryl and David Anderson; to Margaret Boyd, Hope Dunn, and Dr. Willard Boyd (past-president of the University of Iowa) for encouraging me to seek higher education; to Dr. Joseph Richman for his steadfast belief in my ability; to my agent, Richard Marek, who saw something promising in the earlier version; to my editor, Frank K. Darmstadt, who shared that view, and to Charlie Cates and Herman Makler, also of Insight Books, whose patience must be second only to Job's, I am sure; to computer gurus, Kevin Crowley and Al Jagnow, who so willingly shared their time to rescue this manuscript from a disk that had been badly mishandled, and to a hero named Bill Pypes at WordCare, who pulled it all together to meet the deadline; to Professor John McIntosh and

Will Johnson for their help with research; to Professor Kenneth Kuntz, Rabbi Jeff Portman, Father John Boyle, Pastor Paul Hasel, and Reverend David Aananson for religious viewpoints and insights; to Cathy and Mary Fulton for help with organizing and typing; and last, but not at all least, to the Coralville, Iowa, Public Library staff for their outstanding cooperation and assistance.

Contents

Introduction

Authorities claim that survivors of the suicidal death of a loved one are an isolated and neglected group with unique problems and needs. Since the Middle Ages, the suicide victim and surviving family members have been labeled as weak, sinful, criminal, or disgraceful. The resulting stigma, misconceptions, and social rejections make after-suicide bereavement one of the most stressful and difficult of grief processes. Just as the potential suicide victim often struggles alone with a sense of hopelessness and despair, the grief-stricken may also suffer alone. Just as the feeling of rejection may be a motive for suicide, the fear of rejection may also be a deterrent to coping with the circumstances following suicide.

In the moment following my husband's self-inflicted death in 1975, I became a member of a select group of several million Americans, a suicide survivor–victim. The National Centers for Health Statistics and the American Association of Suicidology report that more Americans die yearly from suicide than from homicide, or are killed by drunk drivers, and that suicide occurs every seventeen minutes, making it the ninth leading cause of death in the United States. In the last five years, suicide deaths have exceeded those from AIDS.

According to Christopher Lukas and Henry M. Seiden, in their book *Silent Grief* (1987), the U.S. Department of Health and Human Services reports the approximate 30,000 recorded suicides per year directly affect the lives of at least seven to ten other close family members or friends, leaving 200,000 to 300,000 new survivors yearly. If, as Lukas and Seiden speculate, the possible "unofficial" number of suicides is another 20,000 to 30,000 per year (considering alcohol- and drug-related deaths, accidents, and suicides covered up by family and officials), the number of survivors nearly doubles. There could be as many as 6 million suicide survivors living in America today, and these people have much in common. For example:

Deliberateness: It is the only form of death in which the deceased die on purpose—deliberately—and over and over, we question "why?"

Involvement: Survivors may carry lasting scars, because they are involved in a more personal and violent way than are most survivors of nonsuicide deaths. For instance, most deaths in America today occur in hospitals or nursing homes. We are, for the most part, relatively uninvolved in those deaths. But the majority of suicides occur in the home between 3:00 P.M. and midnight. These are violent deaths, and survivors are involved from the moment they witness the act or find the body. And guess who those witnesses are!

The American Medical Association reports that almost half of all of suicides are witnessed, either visibly or audibly, by the spouse. The next largest category of witnesses is children. Inclusion of percentages of both parents and children as witnesses shows well over 50 percent of immediate family members involved with the death in an extremely traumatic manner.

Legacy: Suicidiologists agree that many of today's survivors will become tomorrow's victims. Survivors inherit a legacy of suicide, including everything from social stigma, to loss of hope, to self-rejection, to becoming an increased risk to suicide themselves. A report from the U.S. Department of Health and Human Services states that survivors are more prone to accidents, alcoholism, illness, emotional disturbances, malnutrition, and a variety of conditions related to extended depression and unresolved grief.

Memories: Many survivors are haunted by the memory of finding the body or witnessing the death. The shock and violence associated with self-inflicted death is quite different than that of natural death, because this grief often feeds on itself through shame, guilt, humiliation, and anger rather than healing over time.

Investigation: Suicide is investigated as if a crime may have occurred. Family members may feel as if they are under suspicion. As a result, spontaneous grief, which must be held in check during investigation, can lead to unresolved or incomplete grief.

Focus: With suicide, the primary focus is almost always on the act of suicide itself, rather than on the survivors' welfare.

Insurance: Some survivors may be deprived of insurance benefits. Regardless of how necessary the insurance company's reasons might be, survivors may feel they are being victimized economically and financially because of the suicide.

Embarrassment: The lengthy searching for answers is also an effort to save face for both the victim and survivors with a justifiable explanation. Feeling betrayed and embarrassed, survivors struggle to restore the family's reputation and reorganize their place in society.

Judgment: We form opinions concerning the right or wrong of suicide and make moral judgments about both the deceased and the survivors, as, indeed, do the survivors themselves. Because of that, shame and embarrassment about the method of death often overshadow the survivors' pride and esteem for their loved one.

Self-Worth: It's not unusual for death, an accident, or any kind of loss to invoke unresolved or delayed grief regarding earlier losses. But when death is by suicide, the resulting shock and searching process can trigger a different kind of unresolved grieving—the kind related to some past trauma which affected one's sense of self-worth, self-image, self-confidence, or well-being; the sort of loss we don't consciously take the time to grieve about, such as childhood experiences which have produced feelings of confusion, shame, isolation, or rejection. The pain of these experiences may have been repressed and unresolved simply because of the helplessness and vulnerability of being a child; now, they resurface.

Self-Blame: It is a form of death where people often judge their own actions, attitudes, and responsibility in relation to the cause of death. That's different than regretting something one did or didn't do. Survivors replay the events preceding the suicide over and over in their mind's eye and fantasize how it might have been different "if only I'd done this or that."

Silence and Confusion: Lukas and Seiden (1987) emphasize that only death by suicide is surrounded by a conspiracy of silence—a cover-up versus truth. We question what to tell children, sick or elderly family members, the community, and the media.

Multiple Losses: Survivors must deal with both the tragedy of death and the trauma of suicide, which are two separate, yet related, issues. Survivors grieve not only over the loss of someone by death but over all the losses generated by stigma and shame; not only the loss of position in the community but of reputation and social goodwill; not only the loss of friends but the loss of face and self-confidence when they know or suspect that they are the object of gossip, curiosity, and speculation.

Relationships: Left unresolved, the psychological aftermath of a death by suicide may continue to undermine the lives of survivors for months or even years, resulting in family dissension and/or alienation. The blow to one's self-image and the length of time involved in working through this grief often causes survivors to feel that relationships with others have been permanently affected.

Terminology: Suicide is a form of death which often may be stigmatized by terminology. We say people commit suicide, commit crimes, and are committed to institutions. We do not say they commit heart attacks or cancer. We say they *died* by a heart attack or cancer—why not say they died by suicide?

Perceived as Preventable: Ellen S. Zinner, at the University of Baltimore, believes that survivors consistently perceive this death as having been somehow preventable, despite histories of sadness, depression, mental illness, suicide threats or attempts, multiple losses, and so on. She's right; they do, and that's why they so diligently search for answers.

Ambivalence: Not all suicides are sudden or unexpected; many have been preceded by threats, arguments, separations, broken promises, and police involvement. And not all suicidal persons were warm, gay, loving, popular, and so on, all of the time. Rather, many were terribly unhappy people whose misery sometimes affected the lives of all those around them. Nor are survivors always patient and forbearing; many lose patience and tempers flare, regardless of loving concern and the best of intentions. After the death, many survivors may be equally torn between both relief and anguish.

Support: There seem to be no "right things" to say to comfort survivors of suicide when they most need comforting, when their grief is compounded by questions and confusion, and denial or secrecy seems the best way to handle it. The usual comments, such as "Well, you did your best for him/her," or "He/she lived a good life," seem inappropriate. Often, it is easier to say nothing or stay away from the bereaved altogether. So what can we do to help?

The best way to help survivors is with the development of postvention programs. *Postvention*, a term coined by Edwin Shneidman, founder of the American Association of Suicidology, refers to all aspects of research and education for suicide survivors, such as conferences, books, support groups, and the like. Postvention care may actually serve to prevent suicide, not just during or after the crisis, but a month, a year, or a generation later.

Learning all you can about survivorship is the best way to start. Fortunately, many good books have been written for and by professional caregivers and survivors. This book is one of those that tries to show what it's like to be a survivor, and what can be done to help understand and deal with it.

* * * * *

Part I, "My Story," is more than the story of Bill's suicide. As I struggled to understand his death and my relationship to it, I found myself examining at length a host of prior losses and hurts, all of which affected my resolution of this one, such as the rejection that marked my childhood and parent relationship, family jealousies, the breakup of my first marriage and it's impact on my children, why I entered into a second abusive marriage, and the influence of alcohol in both marriages. At times, it seemed that all I did was examine my past.

This process was not unique to my experience. Many survivors question themselves in the same way. We examine the event, the circumstances leading up to the event, the personality and habits of the deceased, our relationship with that person, and the development of our own personalities and family influences until a sort of self and family psychological analysis has taken place. It goes beyond looking for an answer to "why suicide?" It's attempting to solve the riddle of why and how we became the way we are, and how we go on from here.

Suicide does not happen out of nothing. Survivors sense early on that recovery depends on confronting many factors, because it helps them to see the multiinfluences involved in their loved one's action and their own reactions. It was my willingness to pursue this in-depth and painful analysis that brought about the understanding and personal healing that was, for me, much more than just solace from grief. This change, or growth, was not the purpose for my search; rather, it was the outcome.

"Voices of Survivors" concludes with other personal stories by siblings, parents, spouses, a lover, a child, and friends. Their stories are best told in their own words.

Part II, "Growing through Grief," serves as a guide, with chapters describing the possible emotions and characteristics of after-suicide grief and the growth that can come by working through it. There are specific suggestions from survivors on how to help one's self, how to help a survivor, how to listen, and what to say or not say. Part II also addresses the questions often raised at meetings about funerals, the police investigation, how to help children, if suicide is a sin, and the value of support groups.

Part III, "Reflections," presents my personal reflections on suicide in moral, religious, and philosophical terms; speculates on the various factors influencing suicide, its aftermath, and cultural attitudes; and poses the possibility that generations of mental, emotional or verbal abuse can impact messages sent—or received—

(either consciously or unconsciously) of self-destruction. I believe self-inflicted death stems from a variety of social, psychological, environmental, and cultural influences and attitudes which should be considered in suicide prevention and postvention programs.

Part IV, "Appendices," lists resources about postvention and grief: books, booklets and pamphlets, directories, newsletters, manuals, magazines, videos, various organizations, and information about Ray of Hope.

Although this book, as in the previous version, *After Suicide: A Ray of Hope*, cannot present perfect solutions, it offers many ideas and insights which have been helpful to me both personally and as a grief counselor for suicide survivors. People have asked me to write about what I think, what I have experienced, and what I have learned both as a survivor and as one who has worked closely with survivors for over twenty-one years. This book presents my observations, along with suggestions from other professionals who work with suicide survivors, and views from survivors themselves.

At one of our first gatherings, a mother and father observed, "Our daughter killed herself because she had lost all hope of a future for herself. We are here because all we've done since her death is look for our ray of hope to go on." Thus the name for Ray of Hope, inc., the title for hundreds of workshops, and the theme for this book, now called *Life After Suicide*, because that is what it's about, and *A Ray of Hope for Those Left Behind*, because that's what it offers.

The book is organized so the reader can turn to the subject of interest rather than to start at the beginning and read through. It is written for you, the survivor, and also for those who want to help you. Although our stories are different, our loss is similar. Your life and mine are forever changed, and we share the same pain, the same legacy, and the same quest for hope.

I

Voices of Survivors

Dear Survivor: A Letter to You

Dear Survivor:

It is said that death is a part of life; the other side of birth. I believe death can also give meaning to life, a meaning that may escape you while your grief is fresh and raw, but which may someday bring a special quality of peace to your spirit. As terrible as your loss is, you can survive even though it seems unbelievable. Once that happens, you will have touched upon a new and incredible inner strength.

But for now, you may have a mixture of thoughts and feelings. Despair, longing, anger, guilt, frustration, questioning, and even understanding strive for comprehensible sense and shape. You seek relief—and you need to heal. It is a journey, and you must work at it.

And so—*cry*. The pain is real, but the tears are healing. Often we must struggle through an emotion to find the relief beyond.

And so—*talk*. Talk to one another about your loss and pain, and ask others to listen. Tell others you need them to listen. The more you deny something or address it in silence, the more destructive power it can claim over you.

And so—*search*. Over and over, you will ask "Why?" It is a question you *must* ask. Although you may never learn why, it is still important to wrestle with the question for a time. Eventually, you will be content to give up the search. When you can willingly let go of the need to question why, it will lose its hold over you. But it will take time.

And so—*speak*. Speak as often and freely of your lost loved one as you need to. He or she will always be a part of you. Not to speak of the deceased denies his or her existence—to speak of the deceased affirms his or her life. Believe that in time, the pain of loss fades and is replaced by precious memories to be shared.

And so—*grieve*. This time of sorrow can be used to draw a family together or pull it apart. Acknowledgment of guilt and anger helps you to gain a more balanced understanding of what happened. Give yourself permission to feel and express nagging guilt and anger even though you or others may think it inappropriate.

And so—*grow*. We cannot control all that happens to us, but we can control how we choose to respond. You can allow yourself to be destroyed by an experience, or you can choose to overcome and survive it. When you grieve constructively and creatively, you come to value life with a new awareness.

And so—*become*. Become all you can become. Enter into a new dimension of self-identity and self-dependence as you come to love others more fully and unconditionally.

And so—*accept*. Accept that in some strange way, this death may enable you to reach out with a new understanding, offering a new dimension of love as you become more attuned to the suffering of others.

I believe in a loving God who offers strength, guidance, and solace as we struggle with our anguish. I believe, as we regain balance and meaning in our shattered lives, we come to see that death can indeed bring a new meaning to life. This is my prayer for you.

ELEANORA "BETSY" ROSS (1983)

I

A Ray of Hope (My Story)

We must wait until evening to see how splendid the day has been.
SOPHOCLES

"Just keep telling me you love me," my husband said on the phone. "I want that to be the last thing I hear before I hang up." As I did as he had asked, he quietly hung up the receiver, walked out of the phone booth, took a rifle from the trunk of his car, placed it behind his right ear and blew off the back of his head. Bill's months of despair and depression had ended; my years of grief and agony were just beginning.

Bill's alcoholism had caused many problems during his life and our stormy four-year marriage. It brought out such ugly things in this otherwise kind and interesting person. I had lived with both love and terror during those years, and that was the reason for our present separation of nearly a year. Before meeting Bill, I'd had no direct experience with alcoholism and did not know what to expect or how to handle it. I soon learned. At first I made all the usual mistakes of trying to control things or to reason with him.

Charming, witty, and affectionate while sober, Bill went through a complete personality change when drinking. On those days, I'd wonder, "What's his mood today? What will he do? Should I hide, or what?" To Bill, booze meant fighting, and if I were nearby, I became the target. I was 4'11" tall, and he was 5'11". I weighed 95 pounds and he weighed 195. Only once did I try to hit him back, and that time I gave him a black eye. Afterward, Bill thought it was funny. He would point to his eye and then hold my hand up for people to see. "Look at that little fist," he'd say. "Sharp as a pool cue. Almost put my eye out." But, most of the time, the odds were not in my favor. I had been thrown through a door and down some steps. I had once driven myself to the emergency room with my lip split wide open.

I learned to anticipate his drinking bouts and lived "perpetually packed and ready to flee." I kept a small suitcase of things I might need near the door. I even left it partially unzipped in case I needed to slip something into it at the last minute. I had extra sets of car keys within reach in every room and outside, where I could find them in an instant and get away before being hurt. I'd return in the morning, when I knew he'd be sober.

One time I miscalculated. Bill met me at the door, still drunk and swinging. A slap caught me off guard, knocking me down. Terrified, I lay as still as I could, with my arms over my head. He watched me a minute, then nudged me with his foot until I rolled onto the grass. "And don't clutter up the sidewalk," he said, before going back inside. After a while, I got up and ventured inside to find he had passed out. Later, he was contrite and apologetic, explaining to me that the reason he drank too much and got upset was because he loved me so much. "I'm so afraid I'm going to lose you and that if you don't love me back, I'll have to beat you until you do," he said with a chuckle, thinking it was a pretty good joke. This time, I didn't laugh.

I loved Bill and wanted this marriage to work but was also afraid of him and didn't know what to do about it. Then one day, I saw a sign on the library door that read, "If someone you love drinks too much, call AL-ANON." I did, and an hour later met with a woman who listened to my story, told me about alcoholism, and gave me some pamphlets. For the first time, I learned our situation was not unique and that I had alternatives other than just to hide a night at a time. Incredible as it seems, I had not known that. I had truly believed to leave our marriage would mark me as a coward or failure. After all, I already had one divorce. I believed

I needed to prove I could make a marriage work—that it was all up to me—and all my fault if it didn't.

I began to attend Al-Anon meetings and learned a great deal about women who stay with men who abuse them. I learned Bill's alcohol addiction was controlling both of us—everything we both said and did. Booze—not Bill—was the enemy. I was told I'd have to make a decision about alcohol—live with it or leave it. I listened at those meetings—I learned—but a part of me didn't quite accept the extremes of "Love it or leave it" as the only possible solutions.

So, I tried a different tactic. I told Bill I'd seen a divorce lawyer and would go through with it if he didn't stop drinking. He replied, "If that's all that is wrong, I just won't drink when we are together. I'll wait and drink only when you are back in Iowa."

I thought this just might work, because Bill and I lived a unique lifestyle. Most of the time, he traveled from one construction job to another in a large motor home. I alternated between spending weekends with him at his job sites and weekdays in Iowa, where David, my adolescent son from my first marriage, attended school. I still had my trailer, which was David's and my home before I married Bill, parked on my folks' farm. Usually David stayed with friends or my parents when I was with Bill. This plan would keep David and Bill separated most of the time. If Bill kept his promise, I'd be safe, David would be safe, and I would save the marriage. I thought I was pretty clever.

To show his good intentions, Bill volunteered—with a great show of "Look what I'm doing for the little woman" to attend an AA meeting. Throughout the meeting, I pretended to be too entranced by the speakers to notice Bill's meaningful, sidelong glances. We were no sooner out the door than he snorted, "Did you see those people? They're a bunch of drunks! And they even admit it! I don't need AA. I don't have a problem!"

To prove his good intentions and ability to control his drinking, Bill rented a beautiful, furnished home near his job so we (David included) could spend the summer together. He then took us both on a vacation to Yellowstone Park, the Rockies, and a working dude ranch owned by one of his old rodeo buddies.

The ranch bunkhouse (remodeled for visitors) was situated so that we slept at night with our feet in Colorado and our heads in Wyoming—a rather unique distinction, I was assured.

On our return from the West, Bill bought me a new car and outfitted David with a little red go-cart, complete with driver's suit and helmet to match. I figured we had these things coming to us.

However, this is something women should ask themselves about if they consistently object to attending Al-Anon, or to leaving abusive alcoholic men. Gifts and material possessions can be a pretty good payoff for submitting to abuse, as can attention and sympathy from being the "long-suffering black-and-blue martyr." Both actions are attempts to control the situation, just as were my own conditional ultimatum to Bill and his resulting extravagance.

Some women try to control the guy's drinking by meeting him at the bar right after work and either drinking with him and/ or exchanging information with the other wives—information such as how to divert his attention so she can rescue some of the just-cashed paycheck and later convince him that he lost it, spent it, or the bartender swiped it.

There's a wealth of information to be shared among an alcoholic's family members on how to shame an alcoholic, thereby gaining favors, get the upper hand, or get revenge. It's not intentional deceit on the wife or family's part—it is pure "gut survival." That's why alcoholism is called a *family* disease. It makes people feel, think, and act in ways they wouldn't if they felt safe and secure. It alters one's mental, emotional, and physical health. The only constant thought, or motivation, is to outwit the alcoholic and avert or control the outcome of his/her drinking.

Within days of settling into the rented house in Michigan, Bill began to complain of nervousness and headaches. "If I drink just a little bit, I'll feel better," he said. "After all, I stayed stone sober for over three weeks, and that ought to prove to you that I can control it. No bar hopping—just a little wine at home in the evenings." He refused to admit his discomfort was from withdrawal symptoms.

The following Friday, when Bill was only three minutes late for supper, I knew the dry spell was over. Before Bill arrived home two hours later, David and I had grabbed food and Ace (his black kitten), ran for David's bedroom, and shoved the dresser in front of the closed door. For two days, Bill shouted and raged, pounded on the door, threatened to kill us both, broke dishes, harassed the neighbors, and occasionally passed out. During the lulls, David and I replenished supplies. Although Bill was a violent drunk, he was not a sloppy one. He always walked straight—straight into whatever was in front of him. He would stop, blink, reaim himself, and walk straight again—into another wall, person or object. The house looked as if he'd walked straight into everything.

Sometimes Bill was extremely jealous of David. If drunk, he would do mean little things to him when he thought I didn't notice or try to convince me to send my son to a military school so "we'd have more time together."

At one point, he had stood outside our bedroom door and shouted, "I'm going to fix that kid of yours, you'd better believe it. Oh, I won't put a mark on him—I'll just slap him on first one side of the head and then the other until he is permanently addled. Then, you won't want him." I believed him, because I had learned by now that Bill had indeed hurt other people in fights and often hit a former wife.

I knew I could never expose David to this again and made the decision to leave for good. I also knew I dare not let Bill discover our plans, or he would have forcibly stopped us, and I finally realized he might permanently harm one or both of us.

We stayed in David's room until Bill left for work Monday morning. That evening, Bill was sober—but defensive rather than apologetic. "Can't a man even make a little mistake?" he'd ask, trying to play on my guilt. I didn't answer him.

"Sometimes you make me so mad that if I was a snake, I'd bite myself," he said, trying to joke. I carefully smiled, agreed, but did not offer a response. David just stayed out of sight. "If you and your kid don't lighten up, I'll have to get drunk again," he warned.

Quietly and slowly, over the next two days, we packed things in my car, got David's things from school, and made other preparations. I went to a doctor and asked for a prescription of Antabuse (pretending it was for myself). I ground it up and put on Bill's sandwiches the day we left, hoping he'd feel too sick to follow us.

Bill must have suspected our plans to leave, however. I had learned that the branch bank opened fifteen minutes before the main bank, so I left the house immediately after Bill left for work and was waiting at the bank's door. I learned later that Bill had tried to close our account just minutes after I withdrew our small savings.

After leaving the bank, I rented a small U-Haul trailer to move my electric organ and David's go-cart. But when I opened the trailer door back at the house, the smell of horse poured out at us. That meant another flying trip to the dealer, and home again where the landlord and his wife gladly helped us load up and get on our way. Just outside of town, David's kitten got frightened and carsick, so I went back to find a vet and some medication. It was getting late, and I just hoped Bill had eaten his sandwiches.

On the second trip out of town, the trailer tire went flat, and I had to go back to get it fixed. The third time I left town, a thick fog rolled in off the lake, and I missed a turnoff and drove east instead of west. I ended up in downtown Toledo near midnight but refused to stop. I turned around and continued the long trip back toward Iowa, despite another low tire, a cranky kid, a recovered frisky kitten, an unprotected turtle, and another wrong turn, which took us through downtown Chicago at 7:30 A.M.

When we pulled up to my trailer hours later, Bill was snoozing on the front steps, hat over his face. (I had never given him a key to my trailer, either before or after we were married.) "Howdy." He waved at us. "What took you so long?" David clutched the dashboard, I clung to the steering wheel, and we just looked at each other.

Bill refused to leave my trailer and return to his job, claiming, "I'm not drunk now." He wasn't, but I called the sheriff anyway, who arrived a few minutes later and tried to arrest Bill. (Trespassing was all I could think of.) Bill shoved his hands in his pockets, planted his feet, looked up at the officer and said, "I ain't goin'."

They argued for a while, and finally the officer said, "Well, I can't beat him up and I won't shoot him, but if he promises to leave quietly after you've talked a few minutes, I'll wait. Is that okay?"

What could I do but agree? I tried to persuade Bill our marriage was over, that I refused to live with alcohol as a part of my life, and that he was a danger to David and me. Finally he left, convinced I would change my mind.

I didn't, despite the following months filled with daily phone calls from Bill, crying, pleading, begging, and bargaining. Soon afterwards, he began to threaten to harm my parents, David, and me. When that didn't work, he began threatening to kill himself.

On Christmas Eve, Bill called me from his company's office in a neighboring state and begged to come home for Christmas. A part of me missed Bill terribly—missed the fun we had and the love that existed in spite of his problem—but I had to say no, because I could tell he was already drinking. "You're dead," he said, and hung up.

The following morning I received a phone call from a young woman who asked, "Are you married to Bill Ross?" I said yes and she said, "Well, I think you ought to know he nearly killed my mother last night." While in a drunken stupor, Bill had taken a woman to a motel, had told her he was going to kill her, and had then beaten her senseless. She survived but was permanently injured. I later learned she was tiny, red-haired and wore glasses. It could have been me if I had let him come home.

An initial charge of attempted murder was changed to aggravated battery. Released on bail, Bill signed into a substance-abuse recovery program. A few days later, he called me from there. "I understand how you feel about me," he said, "and I don't blame you if you hang up on me. But, something important has happened, and no one will understand better than you. Please listen." I hung up.

Every few days, he'd call. Sometimes I hung up. Sometimes I screamed accusations till I lost my voice. I raged on and on about all the things I'd resented and held in for so long. He simply listened and would say, "I know how much you need to say those things. You're right, and I don't blame you. I say them to myself, too."

At last, after three months of this, I listened. Bill told me that while he was sitting in jail, a priest came to see a young man who had wrecked his car (while drinking), and whose wife had been killed. The young man had sobbed and asked the priest for help, who replied that in spite of his actions, God still loved him and wanted to heal his pain if he repented and asked for forgiveness.

"That priest could have been talking to me," Bill said. "In a flash, I realized what I'd done to that woman, to you, to so many others over the years, and to myself. I am so ashamed. I want that healing and forgiveness, too. I don't even remember hurting her. I have only a vague memory of trying to fight off demons or monsters that I thought were attacking me. I always thought my drinking was either a big joke or other people's problem, if they didn't like it. Now, it's hard to believe I've hurt someone so badly. I want to try to do something to make up for all that. At least, I can tell people what alcohol has cost me. If you ever let me come home again, I want it to be right."

I agreed to talk with Bill on the phone during the months ahead while he waited for his hearing. He said he would have to look for another employer, since the assault had cost him his job with a prominent construction company, and he faced a lawsuit by the injured woman.

During those eight months, Bill was haunted by guilt, even though he tried to make amends with the people he had wronged over the years. The prospect of prison frightened him. "I'll go crazy if I'm locked up. I'd rather die by my own hand than lose my mind in prison," he'd tell me.

Often, I'd answer the phone to hear Bill crying in desperation and fear. "I had to call someone. The desire to kill myself is so strong. It's as if something is pushing me, and I'm afraid I can't stop it." Later, he would say, "It seems as if suicide is the only solution. I've hurt myself, you, and so many other people, and I can't seem to fix things. I love life. I want to live, but I know now that I deserve to die. I'm so ashamed, and I don't know what else to do but kill myself. Everyone I love will be so much better off without me. I don't know if I can hold on until the hearing. I've never been afraid of anything before in my life." At some level, I realized this was not an alcoholic ploy for sympathy. He believed what he was saying.

Reluctantly, I agreed to meet Bill on weekends and see him through this, even though we had been separated for over a year by this time. We sought advice from a number of professionals. Most ministers encouraged Bill to have faith, but he didn't seem to understand how to do that. One clergyman flatly stated, "You'll go to hell, you know," and refused to talk with us any longer. As we sat in the church parking lot, Bill asked, "Does God doom a man to hell just because his problems have driven him to a despair he can't handle? I just can't believe He does. Won't God understand that if I kill myself, it's not because I want to die, but because I don't know what else to do?" I had no answer to that.

"We've only started to look for help," I said evasively. "We have an appointment with a psychiatrist this afternoon. Let's hear what he says." That psychiatrist said to me, "Ignore him. He won't kill himself. He's just trying to keep you involved. Don't let him dwell on his problems. Change the subject." He actually advised me to call Bill's bluff and dare him to carry out his threat. I knew better than that and refused to try it.

I tried to help, listen, and reason with Bill as much as I could, but at times I felt as hopeless and helpless as he did. Finally one day, I took the advice of the psychiatrist. I turned to Bill and said, "I'm sick of this. I don't want to hear it anymore."

Startled, Bill gazed at me. I had the sinking feeling I had said something wrong, and started to retract my statement, but he stopped me. "Forget it, honey," he said. "I understand. I don't blame you." He sat quietly for a moment, then added, "There's no point in seeing anyone else. They just don't believe me."

"Maybe they don't know how to help you," I answered, although silently I had to agree with him. It puzzled me that so many knowledgeable people had rejected Bill's pleas for help. On the one hand, I sensed Bill's problem was a threat to them, but I could not understand why. I just knew something was dreadfully wrong, other than Bill's threats of suicide. I suspected part of the problem was Bill's own attitude. He was difficult to counsel, because he wanted instant answers and instant relief.

No one seemed to take Bill's threats seriously. Most people did try, at first, to point out alternatives or to encourage him to be patient, but it wasn't enough somehow. Now I realize the professionals we saw (picked at random for the most part) were not right for Bill's problem. We needed to see someone who was knowledgeable about alcoholism, and suicide, and depression. He also needed a counselor who would have listened more and then encouraged a definite course of action, working along with him. The community in which we lived at that time, in 1975, had neither the right resources, nor a referral service that we knew of.

On the other hand, I could understand why no one took him seriously. Bill's appearance and reputation contradicted his present depression. He was an aggressive, colorful character, who radiated a zestful, adventuresome spirit. A captivating storyteller with a folksy sense of humor, he often referred to himself as a wild Irish–Indian cowboy. In addition, Bill had previously threatened or attempted suicide when he had been drinking. Some of those attempts—or gestures—had been quite melodramatic.

One time he phoned me from a job site near Canada, wanting me to join him there. I refused, because I could tell he was on a drinking spree, but, he accused me—as usual when drinking—of having a new boyfriend. Apparently during this binge, he rented a small plane, flew it out over the lake on half a tank of gas, and dunked the plane in the water when the tank was empty (or so he said). Of course, this happened within sight of a tanker, so he was rescued. And, of course, he just happened to be wearing his new custom-made suit and best boots. He was hospitalized with two cracked ribs but insisted on getting out of bed to call me and tell me what he'd done.

"I nearly died," he yelled over the phone. "And if I had, you'd be a rich woman with plenty of money to have any man you want!"

I listened and then said, "You woke me at 5:00 A.M. to tell me that? I don't need your insurance money to find another man. I already have what I need for that," and hung up. They tell me he screamed, "Bitch!" at the phone, then hung up, turned to the group of silent, wide-eyed nurses, shrugged, grinned, and said, "Oh hell, guess I'll get some breakfast at a fancy restaurant before I go back to work. Who wants to come with me?"

Another time, during a separation, he rented a small plane and flew to a friend's ranch in the West. Apparently, his plan (while drunk) was to saddle up a horse, ride into the desert at night, and sit under a mesquite tree until he could "will himself to die as the old unwanted Indian chiefs used to do." Before riding away from the ranch he called to tell me about his plan. I wasn't worried. I knew he would be back in time for breakfast. (He was.) "Okay," I said sleepily, "have a good time," and snored into the phone. "You'll see," he shrieked, "you'll be sorry," and banged down the receiver. Before he hung up, I could hear masculine snickering and joking in the background. Like many others, I believed Bill's threats of self-destruction were "all talk."

During the time of his treatment at the recovery houses, my emotions were mixed. Our marriage had been tender and violent, safe and frightening, happy and sad. At times, we were like soul mates, but I had been in a perpetual state of confusion and upheaval as I had tried to adjust to continual separations and reconciliations.

Before treatment, his suicidal threats and gestures had been either a nuisance or entertaining and obviously manipulative. But now, there was a new tone: a mixture of sadness and desperation. I wanted to be free of all this stress and anxiety of never knowing what would happen next. I felt as if I were suffering from battle fatigue. To my horror, I sometimes found myself imagining how much better things would be if he did carry out his threat.

Despite his voice of doom and discouragement, and my concerns, I still had hope for his improvement and, "possibly," our future together. During those months of rehabilitation, he looked for work continuously by calling the many construction companies he had worked for in the past. The typical answer was, "Sorry, Bill, we have nothing open now, but we'll call you as soon as we do." Bill was sure the refusals were personal. "They've heard about what I've done, and where I live now," he'd say, "and they don't want me." Whenever someone would remind him that construction activity was at an all-time low, Bill always responded, "I can't wait. I need work now. I'm too old to learn anything else."

While looking for work, he became increasingly active in AA. Gradually, I saw him accept the fact he was an alcoholic, and I began to see the emergence of a new maturity and wisdom. I believed he had reached the turning point many alcoholics apparently have to go through before recovery can begin.

I'd heard, and believed, the myth that people who talk about suicide don't do it, and I talked myself into believing I had talked him out of it. "After his court hearing," I would tell myself, "things will be better." I also believed the aura of sadness I glimpsed from time to time would soon vanish. It did—but only with his death.

Only one hour after last talking with Bill, on that Wednesday morning, I received another phone call informing me he was dead. I just sat—frozen—and stared into the space of my living room, the receiver dangling from my hand. My mind raced with memories and questions, trying to settle somewhere. "Bill killed himself," I screamed silently. "He really did it." With a horrible sinking feeling, I realized I had known Bill would kill himself but I hadn't believed he would. And over and over, the thought hammered at me, "I was not there to stop him. I was not there to stop him. I was not there...."

Immobilized, I sat by the phone and remembered our last weekend together, just three days earlier. We had been sitting in the restaurant where we always met, when he told me his hearing date had been set for the following Wednesday. Bill had dreaded this moment more than anything in his life and had talked about the hearing constantly as well as about the "pull" of suicide and his fear of possibly giving in to it. These past weekends when we had been together, I had often awakened at night to find him staring out the window. I always asked, "What's wrong?" He always answered, "You know." I always held out my arms and said, "Tell me again." And he would.

But that Saturday morning, something about him had been

different. He appeared relaxed, no longer worried and anxious. When I questioned him about this new attitude, he said, "Let's not talk about it. I've been Gloomy Gus long enough. Let's just enjoy the weekend." He grinned at me and told the waitress, "She doesn't really want the coffee. She just likes to hold the cup." I smiled at his kidding and thought to myself, "Now, this is the old Bill."

What a pleasant change to see him smiling quietly at me while I bubbled with optimism for the future. He said he might go live with his married son after leaving the halfway house, while we remained separated for the time being. We agreed it would take time to see if we could put the marriage back together. "I don't like it," he said. "But I'll do it for you."

Later that evening, it was Bill who reassured me by saying, "No matter what the judge says or what happens, you'll be fine. You're smart, you're pretty, and you're a good person." He was quiet for a moment, then chuckled. "I feel like I've been turned upside down, spun around, and not pointed in any direction. I guess that will change in a few days." I had snuggled closer, pleased that he was joking and happy at last.

"Here, I want you to have this—keep it safe for me," said Bill the following morning. I looked up from my packing to see him holding out his most prized possession, a silver belt buckle he had once won as champion bulldogger of the year.

"Oh, no, you keep that." I pushed his hand away. "Anyway, if you are sentenced, I'll get it when I'm here for the hearing."

"No, honey—no," he protested. "I don't want you here. If I see you in the courtroom and I'm sentenced to prison, I won't be able to stand it. I'll fall apart, and I don't want to do that in public. Anyway, I want to know you're safe at home with your family and people who care for you when you get the news, whatever it is."

I argued with him, but he remained firm and I finally gave in. I took the buckle. "I'll see you as soon afterward as possible," I assured him. I returned home, satisfied at last that he was going to face the hearing and its outcome, and I had been in my trailer when he called that morning.

With the phone still in my hand, I thought about Bill's call just an hour earlier. He had been about to leave for his hearing, and had asked me, "If I promise not to kill myself, and if I don't go to prison, will you agree to let me come home right away?" I had sensed the trap in his question, and I wasn't ready to say yes. After the physical and verbal abuse that had periodically marked Bill's alcoholism, I had to be sure he'd stay sober once he was on his own again. I couldn't take any chances. I still loved him, still hoped our marriage might work, but I needed more time. Although he knew how I felt, I explained it to him again. "We've already discussed this," I said.

"Yes, I know—I understand," Bill replied, and paused. "Well," he said slowly, "just keep telling me you love me ..."

Still sitting by the phone, I thought to myself, "If only I'd been there with him, he would still be alive. If only I had realized he had actually been serious." Stunned and confused, I questioned my self-worth, my capacity to love, and even my motives for not wanting Bill to come home right away. "Could it be that I'd wanted this to happen?" I wondered. "Oh, my God! What if that's true?" I had just fallen totally into the clutches of guilt—all-encompassing guilt.

Frantically, I began to question the "why" of his death, along with a dreadful fear I would find no answer. Bill had robbed us of any chance to put our lives back together. He had the last word—the upmanship on power and control. And here I thought I had been in control of the situation. What a farce! I was, in fact, as helpless as he had been, but with no way to reply or retaliate as he had.

Suddenly, my brain did this fast shuffle and everything fell into place: his refusal to talk about the future, his unusual calm, not wanting me with him today, giving me the belt buckle—all were clues of his intentions. He knew he would do it! Damn him! He knew! He fooled me! *How dare he do this to me*! Then, shocked at my own reaction, I asked aloud, "But how can I hate him when he hurt so much?"

At that moment I heard someone reply, "Well, it's for the best. I always knew there was something wrong with him." Startled, I looked around the room. When had all these relatives come in? I must have called someone. Vaguely, I realized hours had passed, and I was still sitting there by my phone. How long had people been there visiting, while I sat isolated with my whirling thoughts? I didn't remember calling anyone, but I obviously had.

I stared at my aunt, my mind echoing her words. For the best? My God, I thought, Bill is dead! Suddenly, the reality of death hit me, and I fled to my bedroom and locked the door. My mother followed me, knocking on my door, wanting in. "Please wait," I pleaded. "Give me some time alone. I'll be out soon."

More than anything else, I needed desperately at the time to be alone. I sank to my knees, pounded the floor with clenched fists and cried, "Please God, make a miracle! Make him back alive!" Then, whispering the scream so no one would hear, "Bill, you SOB, why couldn't you wait?" and "Oh, Bill, I am so sorry," and "Oh, God, help me."

I could hear my mother complaining in the living room. "Eleanora won't let me in there with her. How can she be so mean? We come to be with her, and she runs to her room. We might as well go home and leave her alone."

I pulled myself to my feet, choked back the sobs, and walked into my living room. I realized I'd made a mistake for wanting a few minutes alone to cry and pray—for not letting my mother see me when I broke down. I knew she had a way of sometimes making others seem so much worse, or different, than they really were, but I was just too distraught to have to deal with it then. With all my heart and soul, I wanted to hear someone say, "We understand and we care. You grieve however you need to. We'll all be here for you." But no one did, and I knew better than to ask. I stood as tall as I could and said, "Thank you for coming. I'll be all right." And, oh, how I did try to be.

One week later, I began my second year of undergraduate study at the University of Iowa. I drove over seventy miles a day round-trip to classes, maintained a 3.6 grade point average, paid my own way with scholarships and loans, and worked part-time to make enough for food and trailer payments. David, with his life finally free of turmoil, became busy with school, a bowling league, and helping my dad on the farm. I spent hours shooting and developing a series of photographs entitled, "My Dad's Hands," which won several local awards, and joined our church Bible study group. This hectic schedule was a curse, because it kept me too busy to grieve; a blessing, because it kept me too busy to die.

But no matter where I was or what I did, Bill was always on my mind. Nothing made sense. I understood why he had killed himself, and I did not understand. I felt responsible, but I knew I was not. I could believe he was dead; I could not believe he had killed himself. I wanted to be alone, yet needed to be with people. I wondered what others were thinking. Often confused, forgetful, and unable to concentrate, I feared for my sanity. I worried because I wanted to sleep so much.

I spent endless hours reliving those last days together with Bill, and his last phone call. I replayed conversations and events, going over and over what actually happened, then creating different circumstances in my mind's eye—circumstances in which Bill did not die. Sometimes the fantasies were so strong I could almost believe I had willed them to be true. Then, I'd go through shock all over again, after realizing it was only a fantasy. I think I would have gone crazy if it hadn't been for David and Daryl (my oldest son, who lived and worked in Iowa City).

Both boys helped as much as they could. One Sunday morning, I awoke sobbing and couldn't stop. For nearly an hour, I heard David clattering around in the kitchen. Suddenly, he appeared in my room with a tray: brittle bacon, burnt toast, weak coffee, pretty-good scrambled eggs, and a plastic flower in a juice glass. It was the loveliest breakfast I ever had. David is my artistically inclined and gentle-hearted child—the one who brought home orphaned animals, the one most eager to please and the most easily hurt.

Daryl, in his early twenties, spent hours drinking coffee and listening to me talk. Patient, intelligent, and sensitive, he would often call and say, "I just had a feeling you were not okay and needed to talk." He was always right. But I worried that all this was too much burden for my sons, and was thankful that my daughter had family, friends, and a good job in Florida, where she had moved shortly after her father and stepmother relocated there.

David had suffered from the earlier divorce between his father and myself, as well as Bill's drinking. I worried about him and felt guilty, because I was not doing my best as a mother. I realized he was raising himself, but I had no strength to help him find his way. Sometimes, I lost my temper for reasons he couldn't understand, and I couldn't have explained. I tried to spend time with David, often taking my homework along while he and a friend bowled or attended a movie. But we didn't communicate. Talking took so much energy, my mind wandered, and I had no real interest in life. I simply went through the motions. David needed both his parents, but his father was physically absent with a new wife and her children, and I was emotionally absent with my thoughts and pain.

In his way, David felt (and was) as rejected, betrayed, and abandoned as I. Even in the worst of times, children try to protect their parents. But in only five short years, he had lost his natural father, his older sister, his childhood home, then a stepfather (whom he feared and detested), and now his mother. David had every reason to be angry: angry at Bill because his suicide had put David into the role of my protector; and angry with me, because he still needed me to be his protector. Our roles had been altered, and unable to understand, he naturally resented it. I knew and thought about these things, but somehow my thoughts were always pulled back to Bill's suicide.

My mind groped for order and relief, needing to settle on one belief, one feeling, but every belief or feeling raised more questions. Bill had been bright, talented, and healthy. Why couldn't he have waited for the court decision? Why didn't he give us more time? Why didn't I pick up on his clues? Why wasn't I with him that day? Had I hoped he would kill himself? Why didn't anyone else stop him? Who was to blame? Every question brought conflicting answers. With no answers, I had no sense of direction. "If only I knew something for sure," I'd yell at the air.

I wanted to blame someone other than Bill and myself. I

walked around imagining confrontations between myself and others, whom I perceived as letting both of us down. In my imagination, I scolded the lawyer who had said, "Don't talk to me about Bill's suicidal feelings. I'm not his baby-sitter." And I shamed Bill's relatives, who had known Bill's gun was in his car but had not removed it, even when they could have. I saw myself returning to the psychiatrist's and clergymen's offices and yelling, "See! See what you did? You think you know so much, but you let my husband die! What do you think of yourselves now?" I wanted people to ask me how Bill died so I could retort, "He killed himself, because nobody cared if he was dead or alive. So there and so what! Make something of it!"

I yearned to talk about Bill, our love, our motor home, the fun we had together. But whenever I mentioned his name, family members would walk away or change the subject. Some people only wanted to know the grisly details. I longed for someone to ask how I felt or what I needed. Sometimes I found myself explaining or justifying Bill's act, our relationship, or even myself to people. It seemed as if there was something wrong with me because my husband had killed himself, or because I was grieving.

I wanted another chance to help Bill. I had been afraid for him and afraid of him. Now, I was afraid to go on alone—afraid I couldn't—but I knew I had to. I wasn't ready to let him go, to say good-bye; we hadn't had enough hellos yet.

I was difficult to believe Bill was dead, because I had *not seen* him dead. He died 300 miles away, and I had been unable to attend his funeral. Now, I realized this was interfering with my ability to accept his death. At times, my mind suspected his death was all a cruel trick. Once I phoned the company he had worked for and asked to speak to him. It helped to hear someone say, "I'm sorry. Mr. Ross died some time ago."

I had missed Bill's funeral because there had been no one to accompany me on the trip, and I had been too shocked and confused to drive myself. "Let his son arrange things," my family said. "Anyway, he was an alcoholic, you were separated, and he killed himself. Why do you even want to be there?" No one from my family sent flowers, and I received no condolence cards. Later, some women at church apologized, saying, "We wanted to offer you comfort but didn't know what to do. Your parents said not to contact you, so that's why we never called or visited you." It was as though his life and our love were shameful, worthless, or hadn't existed.

My family's hostility toward Bill—even after his death—was understandable, because his drinking had caused them a great amount of embarrassment and stress. Much of that embarrassment was due to Bill's drunken phone calls, which were gleefully enjoyed by neighbors on the party line. He had harassed my family with threats of dropping a bomb on my trailer. I didn't worry about it if I knew there was distance between us, because I also knew he would pass out shortly after making the threat, but there was some cause for alarm if he were nearby. Once he stuffed crushed flowers in my mailbox; another time, he put a hangman's noose outside my door. Each time, he had driven many miles at night while drunk to do this. My family had had reason to fear and resent him.

But I did not understand their hostility toward me after he died. I needed their support and understanding while going through this painful transition. They had been very supportive of me during the divorce from my first husband, and I couldn't see how this was different. I tried to explain to my parents how rejected, lonely, and hurt I felt, how much David and I needed them.

"I wish you'd forget him," my father said angrily, "and as long as you are going to be depressed and difficult, don't come around bothering the rest of us. Especially your mother. Ever since you were born, I've had to listen to her go on and on about how much you have always hated her, even when you were a baby. You were *born* with a mean streak, and your mother and I think all the family should know it. No one, not even your children, should have anything to do with you." I must have looked strange, because he paused, then added in a softer tone, "That's the only way I know to keep your mother from getting upset, from her upsetting me and everyone else when you are around."

Too stunned to reply, I stared at him, slowly backed away, and returned to my mobile home, closed my door, knelt on my bathroom floor and was sick. I had just been stoned with words. An old sense of betrayal and an old fear of trusting people—that I thought I had overcome—swept over me. Fear of loss, and fear of people, again began to invade all the relationships I had been trying to repair. Bill had lost his life; I was losing my right to grieve, my right to live a normal life, my right to be an accepted human being.

I gave in to my feelings only during the forty-minute drive home from campus. Missing Bill's presence or his arms around me was so painfully consuming that at times my entire body hurt. This pain would suddenly and repeatedly return, as if the same arm were cut off over and over. At those times, I wished Bill had been buried rather than cremated, so I could stomp on his grave. Sometimes that was funny, because I could almost hear Bill say, "That's my little redhead. Even-tempered. Mad all the time."

Other times, my body shook with the deep sobs I had held in all day. I felt useless, different, no good at anything, unwanted. Pounding the steering wheel, I would scream, "Damn you. I could kill you for doing this to me!" or "Come back, I miss you." When I turned into my driveway, across the yard from the farmhouse, I'd turn off all the tears. I felt I could not afford to let my parents or my brothers and their families see my suffering.

It's ironic that as much as I wanted empathy and to talk about Bill, I sometimes couldn't handle it when it was offered. My Aunt Genevieve and Uncle Harry had enjoyed Bill's company; they had compared motor home stories and traded jokes. Weeks after Bill's death, we met on the street, and when my aunt tried to express sympathy, I was so overcome I could not respond. I cut her off. She had lost a son a few years earlier and could have related to my grief, but I did not know how to respond to her expression of concern. I had learned to grieve alone, but it was killing me.

Sorrow seemed to be an entity of its own. It hovered around the corners of my days, waiting to drop over me and take my breath away. I feared these attacks. More and more, I thought I knew what Bill must have been thinking before he shot himself.

I'd lose myself in imagining his every thought and movement up to the moment he pulled the trigger, as if I could think his thoughts and feel his feelings. Sometimes, startled, I thought I actually heard the sound of the gunshot. I wondered if suicide would be a release for me as well, and thought about death. Death would be an easy escape from the dreadful pain of silence and loneliness, but I knew I could not inflict this hurt onto my children.

I was so tired. Not sleepy tired or physically tired—but wasted tired. I had to have relief. One day, feeling especially alone and discouraged, I drove into my driveway to find my parents and older brother walking together in the yard near my trailer. One of them glanced up and asked me how I was. Touched by this unexpected expression of concern and interest, I impulsively decided to confide, and said, "I'm so tired, lonely, and discouraged that sometimes I think I just want to go inside my trailer, turn on the gas, and end it all."

"Well," said my mother quietly, "if that's the way you really feel, why don't you?" They were all eyeing me sideways. As usual, in these situations, I reacted as I had been trained to while still a small child. It was as if I could hear an old tape still playing. "Don't you dare talk back, young lady. You do as you're told. Don't you dare say a word." My heart lurched, and I froze midstep for a long moment, not wanting to believe what I knew I'd heard, but with the words "Why don't you?" swirling around my head.

In a trance, I went inside my trailer and attempted to do just that. Looking back, I don't remember my actions, but I do remember watching myself lock the doors, stuff rugs and towels around them, turn on the gas furnace, and sit down beside it. Then the phone rang, and you know how it is with telephones—they are the boss—even when you're in the middle of trying to die. It was within arm's reach, so I managed to answer it. It was David, wanting to know if he could bring a friend home that evening, and if I'd make tacos. The call was a godsend, because it knocked me back into rationality, but to my horror, after hanging up, I could not get my legs to move from the floor toward the gas handle. I reached for the phone again and managed to call Connie and Warren Lewis, who ran the local ambulance service and funeral home.

"Help me," I cried to Connie, "I can't make myself move," and told her what had happened. In just a few minutes I could hear their siren screaming its way down the road, and a state patrol car pulled up from the other direction. Together, Connie and the officer tore the trailer door off its hinges, turned off the gas, and carried me to the ambulance.

At no time during this commotion did my parents or brother come from the farmhouse to check on me, but as the ambulance was leaving, my brother ran up to Connie and asked, "Will you come and see to Mom? She's really upset!" "You take care of her!" cried Connie. "You people are responsible for this and Eleanora is my only concern!" My family never mentioned the incident and never inquired later about my feelings or welfare.

Connie took me home with her, tucked me in a chair with a blanket, gave me a hot cup of tea, sat down beside me, held me until I stopped shaking, and let me talk (between sobs). By the time she drove me back home, she had convinced me to seek help. It was the first turning point toward my recovery.

I had one special friend from a Bible study group, Joyce Woodring, whom I did talk with from time to time, but I had tried not to bother her too much and had held in many of my really deep feelings. But this was a crisis and I had to have help. I called her the next day, and she responded immediately. She had realized for some time that I was in trouble. When she arrived, she put on coffee, took the phone off the hook and said, "Okay, I'm here—and I'm not budging until you have talked this out—for as long as it takes. No one is going to hurt you—or even try—without going through me first." She meant it—she's a big girl—and it felt so good to be protected. It was just what I'd needed for so long.

I talked about the good times and the bad times with Bill. Joyce and I laughed together over the rodeo stories he used to tell. One of Bill's six brothers, Gene, had been the world's champion bulldogger three times in the late 1930s and early 1940s. Bill was full of stories about Roy Rogers, Tim Holt, Jim Shoulders, and other rodeo stars of those times. "You'll have to meet these people someday," he'd say. "That Roy Rogers is a little fella but a hell of a nice guy. Howard and I carried him all over New York one time. He wanted to learn about cowboys but fell asleep early in the evening. Howard would just hoist him over his shoulder and off we'd go. Roy spent the whole evening like that—draped over Howard's shoulder." Another time, Roy wrote a song about Howard—a parody to "Pistol Packing Mama." "I'd like to meet them," I said. "But when?"

"Oh, there's time," Bill would answer. "Those old cowboys never die. They just sit around and lie to each other." I had taped the stories as Bill told them and now Joyce and I listened together. I had needed for so long to talk about Bill, to reminisce, and once I started, I couldn't stop.

I told Joyce all about the time we were driving the motor home at night through Florida, when Bill suddenly pulled off and parked along the beach. I thought he was finally going to sleep. "I've got something to show you," he said. "Come along." He built a small campfire on the beach, settled me in the sand with a blanket, and disappeared into the motor home. He reemerged with a bottle of wine and commenced to dance—Indian style— around the fire, waving the bottle of wine and singing a song about how "Old Cowboy Pete Roped the Devil." Bill was dressed in nothing but his white undershorts, cowboy boots, ten gallon hat, and a Mexican serape over his shoulders. "I'll never forget that sight," I told Joyce.

I recalled how the thick silvery hair on his chest curled around my fingers and how I loved to trace his facial features in the moonlight. Just after Bill died, I had written a poem about him called "Tracing a Memory," and I shared it with Joyce.

"Tell me how you met Bill," she said. We smiled at each other. She'd heard the story before but knew how much I loved to tell it. My nineteen-year-old marriage was in a great deal of trouble when I first met Bill, and I had been struggling to keep our home intact. My first husband T. J. (not his real name) was involved in another extramarital affair, this time with a secretary who had picked him up at our house in Granite City, Illinois, in order to drive together to Fort Lee, Virginia, for an extended business trip. T. J. had informed me that they would be sharing a room, and I knew I would hear all about how badly I compared with her upon his return.

After they left, a friend called and invited me to a party. "You need to get out of the house, stop all that crying, and laugh a little," she said. I didn't feel like getting out—or laughing—but she insisted, and I drove over to her home for a few minutes.

"Is that your little dog?" asked the tall, good-looking man in a western dress suit to whom I'd just been introduced. He smiled and looked down beside me. Puzzled, I looked around, and the man chuckled, "There's no little dog," he said. "I just wanted your full attention." (The "invisible little dog" would later become a bond between us, and we named him Spook.)

He already had my attention because I'd been staring at him. "I've got a face like the coast line of Ireland, don't I? Rugged."

"You have an accent," I said, sidestepping the question. "Where are you from?"

"There's your opportunity, Bill," laughed the fellow beside him. "Tell her about it."

"It's a long story. Sure you want to hear it?" I did.

"Well, I was born on a ranch in southwestern Oklahoma. The youngest of a pack of twelve. My mother was home alone that day when she saw this band of Indians coming. Well, she ran out to the barn, hopped on this little mare, and started riding as hard as she could for the breaks—that's what we call a patch of bad country out there—near where my dad was. The mare was about to foal, and danged if all the excitement didn't cause them both to go into labor. So she stopped under this mesquite bush where I was born, and the mare dropped her foal at the same time. My mother put me astride the colt, she hopped back on the mare, and we outdistanced the Indians."

He chuckled, smiling down at me again when I laughed. "I knew that was going to be a big lie the minute you started talking," I told him. "But I think, somehow, I almost believe it." "I've got flannel mouth," he said, still smiling, "It flaps like the seat of a pair of long johns hanging on the clothesline on a windy day. That means I talk a lot." He was right.

Something had been puzzling me about the way he smiled. Now I knew what it was. He smiled with his eyes. He'd tip his head a little and crinkle the corners of his eyes as the warmth of the smile filled his face and flooded over on me.

"I think I'm going to call you Betsy," he commented a bit later. "It goes so well with Ross." Before I could answer, he chuckled and said, "Don't you know? You're going to marry me." I think I had known.

Bill explained that his background and lifestyle were far different from mine. "I've rodeoed hard, worked hard, fought hard, and played hard," he said. "And when we Rosses get to drinking, we're apt to take offense right quick and talk to a man by hand. Think you're up to riding the river with a man like that?"

"Anytime you get out of line, you just lean over so I can reach you, and I'll talk back by hand," I had joked with him.

A strong arm folded me close to his chest and he lay his chin in my hair. "I believe this little redhead has a taste for excitement," he said. "When do you want to get married?"

"If you'll choose the month," I answered, "I'll choose the day."

"Next month."

"The first."

"The little dog is a witness to all this," he chuckled. "You can't go back on your word, now." We both laughed. I said "good-bye" to my friend and returned home. My friend was right—it had helped to just be lighthearted and silly, to laugh and joke with someone like that.

Driving home, I could not help but compare Bill's easy humor with the way T. J., together with his sister Blanche and her husband Jud (not their real names), found amusement at other people's expense, and seemed to enjoy their embarrassment or discomfort. There's a big difference between laughing *with* people and laughing *at* people. In addition, when I was dating T. J., my father had remarked at his practice of tormenting animals, but I did not then see the warning signs in those behaviors.

I recalled Bill's joking about marriage, and that, as we parted, I had announced that another marriage was the last thing I'd ever want. In fact, my parents had seen the end coming and were worried for me. On a number of occasions, they had assured me that the kids and I could move back to Iowa and we'd find some way to live.

T. J. had often taunted me, saying, "And don't think you could ever support those kids by yourself. You're too stupid. The only way you can survive is if someone takes care of you." Sometimes, during the following weeks, when I felt really frightened and unsure of the future, I wondered if T. J. were right, and if Bill were serious, but what I really wanted was for my kids and me to be on our own and to be safe.

T. J. was right that I had no skills, and after our separation, it was a struggle to support David and myself, and my parents did feel imposed upon after a while. Perhaps that explains in part why I was receptive when Bill contacted me after I'd settled in Iowa. Apparently, he'd kept track of me through my friend. Even then, I resisted for two years before finally agreeing to marriage, because I was too tired and discouraged to even think about dealing with another man in my life.

I also talked to Joyce about our favorite motor-home adventures; how Bill would stand in the motor-home door, wait until I walked away some distance, then drop a lasso over my shoulders and pull me back to him with the rope for a kiss (we always got applause if there was an audience); and about the time the motor home rolled into a ditch when Bill had pulled off the road in order to use the bathroom at the back—how he tumbled out and rolled down the aisle, trousers around his knees; and about the time I got my arm stuck in the magazine rack and could do nothing but giggle until Bill came and lifted me up so I could get loose. I talked about our separations, his alcoholism, my feelings of rejection, and all my guilt regarding Bill and my children.

As I confided in Joyce, she laughed in the right places and cried in the right places. She never interrupted, never reminded me how others have grieved, never implied my grief was unimportant, and never tried to prove "she had suffered more." The most important gift Joyce gave me was to let me grieve in my own way. When I talked about how responsible I felt about Bill's suicide, I expected her to tell me I shouldn't feel guilty, but she didn't.

She would merely say, "Tell me how that feels," or "Do you really think so?" With that response I could at last explore my feelings, including questions about God. I told her how I was mad at God, because I had turned everything over to Him, expecting it to be healed, but instead Bill had died and my pain continued.

At one time, our minister, Pastor Paul, had asked me if I was praying for Bill's drinking problem to be healed because it would make things better for me, or because that's what God wanted for him. I had to admit, the idea of his sobriety for my own convenience was uppermost in my mind. That's not to say my prayer was wrong, but rather, that sometimes some seemingly very good prayers may not be answered if the motive is primarily a selfish one. I had prayed to be forgiven for that and had then released both Bill and my attitude to God, saying, "You do whatever is your will with Bill, regardless of how it affects our future." Three months later, Bill had killed himself.

Could that have been God's will? No, I don't think so. No painful, senseless tragedy is part of God's divine will. Tragedies happen because human beings have the free will to make decisions, good or bad. As a result, some tragedies may be accidents, some may be mistakes, some due to human frailty, some may be sin, and some we'll never understand.

Isn't it interesting how we give *ourselves* the credit when something goes the way we want it to, but hold *God* responsible when it doesn't, with comments like, "Well, it was (or wasn't) God's will." I think of that when I hear something related to nature described as "an act of God." Just how do you know what's an act of God? I have an old decorator telephone warranty that says the phone is not protected against damage from lightning and other "acts of God." Does that mean it *is* protected from acts of the devil? And if so, how does one know if lightning is, or is not, an act of the devil? And how could I know if Bill was, or wasn't, being punished?

After this time of crying on Joyce's shoulder about spiritual confusion and family alienation, Joyce offered her family as an "extended family" for David and me, and suggested we stay in touch daily. She even installed a longer phone cord, so she could move around her house while we talked. Taking advantage of her listening ear, I told her my story over and over. With her gentle patience and acceptance, I began working toward an understanding of what had happened to Bill, and what was happening to me. Joyce both helped and allowed me to probe all the implications in Bill's death, our relationship, and my present struggle with grief. We discussed the spiritual aspects, searching to discern something of value in all this. As I strove to regain my faith and put it to work, my grief process gradually became a growing experience. Joyce was a gift from a compassionate and concerned God, for with the talking and sharing, healing began to seep into my wounded spirit.

Joyce urged me to continue in our Bible study group and to talk to our minister. "We don't know what sort of spiritual contact, if any, took place in that split-second between the time Bill pulled the trigger and the time death was final," Pastor Paul said. "But what we do know is, God understands better than we do the illness of alcohol and depression. His love, mercy, and healing are greater than any human can offer." He encouraged me to search the Scriptures for answers, and as I did, I discovered verses which comforted me concerning Bill's salvation, and others which gave me permission to grieve.

With these revelations and the support I received from friends and my children, I began to experience a renewal of faith. For the first time since Bill's death, I saw a ray of hope. I was beginning to get the rattle out of my mind. Maybe there was growth in the midst of turmoil—order from the chaos—after all.

It was a year after Bill's death before I could carry out his request to bury his ashes in a special place of our own. Sitting in the warm sunshine beside the tiny grave I had dug, I thanked God that Bill had been part of my life. We had shared the same spirit of adventure, and I'd always miss his special sense of humor. I smiled when I remember how he would stand in the bathroom door watching me primp and say, "Someday, honey, I'm going to build you a bathroom with a house around it." Bill had brought excitement and laughter into my life, but my preoccupation with our relationship was the cause of much of my pain now. I realized I had been grieving on more than one level—not just that of missing Bill, but about many things that had happened to me: some from long ago, some from my first marriage. I was beginning to want to do other things, but grief still dominated my life.

It was time to release him in order to free myself. I opened the canister and let his ashes sift through my fingers. They were so white and clean. Bill had chosen cremation for this very reason. He was proud of his Indian ancestry and believed in purification by fire. The last time Bill brought me here, he had shown me where to bury his ashes. Placing his foot on a tree trunk and leaning an elbow on his knee, he had looked toward the West and talked about how his "tracks" were all over those states. "I loved it out there," he mused. "Bad things always happen to me when I'm east of the Mississippi. I used to try to pick up the world in my teeth and shake it when things didn't go my way. That hasn't worked this time." His eyes smiled down at me. "It's your turn to shake things up now, and heaven help anyone who gets in your way."

I placed the canister of ashes so it pointed east and pushed dirt over it with my hands. Bill's words kept returning to my mind. "You will do something with all this," he had once said. "It's too late to help me, but you will help someone else someday." My thoughts turned to others in similar circumstances, who also must be suffering in confusion and silence. I didn't know what I could do—if anything, but I knew I had to try. I could not ignore Bill's faith in me.

Paul Tillich (author of *The Courage to Be*) wrote that to continue to exist outside the realm of God is a state of nonbeing (not nonexistence). For almost two years, grief had been my companion and my God. It was time to start "being" again, within the realm of God. In *Dwarves in the Stable*, Frederick Buechner discusses his father's suicide and the impact a desperate person's choices have upon others. But he also reflects upon how God may be working in and through those choices.

With that thought in mind, I asked God to take both Bill's burden and mine, and turn them into a blessing for others—something which would give meaning to Bill's senseless death and the rest of my life. I stood up, said good-bye to Bill, thanked

God for whatever He would be doing, and walked down the small hill to my car. (I could have sworn there was a little dog following me.) With that act of faith, my healing process moved ahead in leaps and bounds.

It wasn't as easy as it sounds here. Since Bill's death, I'd been "running to" and "running from," and for that time, I guess it was as good a balance as any. But now, I had to decide how long I wanted to be one of the problems left by Bill's suicide. Misfortune had befallen me. I had to look it in its face and give it a name; then I could put it—and myself—in the right place.

In order to get in touch with reality and with the present, I made a list of questions for myself: "What can I do? What can I not do? What do I want? Not want?" (I knew an answer to that one. I had cried daily for nearly two years, and all it had gotten me was ten years of aging. I didn't want more of that.) What have I achieved? What are my strengths and talents? How often can I pick myself up and start again? (As often as I want to.)

Another list of issues to resolve included (1) my feelings of anger and guilt, (2) the conflict with my family, (3) the stress from my first marriage and divorce, (4) my children's shattered lives, (5) an understanding of Bill's suicide I could accept, (6) painful childhood memories, and, of course, (7) what did I want most for myself. I started with Bill—with trying to answer that eternal infernal question of "Why?"

In the weeks following my burial of Bill's ashes, I read everything I could about suicidal persons but found very little about the plight of survivors other than the book *Survivors of Suicide* by Dr. Albert Cain. There I came across the term *postvention* coined by Dr. Edwin Shneidman, which relates to the care and situation of survivors. As I studied the literature about suicide, especially books by Shneidman and Farberow, I began to understand the workings of Bill's mind as he made the decision to end his life.

Now I realized that Bill's obsessive need to "dwell on his suicidal thoughts" did not stem from a desire to be morbid, but the desire to save himself. He comprehended the seriousness of his self-destructive urges far better than anyone else. He feared the pulling power of those urges and was desperately searching for help in resisting them. Of course, he was seeking attention: justified attention. Without that attention, he simply could not face alone the things he most feared. In failing to recognize this, we let slip by the primary time for even trying to save him.

Bill's suicide was the combination and culmination of many factors. I discovered Bill fit into the category of those most at risk for suicide: a white male, age forty-five or older, divorced or alone, with a drinking problem, and without a job or profession. Even his ethnic heritage, childhood experiences, and background were risk factors.

Of Irish, German, Cheyenne, and Cherokee descent, and tracing his ancestry to Chief John Ross (a part of the Trail of Tears saga), Bill was the youngest of twelve children. Raised on a ranch in Oklahoma, he spent his time trying to imitate his older brothers, who were all rodeo enthusiasts. Somewhere around age nine or ten, he tried to teach himself steer wrestling by mistaking a cow for a steer, and by using the fence for a hazer. "Most of the time I was in the air," he told me, "somewhere between my pony and the ground."

Bill's father apparently observed all this commotion from a windmill he was repairing. He cleaned up Bill's "skinned bark" at the water tank and began teaching the boy the right way to ride, rope, and steer wrestle. Bill adored his dad, basking in the new-found attention and closeness, but lost his father only three years later, when he died suddenly while on a hunting trip. Coming in the back door while his mother was on the phone, Bill mistook her words "heart attack?" for "scout pack."

Bill's scout pack, with scraps of food in it, was missing at the time, and when the cause of his dad's death was shown to be food poisoning, Bill thought he was responsible. "All I remember is that one day, I was a brokenhearted kid of twelve lying face down on the front porch, where I cried myself to sleep, and my oldest brother picked me up and carried me to bed. I remember nothing about the following two or three years. The next thing I knew, I was a man and didn't know how I got there or what to do about it."

Bill transferred his hero worship back to his older brothers, following them to rodeos, working and sleeping in horse stalls, and riding the rails. "My brothers showed me how to drink, how to fight, and that chasing girls could be as much fun as chasing steers."

"I never got over the loss of my dad," Bill would reflect. "I now know his death wasn't my fault, but I still feel guilty, and I'm still mad about it, because I had him such a short time."

Even though Bill had not understood all the factors involved with his decision to kill himself, the information I gathered helped me to understand to some degree. I believe Bill thought he had nothing to live for. He was afraid of going to prison, afraid of never returning to his construction work, and afraid his marriage was over.

The day after his death, the judge told a reporter that in view of Bill's good record, he would probably have gotten a suspended sentence. Two weeks later, I received a phone call from a company wanting Bill to supervise a job immediately, and I had been considering a trial reconciliation. Had Bill waited one more day, he would have had his freedom; two weeks, and he would have had a job in Texas (the place he most wanted to live); one month, and he would have had another chance with his marriage.

He had failed to follow the AA principle of "One day at a time," and he could only see the darkness in his own tunnel. Bill was not mentally ill, not suffering from low-self esteem and did not feel sorry for himself, but he was facing multiple losses: his freedom, reputation, future employment, home, and family. He tried everything he knew to help himself, but he had lost hope. The tragedy is not so much that he killed himself but that he believed he had to. He made the decision to die, but I think escape, *not death*, was his choice. For Bill, suicide was not only a release from pain, but a way toward peace and safety.

At Al-Anon meetings, I learned alcoholics are at great risk to suicide during the first year of sobriety. Alcohol has been their companion, their center of life. Sobriety represents a loss of that familiar lifestyle, no matter how destructive it might have been. I don't think Bill understood that his depression was part of his recovery. I also believe Bill's self-image depended more upon what he had, rather than who he was or could become.

Some people depend upon constant attention, admiration, and approval from others for their sense of self-worth. They gain ego gratification by acquiring material possessions, money, power, position, the perfect family, from their appearance, or by cultivating a certain personality trait, charm or wit. People may have trouble developing a real sense of themselves when their sense of self-worth is achieved only by what is reflected back to them by others and their environment. They constantly demand attention and soak up whatever strength others radiate, often leaving those others feeling emotionally drained.

Problems arise for these people when they must confront tragedy or disappointment. In fact, they may perceive any setback or disappointment as a calamity if they lack the inner resources to cope realistically and objectively. They fall into their own "pit of lack" and cannot see a way out other than to complain; fight; bully or blame others; retreat into denial, depression, or drugs; or give up.

Bill's mind-set was like this in many ways.

Without his job, without prestige, a pretty wife, a new car, and so on, he saw no hope for his future and rejected alternatives that did not offer tangibles. Nor did he perceive his own lack of inner resources. He never grasped that difference between himself and others who take the ups and downs of life in stride. Indeed, if he did compare himself to others at all, he assumed they were no different than he—just "luckier or meaner."

Without incentive to observe others or analyze his own behavior and attitudes, he never learned from his own mistakes and, in the process, deprived himself of inner growth and strength. There's an interesting analogy here between Bill's inner resources and the plane he dumped into the lake. Neither one had a reserve tank of gas.

I decided I would not be defeated in this way. I concluded the answer stemmed not only from the presence or lack of inner strength, but also from recognition of its source. There is mental strength, emotional strength, and spiritual strength. I knew I already had mental strength. I realized my physical image reflected traits of timidity, reserve, and defensiveness, but in spite of these traits and habits, I knew I was of value and had emotional strength.

For myself, my spiritual strength was the primary provider of the confidence and tenacity I needed for survival and self-growth. It's nice not to be lonely or in pain, to have family approval, and to have nice things, but I didn't need these things in order to survive or to love myself. I came to believe I was worthwhile simply because God created me. That spiritual strength was the backbone for my growing self-image and sense of self-worth, and it gave me emotional strength. This knowledge underscored my mental strength. With those insights, I was able to put my own relationship with God to rights and to gain some understanding of both the extent and lack of Bill's faith.

There's a difference between knowing God and just knowing *about* God. Say, for example, you're fascinated with Paris, but you've never been there. You long to go, you've studied the history of the city, learned the language, collected pictures. You're an expert about Paris—you believe it exists—but you've never experienced the spirit of the city. You still don't know Paris; you only know about it.

A lot of people know about God; they believe in Him and in prayer. But there's that special connection—a touching of spirit (when you know that you know that you know)—which I think Bill was seeking those last months but never found. He read the Bible, prayed, went to church, and was baptized, all good things to do, but for the wrong reasons. He hoped to please God this way, to bargain, and in return, get an instantaneous, miraculous solution to his dilemma, without having to work for, or wait for, a solution.

He thought faith could do something for him if he tried hard enough, but he never really let go of his security blanket of fear. He couldn't let go of his fear without conditions, and without evidence from God as to His intentions. The sort of faith Bill was trying so hard to find doesn't happen through negotiation, begging, or doing favors for God. It comes from simply believing—from letting prayer flow *into* you as well as reaching *out* for answers.

I believe what Bill was seeking has to do with surrender—with regarding surrender as a safe release, not as giving up to fate, or as a humiliating defeat, or as a frantic struggle. There's a special peace following the surrender of sorrow or fear which can both free and strengthen the spirit. This feeling comes after the act of surrendering—not before.

Bill was grieving over many losses. Drinking had been his substitute for facing problems. Now I understood what he meant when he said, "Used to be, when I got into trouble, I could lie my way out, fight my way out, buy my way out, blame someone else, or move on to another job. Now I can't do any of those things, and I don't know what else to do." Even though counselors and friends pointed out alternatives to Bill, he had never developed other ways to cope and couldn't be sure they would work for him. He had, in a way, lost his "self."

And in the beginning, so had I. With Bill, I always knew I was loved. He had given me a sense of self-worth I'd never before experienced. He did not make fun of my attempts to express myself or interrupt me. He listened to me talk and was proud of my mind. He bragged about my looks, personality, intelligence, talents, accomplishments, and abilities to friends and co-workers until they ran when they saw him coming. He thought I was beautiful, no matter now I was dressed—or undressed.

Bill's confidence and aggression were the perfect counter-balance for my shyness and fear of people, and he set about changing that shyness into self-confidence. "You don't ever have to hang your head when you're with me," he'd tell me. "Just carry yourself like a little queen, because you aren't put together cheap." This kind of approval was better than all the psychiatrists in the world for my intimidated ego, and I adored him.

I was so in need of affirmation and approval that I even saw Bill's insane jealousy and possessiveness as evidence of love. *Someone noticed me.* In my experience, indifference meant the lack of love, so attention of any kind spelled love. That's why I was so willing to give the marriage every possible chance and overlook violence, until it was directed toward David.

But, in a way, I had become as dependent on Bill's admiration and approval of me as he had been on alcohol. Now without him, I had to build a new identity, one that relied on me. In order to help myself cope with reality, I continued my college education at the

University of Iowa with areas of concentration in religion, psychology, and journalism.

I had begun my experience as a forty-year-old female freshman during an earlier, extended separation from Bill. But before attending college, I had held a small county job. While still employed at that job during the day, I also had volunteered to design and paint scenery for a community pageant. The scenery consisted of a thirty-foot-long reproduction of a small town main street 100 years ago. I had never done anything like that before, but I loved the challenge, and with some other volunteers, worked at it every evening in a large building owned by Hope Dunn. One day she brought out coffee, sat me down, and started to talk.

"You have too much talent and potential to continue in the job you now have," she said. "Have you ever thought of going to college?" Of course, I had always dreamed of that but never thought it possible. "Well," she said, "if you can keep yourself there, I think I can help get you started with a PEO [educational] grant." She didn't have to repeat the offer. I had enrolled the following semester.

Now, as I worked slowly but steadily for my Bachelor of General Studies degree, I earned scholastic honors and was presented a number of awards, including the McCall Life Pattern Award and the Ella Cabot Lyman Foundation award. I was also published in the journal *Death Education*. With these achievements, I began to feel as if I were worth something on my own after all. I was finally dealing with the issues on my list concerning myself.

Although these insights, experiences, accomplishments, and information from books were helpful, I still needed to meet other survivors. I attended some widows' and single parents' groups but felt somehow different. Other widows did not share my sense of anger, shame, and abandonment. Their husbands had died by "natural" causes, whereas my husband had died by his own choice. These women did not feel the need to make "amends," as I did. I had more in common with women who had been divorced. It became obvious to me that survivors of suicide were unique and needed a support group of their own.

I told one of my professors that I had just buried Bill's ashes, and she was astounded. She had known me for years but had not known I was widowed that way. When I mentioned that there should be a support group for suicide survivors—something like Al-Anon—she said, "Well, Betsy, if there isn't, then you start one." She gave me the names of some people to contact, and I did.

Encouraged by Professors James Spaulding and George Patterson, and assisted by Sally Smith at the Campus Ministry Office, we planned a meeting, with announcements in newspapers and on radio. Marlene Perrin of the *Iowa City Press-Citizen*, and the *Daily Iowan* campus newspaper each ran a full story. To my surprise, all sorts of people responded to the announcement and showed up at the first meeting. Some drove over 100 miles to attend the meeting; some said they had waited for years for an opportunity to share with other survivors. We knew we wanted to continue meeting.

During these meetings, powerful things happened. A bond developed among us—something akin to blood ties. Our most important experience at those meetings was the value of retelling our stories, which helped us understand and accept what had happened.

Resolving grief rather than avoiding it is hard work for those who choose to work through it, but it is well worth it. To my way of thinking, the process resembles childbirth. Once the labor pains start, there's nothing to do but go with them. You can't change your mind, postpone them, or turn back. You can't detour around them or give them away. The only way to get relief is to work with the pain. At the meetings, we learned that grief is not an illness, not a weakness, not a mistake, not self-indulgence, and not a medical or emotional dysfunction. Rather, grief is a necessary and healthy process, which we learned to accept and experience.

From the very first meeting early in 1977, we realized the need for a national organization and public education. In August, our group, called Ray of Hope, inc., became the first nonprofit organization of its kind, so named by the group because those who suicided had lost their ray of hope, and because we, through the group, had found our ray of hope.

That first year saw a great deal of experimenting and reorganization for Ray of Hope, as there were no other suicide-survivor support groups at the time to use as a model. With the help of Daryl and Joyce as sounding boards and errand persons, we put together a logo, a brochure, bylaws, and articles of incorporation. I read everything I could find about a 1972 Grief Counseling Service for Contra Costa County for suicide survivors.

We borrowed concepts from that program, from Al-Anon, and from Make Today Count. In Burlington, Iowa, I met Orville Kelly, who, dying of cancer, had founded Make Today Count (the first support group for cancer patients and their families) and authored a book by the same name. Orville instructed me in how to organize a nonprofit group, plan the meeting format, and contact the proper officials, professionals, and media.

With his advice I found an attorney who volunteered the legal work to incorporate Ray of Hope. My uncle, Bob Spera, advised me on how to select a board of directors and handle the finances. A psychiatric nurse, Ronnye Wieland, offered to colead the support group and to instruct me as a leader, as I had no experience or training in the role as yet.

Two things I discerned early on were that part of the survivor's grief is more of a crisis situation than a chronic condition, and the main purpose of a support group is to meet that need. I used those points to shape the structure of the meetings. At first, Ray of Hope received a great deal of attention here in Iowa. I was besieged with requests to speak at hospitals, churches, schools, funeral homes, civic groups, and on radio and television.

Tom Eisen, a reporter for KGAN-TV in Cedar Rapids, Iowa, interviewed us for a two-part special on the evening news. In September 1979, Tom and others at KGAN arranged for the support group to appear on *Donahue*, together with Dr. Ari Kiev, author of *The Courage to Live*. During a commercial break, Dr. Kiev consented to speak at a conference on suicide postvention if I could organize one.

Following the *Donahue* appearance, I received mail from people all across the country, wanting to know about suicide survivors, Ray of Hope, and how to form their own groups. In

November 1979, with guidance from Professor Herb Exum in the Counselor Education department, we formed a committee to organize a national conference on suicide prevention and postvention.

Before our conference date was set, I learned about a national organization, the American Association of Suicidology (AAS), whose members had met for several years to exchange information concerning suicide. While aware of the plight of suicide survivors, they had not yet incorporated it into AAS programs beyond some study groups and reports by Drs. Cain, Fast, Shneidman, Faberow, Schuyler, and a few others. I managed to attend one of their conferences in Albuquerque, New Mexico in 1979, and announce the existence of Ray of Hope.

Our conference, in October 1980, cosponsored by the University of Iowa College of Medicine and the Iowa Mental Health Authority, attracted several hundred participants from crisis centers, mental health agencies, social services, the clergy, funeral directors, police departments, emergency care units, school counselors, and hospitals. We ended the conference with a panel of people who presented each of these services. A highlight of the conference was daily Ray of Hope survivor model meetings.

Featured speakers at that conference included Dr. Ari Kiev, Cornell University; Dr. Albert Cain, University of Michigan; Dr. Calvin Frederick, National Institute of Mental Health; Iris Bolton, Link Counseling Center, Atlanta; and numerous professors and professionals from the University of Iowa and surrounding area. Cassettes of their presentations were available. Today, hundreds of survivor support groups exist, many modeled after Ray of Hope. One bereaved widow at that conference was Teresa (Knight) Crowe, who helped establish the well-known Survivors of Suicide Group at the Suicide Prevention Center, Inc., in Dayton, Ohio.

Also presented for the first time at that conference was a booklet I had written in 1980, entitled *After Suicide: A Unique Grief Process*. That booklet has been greatly copied in the years since but in a way that is all right—it means what I wrote was valid. This book is the third expansion and rewrite of that booklet. The first revision was a 100-page manual entitled *After Suicide: A Ray of Hope* (1986) and was sold primarily at the AAS Conference the same year (I sent a copy to Joan Rivers following the death of her husband and received a nice note from her in return). A study questionnaire concerning the after-suicide grief process, which was distributed at the 1980 conference, is still being used by Ray of Hope.

Ray of Hope was the beginning of a healing process for many who struggle with suicide in their families. For me, it was more— it was the answer to my prayer and a renewing process. For nearly four years after Bill's death, I knew an important part of me had also died. The tiny bit that remained alive had retreated deep inside me, into an icy, protective casing, while my mind searched for reason and order. Had that fragile, vulnerable bit been wounded, nothing would have been left. But it was strong enough to survive while I healed in other ways.

A great part of that healing came with the understanding and insight into my family situation. At one point, I realized I was grieving more over what I perceived as family rejection than I was over the loss of Bill—another major item on my list of issues to resolve. I talked about it with my paster.

"I want their support so much," I said, "but the more I beg to be included, the more I feel as if I'm left out and told I deserve it. I'm accused of doing and saying things I haven't done or said, and it seems as though no one is willing to believe otherwise—or even listen. I feel frightened, just like I did when I was a child. I felt pretty much accepted while I was married the first time, and also when Bill was alive, but now that I'm alone again, this change in attitude toward me actually feels like persecution and much of it is even directed toward David. I can understand why they feared Bill, but why is that reason to reject and malign me and my children?"

"Well, it both does and doesn't really have that much to do with Bill's suicide," he told me. "If the rejection has always been there, this is simply another reason to express it, and without the protection of a husband, you are vulnerable—so it will be more open. Think about all the things, both past and present, that you may be reacting to now. If there are any skeletons in the closet of your memories, bring them out and look at them in relation to this."

Skeletons in my memory closet? Oh yes, like everyone else, I had several, but one in particular came to mind: one of the many times I was shut in a closet as punishment for objecting when my little brother wanted whatever toy I happened to be playing with. Putting me in the closet was a very symbolic punishment with a clear message of "We don't want you around." I realize now that the act of separating oneself from a child in times of stress can be the action of a troubled and trapped parent, one whose own power to offer help through love and healing is frozen, so the parent lashes out at the object of their frustration, or in my case, put it out of sight in the closet.

Outside, I could hear my mother saying to my younger brother, "Yes, I know she's crying and you don't like the noise, but just ignore it. Don't listen to her. Pretend she doesn't exist. You can play with anything of hers you want. She's got a mean streak just like Grandma Miller." I didn't know what a "mean streak" was—I later looked at myself in the mirror but couldn't see anything like a streak. I liked my Grandma Miller, so I didn't mind being compared to her at all. She was tiny like me. Her eyes were sad, but she smiled at me and clipped pretty pictures from magazines for my scrapbook.

I was used to people pretending I didn't exist. I'd heard that admonishment from my parents to others often enough before, but it was the tone of voice—the contempt and scorn—that left me mute. I was afraid of adult voices, because I never knew what would set off complaints or criticism—or when. I thought I really was whatever the voice implied. It would be many years before I learned it was the owner of the voice who had the problem rather than myself. It was easy to understand that intellectually, but it took a long time to believe it.

The closet was one of those long, dark ones under the stair steps, and I crept into a corner, trying to stifle my sobs, and curled up in a basket of clean, unironed clothes; however, my fear and trembling increased as I watched while a small light appeared in the darkness, began to grow larger, and started to move toward me. Then, I saw that it was Jesus. I recognized him, because he looked just as he did on my Sunday school papers. Smiling, he knelt and picked me up, then sat down in the basket of clothes, and I went to sleep on his lap.

It was so good to be held like that. I believe the strength of that protecting presence has always been with me. As I look back, I can see many "guardian angels" in my life who helped to keep me going: a hired girl, who held me on her lap and played with me; my uncle Jerry, who carried me on his shoulders; the fourth-grade teacher, who discovered I frowned because I couldn't see, not because I was "always mad"; my aunt Genevieve, who once included the celebration of my birthday together with a party and cake she had for one of her kids; my aunt Edie, who treated me to ice cream after I was in a tap dancing recital; an unfamiliar young couple with their baby, who suddenly appeared and gave me a ride home from school just as I was about to lie down and rest while struggling through a snowstorm; and Ann Geppert, a land-lady who taught a young wife and mother how to look at others with empathy and compassion—to think and see within and beyond myself.

While I was still young, I protected myself with an almost catatonic withdrawal from the possible disapproval of adults and other children. I spent a lot of time repeatedly drawing pictures of pretty girls. I think the drawings were my way of saying to myself "You, Eleanora Charlene Miller, are alive, and are a girl, and it's okay." My therapist later told me drawing was indeed a safety outlet for my shaky self-image and social frustrations. And I watched people a lot. I learned to read faces, actions, and voices, and to sense vibrations by looking deep into a person's soul, although, I have discovered, that makes some people uneasy.

Years later, I met the woman who had been my first-grade teacher in a tiny, rural, one-room school. "You looked so tiny, frightened, and forlorn," she said. "At first you wouldn't talk to me and jumped whenever I talked to you. Then, you just watched me. At recitation time, I asked the questions and I answered them. Sometimes you'd nod yes or no. One day in December, I was drawing a barn on the blackboard and you said, 'I can draw a better barn than that,' and you did. That was the first word you said that school year, and one of the *few* times you *ever* spoke."

Well, she was an adult, and I had to watch her for a time before being sure I could trust her voice, and that she wouldn't hurt me for speaking aloud. Once I knew I could, there was nothing more I needed to say. In those days, I didn't talk much to anyone. I had learned that if I asked for something, I'd probably not get it, or my younger brother would.

When I was older, I discovered I could protect myself in several other ways as well. I escaped family interaction through daydreaming or reading, substituting the lack of family acknowledgment and approval by gaining those very things from others through artwork, good grades, 4-H awards, and so on. I thought if I achieved much and asked for little, I could be loved and accepted as much as were my brothers. I ignored being ignored and pretended I felt no pain. I watched my brothers receive bikes, radios, record players, clothes, and cars; I saw their emotional and comfort needs being met and pretended I didn't want those things also. All this pretense of not caring was a cover-up for the feeling of not measuring up, for the shame of wanting my needs met, even if I "didn't deserve it," and the fear of being shamed more, if and when I did speak up.

I had to do something about all this unnatural and unhealthy shame, and I had to find out why I felt so guilty, responsible, and grief-stricken over the suicide of a man who had frightened and harassed my son and me. Why did I go from an emotionally and verbally abusive marriage to a physically abusive one? Why was I so needy and at the same time so afraid of certain people, afraid to speak up and defend myself, afraid to be hugged or touched, afraid to reach out to people? I'd find out if it meant dragging every crumbly, moldy, dusty skeleton out of my memory closet and examining every painful memory.

I went to work. I discovered you've got to be careful about ignoring your memory closet; those old skeletons in there have a way of rattling around until you spend all your time holding the door shut. Sometimes they slip out under the door when you aren't looking or pop out and surprise you when you least expect it. They can hide in the shadows, waiting to haunt you when your guard is down, and follow you around in such a way that you don't see what they are doing to you. That's not the way memories are supposed to behave.

So, show them who's boss. Open the closet door. Invite them out and look them over closely. Look for bits of unwanted gunk on your memory skeletons, and if you find it, set those bones aside. Take time to clean off any mess caused by strong, persistent, negative emotions. Even though we may consciously forget an early traumatic event, our subconscious remembers the emotion of that event, and as a result, it often controls our present and future actions and opinions more than we realize.

Think, perhaps, of this "gunk" as active "spirits" that might cling to troubled memories such as fear, complaints, jealousy, self-pity, spite, rage, anger, scorn, deceit, resentment, vindictiveness, envy, bitterness, conniving, arrogance, bigotry, denial, idolatry, greed, or, one of the most curious, grudges.

Have you ever noticed how some people proudly display their "spirit of grudges" like a badge of honor? I know a large family that specializes in grudges against one another and their in-laws, continuously clutching a list of relatives they "punish" by not calling, seeing, writing, or speaking. They even marry people with preexisting grudges and gladly shoulder the new ones. I once saw one of them walk out of church just because another family member walked in. When they do encounter the detested object of a grudge, they tilt back their head, narrow their eyes, and shoot a withering look over their glasses and down their noses, sweeping this chilling gaze from your head to your toe and back again, before haughtily turning away with an indignant "sniff" or "hummph." It's quite a show.

Carrying a grudge can serve a purpose; it provides an excuse for being angry, for continuing a vendetta, for blaming others and avoiding one's own guilt, for labeling one's self as a victim, and for hanging onto a state of unrepentance and unforgiveness. It can become addictive. Like the alcoholic, persons addicted to self-pity or carrying grudges will create—or interpret—a situation or crisis which justifies finding something else to resent, so they can then indulge in self-pity, just as the alcoholic finds a reason to drink and have a hangover. Like the alcoholic, they will destroy the reputation of themselves and possibly the happiness of others to satisfy the addiction. The trouble is, all this only brings temporary satisfaction, because the craving (as with alcohol) for a new grudge (or self-pity) will always return.

I think Christians need to be very careful to not use religion as a self-righteous justification to indulge in grudges, unforgiveness, or judgment. It's no wonder some people regard Christians as hypocrites, if they use God as an excuse to avoid or condemn someone of whom they are jealous, or are carrying on a vendetta. One might consider asking oneself, "What good is this grudge doing for me? Do I really want to demean myself by carrying around something this ugly?"

These nasty little spirits, sticking onto our memory skeletons, can keep a body so busy kowtowing to them that there's no time left to enjoy life. They suck a person into their skullduggery until his or her soul is dead long before the body reaches a decent age to die. So, clean off the gunk and throw it away, not the bones themselves—you need them.

Think about it. Without the skeleton you are currently hanging around on, you'd settle down around your feet in a lumpy pile, with nothing but your little ole eyes bugging out. Sometimes, we need our past memories, even the bad ones, as a structure to climb up on, look about, get our bearings, and go a different direction.

Another skeleton I tackled was that of my constant thoughts about Bill. They had become a haunting presence in and of themselves. This really came to my attention one day when I was wandering through a mall. Window shopping had been a favorite pastime for Bill and me, and I had paused in front of a display of menswear. Suddenly, I heard myself saying, aloud, "That suit sure would look good on you." I heard a gasp and turned to see a man and woman standing nearby. They were staring at me, wide-eyed and open-mouthed. Then, as one, they turned and scurried away. I had been so absorbed in the memory of Bill and me together that it had become too real for that couple's comfort.

Driving home, I talked to Bill as if he were in the car beside me. I said something like, "Look, you're not here anymore, and there's no way you can be here again, so you've got to stop trying, and I've got to stop encouraging you. I will always love you. I know you love me and didn't want to leave me, but you did. And since you did, you have to keep going. Maybe there's someplace you're supposed to be and something you're supposed to be doing. You can't be part of my existence anymore, and I'm not part of yours, so instead of wishing you were here, I'm telling you to go." Maybe that conversation was silly, but it seemed to help. Eventually, the memories of Bill ceased their haunting aspect and, in time, became a precious comfort.

This experience of "releasing Bill" had such a profound effect upon me that I asked my therapist if we could explore other, earlier experiences that I'd heard about but didn't exactly remember. Dr. Stewart explained how we could use a variety of techniques to reach the source of unidentified and unresolved fears and feelings. We focused on some stories I'd often heard my mother tell about my infancy and childhood.

Apparently, my mother was unable to breast-feed me, so I was put on a four-hour-interval schedule. I was to drink four ounces of milk between every four hours of sleep. But I didn't cooperate; I neither slept the four prescribed hours or drank the four prescribed ounces, much to my mother's distress. After some weeks of this, she complained to the doctor that I only slept for two hours, then cried for two hours until she fed me, and that I only drank two ounces before falling asleep, and "she's so thin and scrawny."

The doctor replied (so the story goes), "Of course the baby doesn't drink four ounces of milk; her stomach isn't big enough to hold more, and of course, she wakes up early—she's hungry—so she cries until she's fed, and of course she soon falls asleep. She's exhausted. And yes, she's thin, because you're starving her to death."

It's my understanding that she then fed me when I needed it, but a few months later, my "mean streak" surfaced again. I learned that I could toss objects, as babies tend to do. Apparently, I threw my toys and bottles out of the playpen, laughing at the time. When the second bottle broke, my mother said, "All right, young lady, if you're going to do that, you just won't eat until you're hungry enough to use a cup."

Over the years, I tried to laugh along with my brothers and their wives whenever my mother told this story and would add, "That sure fixed Eleanora. She never threw anything and laughed about it again." But inside, I didn't share my family's amusement and often wondered how long I may have gone without any food at all. Just hearing the story, it didn't sound so bad, but the way I physically reacted did. Sometimes my stomach hurt—and always—I felt such a vast ache in my heart at hearing these "funny" stories of my infant and childhood distress, misbehavior, and punishments, that I often had to leave the room until I recovered.

With the help of my therapist, I could see a pattern to these physical symptoms. They occurred whenever I perceived that someone seemed to get a kick out of the pain or distress I had or was experiencing, and many years passed before I learned to avoid those situations if I could, rather than try to fix them.

Also during therapy, I came to understand the lasting stress and reactions of those infant events connected with nourishment. I learned that a baby's sense of trust is either developed or destroyed in the first weeks and months of life, when the primary needs for survival (nourishment) are met, along with the warmth, comfort, and gentle handling that make an infant feel safe.

Those hours I lay crying from hunger and discomfort, and the accompanying frightening sounds and rough handling had created the basis for my deep, long-term fear of people, fear of being touched or hugged, the belief I could not help myself, and my heightened awareness of people's tone of voice and implications. The punishment I received for expressing myself as a normal baby discouraged autonomy and reinforced the message that it was useless for me to expect to have my needs met—that if I were, indeed, to survive, it would be on my own and by happenstance.

These infant experiences, harmless as they may sound, were serious enough to result in what is called "early attachment disorder," which affected my ability to love and trust without fear and created the feelings of despair and helplessness.

Dr. Stewart warned me that it might be a long road to well-being, and it was. Although therapy was stressful at times, it explained a great deal and revealed so many possibilities for relief and release. I learned that the lack of nurturing care, and of guidance, can be as harmful as broken bones, perhaps more so in some ways, because it can be so insidious. Physical abuse resulting from an angry reaction is doubtless harmful, but calculated abuse can be especially cruel, because it is deliberate. There's a subtle but important distinction between indifferent neglect and deliberate deprivation. Things may seem one way but be another. In my case, I had developed "learned helplessness" from constant discouragement and punishment.

I struggled with that concerning my mother's way of leading me to believe things: that I'd be told the truth about family plans; that David and I would be included; that I could safely store some antiques in her house; that she was saving my Aunt Leora's diamond ring (which my aunt had willed to me) or other family heirlooms especially for me. I eagerly believed each promise.

Sometime later, I'd find I wasn't informed of plans because they "forgot," or "didn't know if I was home." My stored items (a tiny chest of drawers, David's Tonka trucks, a braided rug from Ann), the ring, and other promised heirlooms either disappeared or someone "took them," or they were given away with the comment, "Here, you take this so Eleanora can't get it," and would eventually show up in a relative's home. These events seemed to increase with unexplained and puzzling frequency after Bill's death.

It was pretty difficult to believe this repeated action over those years, always connected with material things, was not deliberate and malevolent. It wasn't the lost objects that hurt so much, but the action itself of offering—of enticing me to trust and hope—then of taking away, and the resulting scene about something or another.

The tension between my family and David and me finally became so great that David quit school and moved into Columbus Junction, and I put my trailer home up for sale and rented a house in Iowa City. While I was packing, my younger brother and sister-in-law, Irving and Jude (not their real names), arrived in order to remove and take home with them the shrubbery growing in front of my trailer and to examine the things I was either taking with me or discarding.

We had all been very close when I was married to T. J., but in the years since my marriage to Bill, they had very little contact with me whenever they had come to visit with our folks on the farm—until now. While there, Jude suddenly turned to me, started to cry, and said, "Oh, Eleanora, I'm so sorry. I've been on a hate campaign against you for years. I've done and said everything I could to make the family mad at you and David. Will you forgive me?" Startled, I asked her why, but she mumbled something about David and me living next door to the folks.

Irving and Jude usually converse through implications, insinuations, and inferences, and I was simply too busy at the time to play guessing games, so I said nothing. Later, other relatives confirmed to me that Irving and Jude were afraid Mom might give me some antique dish or piece of furniture that they wanted. Jude's hate campaign was motivated by incredible jealousy and greed and her opposition to my divorce.

More important, I was able to see our family problems in a totally different light, as her revelation explained so much that I'd been puzzling over. All these years, I'd been blaming my parents for everything, totally unaware of the pressure they'd been subjected to as they were caught between wanting to be close to their daughter and her children, and the turmoil of having suspicious ideas about us planted in their minds.

Now, I understood why it had so often happened that when my mother and I had been together, and seemed to be getting closer, she'd later change—becoming defensive again. When, in fact, my mother had been manipulated by Irving and Jude, who had used Mom's old fears and resentments to plant suspicion and discord for their own jealous or vindictive motives. It must have been as painful and confusing to my parents as it was to David and me. What a relief to have much of the rejection explained at last.

I told Dr. Stewart about my sister-in-law's confession and asked, "How can I forgive her and Irving when I feel so unjustly tricked and discredited?

"It was unjust," she replied, "for her to destroy you and your small son in the mind of others, to pit you against your mother and father; for you and David to stand maligned, accused, and punished for things you haven't said or done. It is unjust when your mother promises you something, then withholds it and also scolds you for objecting, and for your brothers to take things belonging to you and David. It is horrible to be or feel ostracized by your entire family because of one parent's hell, or a sibling's jealousy and greed, but that's the way of dysfunctional families. If your mother or sister-in-law is using material things to control people, other family members will follow their lead and may be afraid to defy them, or don't even realize what they are doing. People can become insensitive to abuse, deny it's very existence, and even begin to act the same way. Look at examples of that in history or gang activity.

"Your parents may have," she continued, "early in life accepted and believed some terrible messages about themselves, and they continue to operate on them. But, remember this," she added. "It's not really you they hate. What others in your family do hate is what they have decided you represent—whatever ugliness in their own lives they have transferred onto you, although they would probably not see that. And the longer it isn't confronted, the longer it will continue, and the more there is to cover up, the more you, or someone else, will be made to look bad, rather than for others to admit they've been mistaken.

"Closed families tend not to give others a chance; they don't check out facts, and they usually believe what they want, regardless of what others say or the facts show. Denial—and denial of denial—is the only way they know how to fight for their own survival. That's why your nieces will accept something from your mother even though they know it's yours. Jude knows that and knows it will hurt you, so she encourages them to take your things and David's toys. That's how she gets even with you for living closer to your folks than she and Irving do, and that's how she gets you and your children out of the way. She's afraid and uses subterfuge to control her fear. However, I realize that just explaining and understanding the situation doesn't repair the crippling damage that has been done to you.

"You, for example," she continued, "don't have to believe something is wrong with you just because your parents or family believe it, or if your sister-in-law says so. If others believe negative assumptions about you or David without giving themselves, or you, the benefit of a doubt, or without asking you about it, that's because of their sickness. But, you can choose to operate from a different point of view." She was right. I would have to heal myself, because the past couldn't be undone, but the explanations and understanding did help me begin to forgive.

I knew I had to forgive in order to not pass along harmful feelings—to avoid placing my children in bondage to my own negative emotions. I also knew that I had to empty myself of bad feelings in order to make room to feel forgiving—that the act of confession and repentance leaves open space for new habits of behavior. It is not enough to just intellectually comprehend this.

For example, the AA principles of confessing to a higher power that one is powerless over alcohol, of admitting this to others, and of being open to receive help are all actions designed to bring about change. Consider further that if we are powerless to control feelings regarding abuse and/or victimization, we will also then be an abuser and/or victim as long as we are beset with negative feelings toward our victim or abuser and do nothing to change. It's not enough to just say, "Forgive me," or "I forgive you"; you have to *do* something to confirm it such as changing an action or attitude. You might ask yourself, "What would I be doing, saying, or feeling if I really have forgiven?" It's *action* and *affirmation* that break the cycle.

I knew this had happened for me when I could recall formerly painful incidents without feeling any painful emotion. I knew I had forgiven when I no longer felt the hurt or a desire to hurt back.

I also understood why it had been so difficult for me to teach my children problem-solving and coping skills; I had just not learned them myself. I could see the basis for parallels and implications between so many losses and rejections, and the self-defeating ways in which I reacted to all of them. At last, here was a pattern that I would use to examine my feelings and actions. The resulting self-knowledge supplied references and points of direction on which I could base conscious, deliberate changes in my beliefs and behaviors.

In their book *Happiness Is a Choice* (1978), Frank Minirth and Paul Meier claim that once we are into adulthood, we are the primary source of much of our own unhappiness until we grow in wisdom; once it develops, we gain insight into our own self-deceit, and happiness then becomes a choice. For me, this came about by continuing to yank the bad "memory skeletons" out of the closet, cleaning them, and putting them back. With that in mind, I pulled out a twenty-year-old one marked "First Marriage."

My first husband and I had no idea of what was really in each other's minds, not at the time of our marriage or anytime afterwards. I believe we married out of loneliness and unrecognized needs rather than mutual love and respect. Habit and duty helped hold the marriage together. We both meant well, but because of our backgrounds (he was the child of an alcoholic parent), we both lacked skills in communication and personal interaction. I was comfortable; I liked being a homemaker, but I was more alone during those twenty years than I have ever been while living alone. I think he was too. That loneliness and frustration resulted in depression for me and his first affair with another woman.

For many years, I had believed my marriage was as sound as any. Although I knew T. J. found this woman attractive, it never occurred to me that he was not as content in our marriage as was I. This affair, with a woman I trusted and loved as much as a sister, began around the time David was born. It ended a few years later when my father and uncle observed them in my dad's barn, literally rolling in the hay, and my dad made it clear that he would not allow this to continue in his home. This was a terrible betrayal of my parents' trust. They had taken T. J. into the family, despite earlier reservations, and treated him like a son.

Apparently, many people had known about the affair all along, and my parents advised me, "Now just don't say anything and let it blow over." I followed their advice because (1) there were five innocent children to consider, and (2) I wouldn't have known how to confront T. J. anyway. Actually, I didn't need to, as T. J. let me know about the affair anytime I did not respond sexually as he wanted. He would remind me, rather smugly, that "*she* was willing." In addition, when with his favorite sister and brother-in-law, Blanche and Jud, T. J. would laugh and joke about the woman (and her unsuspecting husband) when they thought I didn't catch on.

I was so willing to accept anything, that a few months later, I agreed to be present at her new baby's christening in Illinois. I noticed, but never commented upon, her baby's slight foot defect, similar to one shared by T. J., several of his siblings, and our own three children.

I reacted to all this with my usual denial of reality, pretending everything was all right, and constantly trying to be a better wife and mother. But permanent damage was done; that affair was the beginning of the end of our marriage, and the beginning of irreparable damage to my children's lives. T. J.'s appetite had been whetted for women who were willing to do anything he asked, and eventually he married one of them.

In 1962, two months before David was born, I had entered a psychiatric hospital to be treated for prenatal depression and complete physical and mental exhaustion. Pregnancy was not easy for me. Following the birth of Daryl, who nearly died, the doctor told T. J. that I was too small to continue having babies, although my daughter's birth, two years later, was much easier. But, with this third pregnancy, my weight soared from 94 to 167 pounds. I had toxemia and varicose veins. I couldn't sleep and could barely walk, but I helped move into a new home one week before Christmas (in my sixth month), made the 600 mile round trip to Iowa from Granite City at Christmas, and got the older kids settled in a new school after Christmas, before I collapsed and entered the hospital. I hoped this baby would be a boy so I could name it David Ray—"Ray," because it was my special little Grandma Miller's favorite name. I liked the idea of having another baby to cuddle, but I sure needed some rest first.

My doctor, David Friedman, prescribed at least four weeks of rest and daily counseling. I was pampered, complimented, and respected, and people listened to me. There, for the first time in my life, a counselor told me that I had the same right to respect and affirmation as everyone else, that I was just as good as my brothers and sisters-in-law (I had already accepted the fact that my mother considered them "her daughters"). I was amazed. It just never occurred to me that I could even begin to measure up to my brothers or their wives. I always thought they were all very special and not a burden like myself. I began to see myself with different eyes.

The counselor also told me that I was not responsible for all my parents' problems, or all my husband's moods. "Your father loses his temper because he lets himself, not because you make him do it," he said. "Your mother shook you when you were little because she chose to, not because you made her do it. Both your parents claim you are mean, because it's the way they cover up their own actions and guilt, not because you are. Your husband pouts, bullies, and intimidates you because he chooses to, because he feels powerful when he does, and because he gets away with it, not because you make him do it. They are responsible for their own words and actions. Not you."

"But," he continued, "if your husband keeps modeling the idea in front of your children that you are an object of contempt and are to blame for everything, your children will eventually see you the same way and will copy his technique of blaming, ignoring, and making fun of you. Things will change only when you refuse to believe the worst about yourself, and refuse to respond the way you have been. You have a choice, just as the others have, and are just as responsible for your choice of action as they are for theirs."

What a revelation! Here I was, thirty years old, and didn't know something that simple. But I learned quickly. I went home from the hospital with a new vocabulary: words and phrases such as "Do it yourself," "I don't care," "I won't," and the most un-forgivable of all—"No." Sometimes I practiced saying "no" when I was alone just for the sheer joy of hearing myself.

However, before I went home, T. J. decided that four weeks was too long for me to be away from my "wifely duties," and while my doctor was out of town, he persuaded a resident physician to use treatment that would enable me to be released earlier. Dr. Friedman was furious when he returned to discover that the resident had, although against her better judgment, authorized a series of five electroshock treatments. And I was over seven months' pregnant. I never even knew what was coming. No one told me. They just got me out of bed one morning, took me into a room, and zap. I was left dazed, confused, and weeping.

On the morning I went home, the resident physician stood in the hospital entry, watching us. Just before leaving the building she had asked me, "Are you sure you want to go home now?" "Yes, she is," T. J. replied for me, while I nodded assent. Inside I was screaming, "No, no, not yet! I still don't know what to do—how to act!" But I said nothing. At the curb I looked back. She was still watching; I was still silently screaming for help.

I went home ahead of schedule all right but shocked into a changed person, as well as shocked out of depression. My energy was renewed, and a positive self-image had taken root, but so had a new concern.

I had to take a good look at this man whom I had previously so meekly and willingly obeyed, served, trusted, and respected. Here was a man who was quiet and stoic, but steady, intelligent, industrious, a good provider, and usually good natured, although inclined to pout or "let" me see him cry when he wanted me to feel sorry for him. I also saw a man who had jeopardized our unborn child by subjecting me to violent treatments that may have harmed either one or both of us, simply in order to keep me at home.

This was not the first time T. J. had compromised my health for his sexual desires. I recalled that I had become very ill when Daryl was five weeks old. It hurt to walk, I was bloated, and the pain increased each day. Alarmed, our landlady, Ann Geppert, begged T. J. to take me to the doctor. "Oh, she'll get over it," he'd say. Finally, Ann announced that she was going to call a cab and take me to the hospital herself if he didn't. T. J. told Ann to go on home and call a cab and that we'd be ready soon. While waiting for the cab, T. J. insisted I perform my "wifely duty" just in case I had to stay in the hospital for a while.

In the emergency room, Dr. Friedman realized I'd just had sex. "Didn't it hurt?" he asked. "Yes," I answered. "I thought I was going to die," I cried. After a silence, he said shakily, "Your appendix has been ruptured for several days, you have gangrene and peritonitis. We need your husband's signature for emergency surgery."

A few minutes later, I could hear Dr. Friedman yelling at T. J. in the hall. "What in the hell is the matter with you? You admit that you had sex with your wife when you knew she might be dying! Are you crazy?" I heard T. J. say something about "wifely duty" as I drifted off to sleep. I honestly did not understand at the time just why Dr. Friedman was so upset. The terms *spousal abuse* and *spousal rape* were unknown in those days, and I was used to doing whatever T. J. asked of me.

Not only did my trust and respect for T. J. begin to wane, it became tinged with fear. I reacted the only way I knew how—by pretending that everything was fine and withdrawing from him emotionally. I now knew that I had a right to my feelings, but I had left the hospital before learning the conversational skills I needed to discuss those feelings. I still didn't know what to say to my husband, and I was afraid to try.

But, my newfound confidence was working in other ways. I began to venture out of the house. I helped start our church library, began to visit with neighbors and other women, attended an art class, and took a part-time job. However, the more I gained courage and self-confidence, the more T. J. became threatened and reacted with criticism, scorn, and belittling, techniques which, at one time, would have stopped me cold in my tracks. But not this time; I'd cut my teeth on that stuff and was outgrowing it.

I chose a different way to react—no more tears or begging for forgiveness, but more independence and passive resistance. This was too much for a marriage that might once have been saved with counseling and involvement with Adult Children of Alcoholics. T. J. never seemed to realize that contempt and intimidation would drive us farther apart, not save the marriage.

In the years following the affair T. J. had with my "friend" after David's birth, he became increasingly obsessed with sex, often staying home from work for just that reason, and I once had to have surgery for a sex-related injury. But it wasn't enough. He approached people in our Young Married Couple's Club from church, wanting to swap wives. They refused. He wanted me to pick up men in bars and have sex on our bed while he watched from the closet. I refused.

Over and over, he listed all the things that were wrong with me. At first, I would protest, then, overwhelmed, would cry and apologize, thinking that might stop the onslaught of criticism. But my tears aroused him, and wiping them away, he'd whisper in my ear, "Hubby woves wittle wifey. Hubby will be good to wittle wifey when wittle wifey obeys hubby." My skin crawled.

He insisted that if I loved him, I'd obey him. Finally, I said, "I can't love or respect you when you ask me to do these things. I'll cook, clean, raise the kids, be a "dutiful" wife in every other way, but I will not take part in these things that are painful, dangerous, immoral—unnatural, and humiliating. I *will not obey* you."

He stared at me a long time, then grabbed me by the throat and yelled, "You'll be sorry for this. You aren't a wife. I'll see that you pay." Our daughter heard the commotion, saw him choking me, and called the police. I did not press charges. But his tactics changed.

After that, when he stayed home from work, it was to follow me—everywhere—and stare—not speaking, but just staring at me. Sometimes, he'd chuckle softly to himself, and at first I'd ask, "What's wrong?" or "Why don't you speak?" Later, I just ignored him. If I closed the door to the bathroom, he'd crash it open and watch till I was finished. When the kids came home from school or someone else happened by, he'd turn on the TV or sit down and visit as if nothing were happening.

He once followed me to church and leaned against a tree, staring through the window as other women and I worked on new library books. Finally, the pastor's wife went out to talk to him. When she returned, she told us that T. J. was worried that I was going crazy and might hurt someone, and if I ever lost control, would she help him admit me to the state mental institution?

When I drove T. J. to meet his carpool driver, the silent wall of hatred was so thick in the air, you could cut it with a knife. He made no attempt to be civil unless someone else was around. By this time, I had lost weight, cried when alone, was taking tranquilizers, and had constant stomach pain, but never lost control. Both T. J. and I took out much of our tension on Daryl. Nearly every evening meal ended with Daryl being scolded for something. Or T. J. would say to the kids, "Ignore your mother. You don't have to mind her. She doesn't deserve respect."

At night, in our bedroom, I would often awake in the early morning hours with a bright light in my eyes and T. J. on his knees beside me. "You're ugly," he'd say in a soft voice, gently stroking my face. "You used to be pretty, but you're ugly now. No other man will ever want you. You think you're so smart, but everyone knows you're stupid and laughs at you. No one likes you. Your children hate you. Your daughter doesn't want you for a mother. You're going to kill yourself. Maybe you're going crazy." His hand would come to rest on my throat.

I knew he wanted me to lash out at him, cry or something, but I lay there like a rock—never moving—and I never lost control. Soon, he'd jump up, run from the house, and go tearing down the road in our car. My daughter would sometimes ask, "Where did Dad go last night?" I didn't know then, but years later I discovered he went to see a woman he wanted very much to marry. Always in the past, he'd let me know when he was involved, such as the "friend" and the secretary, but this time he'd kept it secret. Now I know it's because he was serious about this one.

I had to do something as our family was headed toward disaster. We needed a separation—I needed time alone to think. I phoned my parents, who arrived from Iowa within hours; they had known for a long time that things weren't right. After they arrived, T. J. continued his "staring" at me, and when my dad asked him about it, he said, "She's crazy. You should see her sometimes. I think she's going to commit suicide or maybe hurt one of the kids or me. I've talked to neighbors, who've agreed to help me have her institutionalized if she needs it. I never know what she's going to do." My parents were horrified. They knew this simply wasn't true. As I protested, he said, "Just listen to her. She doesn't even know what she's like. She's not a 'wife.' She's worthless."

Mom and Dad left the house, and as I watched them from the window, talking together, T. J. hissed in my ear, "You think they don't know what you're like, but they do. They've always hated you. We both know that. They'll help me put you away." Then he sneered, "You'd better not try to pull anything while they're here, or you'll be sorry."

When my folks returned inside, Dad said to T. J., "We have a suggestion. We'd like to take the kids and Eleanora home with us for a couple of weeks. The kids haven't yet had their summer visit to the farm, and Eleanora could spend time alone with her mother." (We had discussed this on the phone before they left Iowa for Granite City, and I was already packed.) T. J. had never before allowed me to visit my Mom without him or even be away from him overnight, but he reluctantly agreed, provided he also had some "time alone" with me first, and I could follow by bus a day later. He insisted, saying that if I didn't stay, the kids couldn't go to the farm. I desperately wanted the younger ones away from the house in case something happened, so I told Mom and Dad to go on. "Daryl is still here, so I'll be all right," I assured them.

T. J. promised my folks to put me on the bus the next day, but laughed, saying, "In her state of mind, there's no telling where she'll get off. She's likely to take a notion to go anywhere."

After they left, T. J. was surprisingly pleasant but did not come inside as I had expected. Instead he puttered around in a little lean-to shed he'd built off the garage. "I think I'll get ready to cement over the dirt floor in there," he had said. I watched from the window as he moved things to and from the shed: mower, wheelbarrow, bags of cement, tools, and so on. I was thankful he was working outside. Near dark the phone rang. It was my folks, saying they had arrived home. The phone rang again—it was T. J.'s sister. As he came in, he said, "I'll take this call in the bedroom, then let's take advantage of our privacy. I'll be waiting for you in there."

I hung up the receiver and started to follow him, then stopped, staring at the bedroom door. We were really alone; Daryl would be at work for hours. I heard T. J. finish his phone conversation and hang up. I could hear the silence—could *feel* him waiting for me in that dark room, and suddenly, my blood ran cold. I couldn't move; my feet were rooted to the floor, my mind racing with possibilities.

Slowly, quietly, I backed into the hall, paused by the desk, and scribbled a note that I was "sorry for everything and was leaving." I grabbed my suitcase from the laundry room, fled for the car, and drove to a friend's house. When the shaking and babbling stopped, my friends, Marian and Otto Shelton, followed me in their car so I could return ours to T. J. (who would need it for work) and then put me on a plane for Iowa the next morning.

Chaos followed. I never returned to live in my home but remained with my parents and with my mom traveling with me on the many trips south for court hearings and visitations.

Bit by bit, as time passed, I learned things that shed light on T. J.'s behavior those last horrible months of our marriage. When I told T. J. that I could not love or respect aberrant sexual behavior and refused to obey him as things were, it was the final rejection for him. He no longer wanted to save the marriage; he wanted to get out of it.

Around that same time, he had also met Inez (not her real name), the woman he married only weeks after our divorce was final. She wanted my house with its four bedrooms for her five children, and T. J. vowed to give her that, regardless of the sacrifice. Obviously, she offered him something he wanted much more than he wanted the home and family we had built together. She made no secret of their plans and announced around the neighborhood, "He won't intimidate me." She was right—he didn't. Inez was a much better match for him than I was.

I also learned that in our state at that time, T. J. could only have divorced me if he could make it look as if (Plan I) I were insane, or (Plan II) I had deserted him. In either case, he would have automatically received the property. But I messed him up. I wrote and used Plan III—gone, but not missing. Now, in order to gain possession of the property, he needed custody of the children, not exactly what he and Inez had planned. The battle over the children began.

At first, unaware of Inez in the picture, I agreed that the

children were probably better off in their own home than in a room with me at my folks' house. But on one occasion, when I had temporary custody of David and his sister, I sent them to visit their Uncle Irving and Aunt Jude in Rockford, thinking they would be safe while I looked for work and a place for us to live. They immediately phoned T. J. to come and get the kids (without my knowledge) if he wanted to. T. J. did and "hid" them with a sister in St. Louis until I located them. Apparently, my brother and sister-in-law's eagerness to meddle outweighed any concern over the risk of participating in the federal offense of aiding a kidnapping! With Irving and Jude's help, my kids were gone. It was the last time I saw them before the divorce, and the last time my daughter was ever able to visit her grandparents. Jude had put an end to any competition from that niece once and for all.

Other relatives were kinder and tried to repair the damage following this episode. My Aunt Edie and Uncle Charles offered their home to my daughter until I was settled. I phoned T. J., who said he'd give our daughter the message. I was really pleased about this, and I was sure she'd be excited about living with this aunt and uncle she adored, but she never responded. When I phoned again, T. J. said, "She doesn't want to hear from you anymore, and doesn't want to live with any of you. She hates you and wants Inez for her mother." (I suspect she was never told of her aunt and uncle's offer.)

Much as I disbelieved that, I could not break through the barrier. T. J. changed the lock on the door, got an unlisted phone number, returned all the mail I sent the kids, and enlisted his sister Blanche to help in the brainwashing. Blanche is at her best when she can be mad at someone, so she gladly complied, and T. J. soon afterward called to tell me that David also never wanted to see me again. I couldn't believe that either and tried to see David at school, but the teacher stopped me on T. J.'s orders. So, I waited until the next morning.

After T. J. and the older children left, David was with a sitter for ten minutes before he took his bus to school. The sitter saw me coming and locked the door. I broke the window with my fist and gathered up David's clothing and some toys. When in the car,

David said, "I can't be with you, Mom. If I go with you Daddy will spank me." He didn't realize he didn't make sense. We returned to Iowa, where I enrolled David in school.

Two weeks later, T. J. again took David, this time from school to his sister's home, where he phoned me to say he had David again. With my parent's help, I went to retrieve David a second time. I broke another window with my fist to get back into the house after T. J. grabbed David and pushed me out. Before we could leave David, my dad hit T. J. on the jaw after T. J. slapped me, while my mother grabbed David and ran. At the final custody hearing, the judge said, "This woman has been very much ma-ligned and manipulated, and she deserves to have her son." T. J. offered me custody of David in exchange for my share of our house, and my daughter, thoroughly confused by now, chose to stay with her dad and Inez, believing I didn't want her.

Also, at the divorce hearing, T. J. offered into evidence (as proof that I was a bad wife) two items I had hung on the refrigera-tor door: an article by Erma Bombeck about the drudgery of housework and a novelty pot-holder showing a harried woman jumping up and down on her broken broom and yelling, "I hate housework!" As we left the court house, T. J. said to me, "It cost me thousands of dollars to get rid of you, but it was worth it."

My children, once they had served the purpose of securing the house for Inez, were expendable. Daryl, whose room was overrun by two other boys, and his things destroyed, loaded what was left of his belongings into a rickety car by himself after gradu-ation and left for, Ames, Iowa, where he believed his dad had made arrangements for him to live with his Uncle Harry and work his way through college. But Harry had never heard from T. J., so Daryl went to his Aunt Blanche and Uncle Jud, who also turned him away. My eighteen-year-old son then disappeared, and for over three years, I was never sure if he was dead or alive. I later learned he had lived in his car, jobless and homeless, for much of that time. Calls to T. J. were heart-breaking—he said it was Daryl's choice to leave home and come to Iowa and he didn't care what Daryl did or where he went after that.

But, I heard rumors of his whereabouts, and so I kept hunting for my son and finally learned that he was nearby in Iowa City and had driven by the farm, but was afraid to stop, believing he was unwelcome in my family as well. I left messages and packages, and eventually he showed up at the farm, where he was welcomed by my parents, David, and me with open arms.

Daryl has managed to overcome those years and, despite one brief unsuccessful marriage, is a contented and thoughtful man.

My daughter, her life equally disrupted, managed to finish high school early, find a job, and move out. She tried, at first, to bridge the gap with an occasional trip to Iowa, and a special one for her sixteenth birthday dinner and cake from Grandma. She might have stayed here, I believe, but at some level must have known how it would be interpreted by T. J., Inez, and her Aunt Blanche, and that she would then be as ostracized as were her brothers.

When T. J. and Inez traveled to Florida with plans to sell our house so Inez could live close to her mother (whatever Inez wanted, Inez got), my daughter phoned, asking me to come to Granite City to see her. Happy and excited, I accepted, but just as I was leaving, Bill intercepted me—drunk and accusing the both of us of conspiring for me to rendezvous with T. J. Insanely jealous, Bill threatened to follow me and "hurt" all of us. I knew well, by then, of the guns he carried, his strength, and what he could, indeed, do when drinking. I called her back to say I couldn't see her while Bill sat next to me, cleaning his pistol and detailing what it could do to a person. I began to hate him.

That night I dreamed that my daughter was wearing a warm sweater I had given her, but when she saw me, she removed it and handed it back to me. It was a prophetic dream; she never asked for me again, much as I yearned for her. I still believe that, at some time, Bill would have accosted her. In Florida, she was safe.

But Florida was not idyllic. When my daughter stood up to Inez, Inez slapped her, and she left home. T. J. merely said, "Inez was right to hit her, she deserved it, and I don't know where she is." The final child, no longer needed for material gain, was expendable and homeless. T. J. finally told me where she had gone only after I threatened to call the police and list her as missing.

Eventually she returned to Florida and has done well. The mother of my only grandchild (a blue-eyed, long-legged beauty with brains), my daughter is bright, capable, tenacious, determined woman, armed with an "I'll-never-be-hurt-again" defense, but blessed with a contagious zest for life. I miss her.

In the beginning, David kept in touch with T. J. I helped him write letters and showed him how to make long-distance calls. In turn, he waited for calls and letters that soon tapered off. Once, he sent gifts for all seven of them from money he'd made selling Christmas cards, but there was no acknowledgment of their receipt.

But a part of David still wanted to be a part of that family, and when he was nineteen, he quit his job, sold or gave away his things, loaded his prize possessions into his van (including a rolltop desk he had assembled and refinished at age eleven), and left for Florida.

I never expected him to return, but he did—a year later—depressed, discouraged, and filled with anger toward me. David's trust, love for his dad, and need to be accepted provided fertile ground for those bent on instilling resentment and distrust. Nothing can destroy the innocent and unwary more thoroughly than the teaching and practicing of hate within the family fold. Once that was accomplished, David was no longer welcome there. As had Daryl, he left for Iowa alone; no one saw him off or offered gas money. He sold his beloved desk to make the trip.

David is the artistic one of my children; the one who brought home orphaned animals; the one most eager to please and most easily hurt. His life has been marked with setbacks, disappointments, ill-health, and criticism from cousins, aunts, and uncles of both families, but his spirit is blessed with a dauntless will to overcome and survive. My Uncle Bob often said to me, "Eleanora, you will make it in spite of your family." And so will David.

When the dust finally settled, both of our older children had been missing and homeless, and David had ulcers. Three children's lives were forever damaged, and all in the name of adult obsessions with lust, greed, jealousy, alcoholism, and fear. Inez had T. J.'s children out of their father's life and his children's home filled with her children. Irving and Jude had my children out of their grandparents' lives (except for David) and their home filled with other people's things: mine, my mother's, and David's.

Sometimes I just sit back and shake my head in mute amazement at what "good" people will do when a divorce or death takes place. In my case there was an incredible fear that one person might be in a favored position over another for some antique dish, furniture, jewelry, or whatever; and the lengths to which people went to move in on another woman's home, oust her children, scramble over their things, carry out vendettas, and then staunchly deny it all or blame someone else. It's as if there are understood agreements to work together in order to violate one another. Amazing. Just amazing—and, such a silly waste of time.

In retrospect, I realize that neither T. J. nor I had the presence of mind or ability to objectively explain our position to ourselves, to each other, or the children, so it must have looked to them as if they were suddenly and for no reason rejected and abandoned by both parents and both extended families, as well as possibly at fault for their own predicament and forced to choose between them. It's a miracle families survive things so immensely unfair, and no wonder so many of them don't. This is why marriage and family counseling or a mediator is so valuable if divorce absolutely must happen.

When T. J. developed a fatal illness, both David and Daryl journeyed to Florida to see him despite being unasked and unwelcome by Inez and Blanche. Daryl was able to get time off from work and my church helped finance David's trip as he was ill and unemployed at the time. When Blanche heard that I had encouraged them to go see their father, she flew into a snit. She spent 25 years berating both boys because they chose not to turn their backs on me, and in encouraging T. J. to continue the silent treatment toward them because of it. She had hoped to keep T. J.'s illness a secret until after he died and then rub their noses in it. A sadly bitter person, Blanche really only needed very much to blame or punish someone.

If Inez and Blanche had really loved T. J., they would have encouraged him to contact his sons through the years, regardless of circumstances, and would never have wanted to cheat him out of the pleasure of seeing his sons become men.

But mean-spiritedness prevailed, and T. J. never did reach out to his sons although they did to him. Our daughter was at T. J.'s side when he died, and he got to see his sons before he died, which may have pleased him more than he dare let on. It's interesting that the man who intimidated the daylights out of me could be equally intimidated by Inez and Blanche. David and Daryl can stand tall and proud for giving their father the gift of forgiveness. It takes a bigger person to forgive than to nurse a grudge.

Years after the divorce, when I attended Al-Anon meetings because of Bill's drinking, I realized that alcohol had played a major part in my marriage to T. J., even though he was not a drinker. The children of alcoholics often live a dreadful life, never sure who will be beaten or when or why, never feeling secure, always vulnerable. As a result, they will do anything to secure a dependable environment when they are grown. Maintaining control is paramount, and any change (such as my growing independence) brings back those old fears.

T. J.'s father had been the "town drunk," usually unemployed and often jailed for drinking or disturbing the peace, or for accosting some woman. He was once hauled out of his wife's bed in the maternity ward just a day after she gave birth, and whining, "But I haven't been with my wife for two days." Ridiculed by the community, he was a great source of shame and humiliation to his family. Seeing his father vomit all over the house, force sex onto their mother, and pick fights is what T. J. had grown up with until their divorce when he was a teenager.

When I first met T. J., he bitterly hated his father, and from his point of view, with good reason. Near the middle of nearly a dozen children, T. J. was often the target of his father's rage. He had blackened T. J.'s eye as he was on his way for his high school graduation picture, and he turned on T. J. if he defended his mother, a tiny, gentle woman who silently endured the abuse.

I had known the family all my life and in spite of their father's problem, they were accomplished, well-behaved, respected kids who finished school, won college scholarships, worked hard, married well, and looked after their mother. I was proud of them.

T. J.'s emotional development had been sabotaged by alcohol.

Surely this background explains his indifference to his own children's emotional needs, his fascination with unnatural sex acts, his need to see me cry during sex, and his great need to control and dominate me. He must have had repressed rage toward his mother as well, who was too busy just surviving to be there for him. That could account for the fierceness of the hatred he transferred away from his father and onto me and our sons. He saw us as having let him down, as had his parents, but I'm sure he never realized how much like his father he had become.

A father's abusive use of alcohol had reached down through the generations, damaging not only T. J.'s childhood and emotional development (as well as his sister's), but also T. J.'s own marriage and parenting abilities. It had reached out to effect my judgment and actions, both during and after our marriage, and spewed onto our children. I had tried to protect my children at all costs, but my dream of building a home for them was shattered; their lives were shattered.

The effects from alcohol abuse may differ, but the results are just as destructive. There are connections regarding alcohol, both men, and both marriages. One husband was alcoholic; the other was the child of an alcoholic. Bill wanted me back; T. J. wanted me gone. Bill's anger was turned inward upon himself; T. J.'s turned outward onto me and his sons.

I think it was more difficult for our children to accept my position in the divorce. Their father had been the vocal parent and often absent; his behavior was already unpredictable. But I was always there. I had been the typical "super-mom," providing rides, money, stylish clothes, a clean house, well-balanced meals, and social and educational opportunities. Even though I might lose my patience at times, I was still the available parent.

Our children saw me as pleasant and subservient. I did my crying when I was alone or in the bathroom at night, with the door closed so no one could hear me. I really believed no one should know when I was in pain or distress, and I never thought about the consequences of that. I'd learned long ago to hide my pain for fear of more pain through disapproval.

Perhaps I should have yelled and screamed in front of them. If the children hadn't believed things were always okay, it might not have been such a shock to them when I moved out. It had become a loveless home, but by trying to hide all unpleasantness, it looked to the children as if I had become insincere, deceiving them all those years, when my only intent had been to protect them from marital problems which I believed (and had been told) were all my fault and would blow over with time. Instead, they saw my action as betrayal and responded by rejecting me. The more they rejected me, the more unsure I became of them and of myself, and I withdrew even more.

Parents have great power over a child who trusts them, and an unscrupulous one can take unfair advantage of this by maligning the absent parent with insinuations, vague remarks, body language (rolling eyes, shrugging shoulders), and/or outright dismissal. It's then easy to plant suspicions into a child's mind which can destroy the relationship especially if the absent parent's silence (from trying not to cause more conflict in the child's life) is then misinterpreted by the child as a "lack of caring."

That's much different from the parent or person who refuses to speak or make any contact, never writes or calls, and makes no attempt at all to understand, reconcile, or forgive, all without any explanation. That action, if indeed deliberate, is the cruelest of mental cruelties when directed toward a child, parent, or spouse, because with vindictive emotional and mental abuse, no one wins—everyone loses. To plant hate, suspicion, and distrust in a child's mind is a most insidious and malicious form of child abuse. It serves only to deprive the child and leaves lasting scars on his or her heart. T. J.'s intent was to hurt me, but by deliberately damaging the mother–child bond, the children suffered the most.

The responsible response is not one of total withdrawal or total smothering, but a balance of unconditional love, acceptance, and attention—a message that says, "I'll always be here for you no matter how you feel about me," rather than the damaging ultimatum: "I'm on your side only if you accept me and reject her (or him)." Both parents, when separated, should reinforce love for the absent parent. That natural bond should be nurtured for the child's sake, not destroyed for vengeance's sake.

I had married Bill two years after my divorce, while my two teenagers were still in turmoil. I was trying very hard to rectify my relationship with them at the time but with little success. "What can I do?" I wailed to Bill. "Well, you just love 'em, honey," he had answered. "You just love 'em and wait for them to know it."

Following Bill's comment, I had confronted Daryl, who had suffered the most during childhood from his father's and my anxieties. I had explained that it was important to him that he not go through life "dragged down" by crippling memories and invited him to tell me everything that I'd done or said throughout his life that had hurt or angered him. I wanted to understand how he thought and felt, and why. I listened to everything he said without interruption except to affirm or acknowledge, and asked only that he listen to me in return.

I told him, "While I may not be the parent you wanted or needed, that doesn't mean I don't love you. There were things I thought I had to do in order to survive; I may have reacted out of fear or ignorance, but it was never my intent to hurt or deceive any of you. I've never plotted to deprive you of anything or laughed at your pain. Yes, you've suffered in some areas, but if you think about it, you may see that you have profited in others. In any case, it serves no purpose for you to carry endless resentments other than to make yourself bitter."

I explained to him what sort of a mother–son relationship I'd like for us to have if he could or wanted to, and I gave him permission to refuse any part or all of it. I didn't mean it was okay to treat me shabbily or disrespectfully (certainly I wanted to know how he was, and to be remembered from time to time). My goal was to offer him unconditional love and acceptance, and respect his right to accept or refuse it without incriminations, demands, or expectations from me.

I gave him time to think about it and test me. As a result, our relationship took a major turn and is still healing. The time and risk invested were worth it. During those times just before and after Bill's death, Daryl was more than a son; he was a best friend.

Sometimes, we can clean up those skeletons ourselves, and sometimes we need help. A very special childhood memory just refused to heal and needed special attention. A counselor-friend guided me through a process of healing of the memories concerning one very painful childhood Christmastime memory. I recalled I had spied a large tricycle just like the one I wanted and had asked for under the tree. Thrilled with delight, I ran toward it, but before I could reach it, my mother stopped me and said, "Maybe that's not for you. (It was, in fact, for my little brother.) This is what Santa left for you," she said, and held out one of my long brown stockings filled with willow tree branches shaped into switches. My father pulled one of the switches out, when, hands behind me, I backed away from my parents and refused to take out the switch and hand it to him myself. When my maternal grandparents arrived later for Christmas dinner, I heard my grandmother ask, "What's wrong with Eleanora? She looks funny, and she won't let us touch her." "Oh, you know how spoiled and contrary she is," my mother answered. "She's mad because she didn't like her Christmas present. Don't pay attention to anything she tells you. It's all in her head."

My friend helped me to imagine the scene with a different ending. In this case, we visualized God in human form, who stepped in front of my parents, caught their hands, took the switches away from them, and said, "No! You will not hurt my child!" We then visualized God holding and comforting my parents as well as myself, because they couldn't have done that unless they were troubled themselves. If I could see God forgive them, then so could I.

Imagery of all kinds is centuries old and has often been believed to have various degrees of power. We have to be thoughtful when using this technique of healing of memories, because it is part of a process, not a cure-all for all disorders. But, used this way, coupled with special prayer, it was very helpful to me. I can still remember the Christmas incident in my mind, but I no longer feel the pain in my heart.

Following this memory healing, I knew that in order to understand my childhood and relationship with my parents, I must also understand their background, and I discovered that both of them had been abused and victimized as well. My paternal grandfather's back was injured at birth, and with his back slightly bent, he was the object of childhood curiosity and ridicule. A similar fate affected my grandmother, who at age three lost an eye when her father, in a drunken rage, knocked her into a knitting basket. A few years later, she was orphaned and sent to live with an aunt and uncle who were already raising one orphaned niece. My grandmother was young, alone, uneducated, naive, disfigured, and unwanted.

In that day, people with disfigurements were often ignored, hidden away, abused, or tolerated, rather than taught to overcome their handicap. Both my grandparents were rejected people, filled with anxiety, fear, shame, and anger, but also, I believe, endowed with good hearts and a deep respect for values and principles.

My grandmother, a petite, bright, artistic, curly-haired blond, found herself pregnant with my father at age sixteen, with no alternative but to spend the rest of her life in a tiny, four-room farm house. At the time of her death, she could count on her fingers the number of times she had been out of the county. She directed most of her repressed rage, grief, and frustration upon my father when he was still quite young.

In fact, all my mother had to do to make my father see red was to point out that I resembled his mother. It always worked; he would remember the pain of his childhood beatings and react. Just as my grandparents projected their pent-up rage and emotion onto him, my father projected much of his onto me when the resemblance was brought to his attention, and out came the razor strop. Somehow, though, even while still a child, I seemed to know in my heart that he was not really angry with me but was striking out at something else.

My mother's home life was quite different from the sometimes violent atmosphere my father and his brothers experienced. Her family's lifestyle was one of being proper, well-bred, always making a good impression. You could say anything you wanted behind someone's back, but never to his or her face, because "it might hurt their feelings." They truly never realized that what they thought to be considerate and proper was actually polite deceit.

While I was still a child, I observed that these relatives were very competitive for attention. At gatherings, they spent a great deal of time arguing over who was the poorest, sickest, had the most (or least), and who knew the most (the winner was usually the one who talked the loudest or longest). Another chunk of time was spent in bashing whoever was too absent or too dead to defend themselves. Once all that was settled, people relaxed and enjoyed themselves. They were well-educated, accomplished people and could be quite interesting.

To complicate matters, my mother contracted smallpox at only six weeks of age. The doctor had pronounced her dead, but an aunt disagreed and ordered two large basins of water—one hot and one cold. She then dipped the baby alternately into the basins. In a few moments, the shock of extreme temperature exposures began to work, and the baby began to wail. The baby, later to become my mother, had almost been buried alive.

One can look with horror at what nearly happened, but I believe her experience was much like being reborn. I once told her that God must have considered her special and wanted very much for her to live. She really liked that idea.

She recovered, but the pox left huge red pits on her face where it had not been bathed in the water. These scars faded with time, but as a child they caused her great suffering as an object of torment, teasing, ridicule, and shunning by other children. Her own younger sister joined in the jeering and often refused to walk on the same side of the street with her. She was left out of games, called names, chased, or avoided. Older kids threatened to "sell her to the Gypsies" and once tied her to a bridge support while the water was rising. She must have longed for friends who would be on "her side" to help her pay them back, or that her tormentors didn't exist. There is no pain like the pain of not being accepted by one's childhood peers.

My mother's parents were not physically abusive but must have been embarrassed with this disfigured child who was an object of curiosity. But either unable or ashamed to admit or express any negative feelings, they overcompensated, unaware of a subtle but strong, underlying message that quietly and politely pitied and shamed her for being as she was. Being shamed for the way one looks is the same as being shamed for existing.

Their response to her distress over the teasing was to tell her,

"Now, don't say anything back. Just let it go in one ear and out the other. Pretend it doesn't bother you." When she complied, she was told, "Now that's how good girls should act."

When her sister romped outside with other children and my mother was left to sit in the window and watch, her father only knew to give her pity rather than encouragement and skills to overcome her affliction. When her younger sister received new clothes because she wore the old ones out, my mother got new clothes because her sister did. Her sister received attention from their mother when she laughed and joked; my mother got their mother's attention when she was disruptive, emotional, or sick.

To my mother, material things came to mean love. She developed a variety of diversionary and defensive tactics, and built an impenetrable protective armor against an outer world she perceived to be cruel and threatening, and against a real inner world she couldn't or wouldn't face. From there, she could survive despite her childhood tormentors. Also, by transference, perhaps, she could hang onto an unforgiving spirit toward those early tormentors.

Her parents' inability (whether from ignorance or indifference) to help her feel lovable and accepted, and gain insight into her situation, prevented her from developing a sense of self-worth, pride, and the ability to handle life without strife; she did not learn to focus on her many creative talents; her love for beautiful things, her knack for entertaining, her stamina, strong spirit, and intelligence. Many of her life choices and actions were based only on her feelings, not objective judgment.

Early psychological and mental wounds, when left unattended, can produce a person filled with repressed remorse and jealousy, and afraid of growth or change, which can lead to a crippling self-centeredness in which one never sees one's own guilt or learns to forgive one's self or others. As long as one fails to forgive, the appetite for revenge will not be satisfied. But it seems to me that regardless of the past and its influence, there should come a time of accountability, when excuses should be put aside. Perhaps the greatest mistake one can make is to be unwilling to be open to insight and self-assessment.

It is normal to be angry with anyone who shame or ridicule us for having a defect, for not measuring up, or whatever. It is normal to be angry with oneself for having the perceived defect. It is also normal to resent being unable to express those feelings—whether from inner fear or outward circumstances—and to resent being unable to retaliate against an injustice or oppressor.

Unfortunately, it is not unusual for one to project that frustration and shame in devious or vindictive ways upon someone who resembles one's self or symbolizes the resented persecutors from the past. After all, that repressed rage has to come out somewhere. Suppressed rage, from this kind of early teasing and rejection, can sink its fangs into a child's spirit, gaining a lifelong stranglehold of hate. Sometimes, hate festers until it kills someone; other times, it compensates by finding a symbol to punish.

For example, for my mother to pretend that I "didn't exist" was symbolic of pretending her childhood tormentors didn't exist. In hurting or laughing at me, she could at least experience the satisfaction of hurting or laughing at them in return. Perhaps she imagined what those girls might have felt if she were to die while they were teasing her. I think that's what she may have meant the many times she said to me, "You'll be sorry, someday. When you see me in my casket, you'll know you killed me." When I sat alone in my trailer, longing to be included in some family gathering, it was the reversal of her experience. Now, she was part of a crowd and the symbol of her tormentors was left out and alone, watching from the window.

I can understand why I would be a likely symbol, because I was a girl and I was small, as were all the threatening females in both my parents' lives. When the doctor told my mother that she was going to have a girl, her response was an emphatic and furious "Oh, no, I'm not!" And here I was a girl after all, like her sister and the other little girls who whispered and snickered, and whose cruelty she always remembered.

For most of my life, I tried to make things easier for my parents to make up for having been born and for what it cost them to raise me. T. J. was aware of this and did not mind using his vacations throughout our marriage to help my parents with farmwork, remodeling, and so on. I think he very much enjoyed being with my dad. But, after fourteen years, he called it quits. "Your dad always thanks us for our help," he said, "but your older brother has never lifted a finger to help like your dad and your younger brother do—so now it's his turn. I think your family accepts you now because you've got me to do things for them. Without me, you'd be of no use to them." (I now know that T. J. made this decision just after being discovered in the barn with our "friend.")

I heard him but couldn't believe the rapport I had finally achieved with my mother, after becoming a wife and mother myself, was simply because I had a husband and not for myself. Still in the back of my mind was the hope that, maybe now, I would be good enough; that my love for my parents would be as pleasing to them as that of my brothers and my two sisters-in-law.

Favoritism is as unfair to the favored person as it is to the unfavored. Siblings who witness abuse may believe they must keep it secret (thereby becoming unwitting accomplices), which in turn, encourages their denial of the situation. Some favored siblings may find themselves in a position, where, in their own best interest they feel they must conspire with the troubled, abusive parent. To defend the unfavored would be to risk their favored position, and be forced to choose between their conscience and their own need for acceptance.

For me, knowledge is always a key to understanding and forgiving. Knowing my parents' backgrounds, I could empathize with the pain they had suffered, and that helped explain how they related to me. I could understand, sympathize, and make allowances—but it didn't justify things or stop them from hurting.

Then, as I said, sometimes God takes a hand in the healing of old memories. It happened years later, when my father was hospitalized regarding a heart problem. One morning, he called and asked me to come and see him. Surprised, pleased, and curious, I went to see him. He seemed ill at ease but glad to see me. We discussed his condition, the weather, and all the little chores on the farm that he had finished up prior to this hospital stay. "I got the porch trellis fixed but didn't have time to dig up the garden," he said, then fell silent.

Finally I said, "I was really surprised when you called me. Do you realize we've barely talked to each other since I graduated three years ago, sold my trailer, and moved into town?"

"Yeah, I guess that's right," he answered.

"I figured you and Mom disapproved because I went on to graduate school. I know you approve of education, because you went to college—and there are nieces and cousins who are getting an education. I never could figure out why you were so opposed to my being in college."

"Well," he said, "it seemed like it should have been the boys—Mom and I gave them everything we could, and they didn't get to go." He paused. "We also thought you were too old. But I noticed several other older women in your class." He paused again, started to say something, and then stopped. "Is there anything you want to talk about?" he finally asked.

I couldn't believe my ears. He usually stopped me from talking—now he was encouraging me. I decided to take advantage of the chance and took a deep breath. "Yes, there is something I want to ask about. I've never understood why you, Mom, my brother, and his family all went out to eat after my graduation ceremony and didn't want me to come along. That really hurt."

Sitting there in the hospital room, waiting for him to answer, I could remember the incident as if it had just happened. My parents, older brother, and his family had been standing in the lobby following the ceremony when I joined them, carrying my cap, gown, and certificate. We stood around and talked a bit, and then my brother said, "Well, we're going out to eat." He hesitated. "What are you going to do?"

My breath caught in my throat. Then I stuttered. "What do you mean? Are you saying you don't want me to come along?" They looked at one another and finally my mother said, "We figured you had other plans."

"No, I don't," I said. "I just assumed I'd go with all of you." More silence. "Well, I guess you can come if you want to," said my brother.

"Noo-no," I said, tears welling up in my eyes. "I guess I'd better not."

"Well, let's go then," someone said briskly, and like a flock of birds, they were off.

I don't know how long I stood there. I had been so excited—so sure I'd done something right—so sure they would share this triumph with me. But, it had happened again. I had fallen right into the role of rejected Eleanora, without the nerve or foresight to have reacted any other way. Why hadn't I laughed it off and gone along anyway? I despised my helplessness and willingness to be so easily manipulated. "When am I ever going to learn?" I asked myself. "Here I am, over forty-five years old and still crying over my family's behavior."

Then suddenly, while still standing in the lobby and watching them head toward the door, I had found myself being drawn farther back in time to a similar memory of bewilderment and desolation. I was almost five years old and was standing on a wooden porch behind my mother, watching her play with my year-old brother. Just learning to walk, he was toddling around her; they were laughing and hugging each other. I wanted with all my heart to join them but held back, fearing something—I don't know what.

Finally, the desire to show her that I loved her, too, was so strong that it overcame the knot of fear in my heart. Looking back, I could see myself walking forward, putting my arms around her neck, and kissing her cheek. "Oh, no," she had yelled, jerking away, and upsetting my brother, who started to cry. "Watch out, will you—what are you trying to do?" She shoved me back with her arm, picked up my brother, and ran into the house. As the screen door closed, I heard her saying, "There, there, now. That was a bad sister. We'll leave her out there, and Daddy will spank her when he comes home."

The memory of this intense feeling of despair overwhelmed me again, standing there alone in that huge lobby, watching the door my parents, brother, and his family had gone through. I felt erased—blotted out. Tears finally streamed down my face as I sobbed for both the lonely and bewildered little girl *and* grown woman who stood—stunned and mute—staring at closed doors— anguish and heartache a monstrous hovering thing.

Why am I trying so hard to be part of this family? I wondered. I'm no longer a dependent child. What, other than blood ties, keeps bothering me? "Could it be," I asked myself aloud, "that it's important to me to be accepted simply because I'm not? Is that what I'm trying so hard to control?"

As I pondered that question, I felt something snap—and then a tugging or pulling, an insistent moving away—like the shedding of a lifetime. Something tremendous was happening to me and for me. In a new light, I saw my belief that "if I changed my attitude toward them, they'd change their attitude toward me" begin to fade away and be replaced with the knowledge that what I needed to do was change my attitude toward me—and separate my real needs from what I thought I wanted.

It was an old lesson, first heard in the hospital fifteen years earlier, and seemingly needing to be learned over and over. I *knew* I would never feel hurt by any of them again; *not* because my heart had hardened, but because it had healed. With that insight, I was finally, fully released. I really wanted to live my life for me, at last.

There in the hospital room, with my father, I recalled those two moments of rejection and the extreme opposite changes they had brought about within me. "But, it wasn't right to leave me there like that," I said aloud to my dad, pulling my mind back into the present.

"I know that now," he answered, thinking I was referring to just graduation. "Mom and some of the others said you didn't want to be with us because you think you are so much smarter and better than the rest of us."

"That just isn't true," I said. "I wanted to be with my family."

"Where did you go?" he asked after a short silence. "I went to Faye's house and helped her." Faye was a friend, who, together with Joyce, had planned a graduation reception for me that afternoon. "Well, we came to that, didn't we?" he asked.

"Yes, you did, and I was glad to see all of you," I said. "By the way, do you remember what my aunt said to me there?" He didn't. "Well, as she was leaving, she said, 'Now, Eleanora, do you think maybe now you can settle down like a woman your age should, and get a job, maybe in a factory or something?'"

"Oh?" he said and glanced at me sideways. "I didn't know she had actually said that to you." Apparently the subject had been a matter of family discussion, for my dad was surprised not at what she had said, but that she'd said it to me.

"In fact," I told him, "I probably would have found a job then if she hadn't said that. I had been undecided about graduate school, but because of that remark, I enrolled the following week." Suddenly, he was chuckling, and his expression surprised me. It occurred to me that perhaps he had never really disapproved of my spunk after all; maybe he felt pressured to go along with the "family tide." Then I recalled other times when we were alone like this and had talked—when he didn't seem to be mad at me at all, as he was when the family was around.

Now, I saw he was inviting me to talk again. I plunged ahead. "You were right when you agreed I shouldn't have been left that way," I said, "but I've turned some things like that around and maybe wouldn't have accomplished some good things if it hadn't been for events like that in my life. I've always felt as if you and Mom did all you could to keep me from existing in the minds and lives of the family, and when I protested, you blamed or punished me. I can't help it I was born a girl, but how long will it take to get even with me? Does anyone realize how self-defeating it is when people 'choose sides' against others? What will it take for the family to want to understand, reconcile, and repair the damage to everyone?"

My dad continued to sit quietly and listen—not scolding me as he usually did when I tried to talk. Finally, he looked up. "But what could I do?" he blurted out. "I know things have been done and said that weren't right, but what else could I do? I always just tried to keep peace, to keep people from scolding your mother as well."

Having finally gotten up the nerve to speak, he continued in the same forceful tone of voice. "I want you to know, I've told Mom that all three of you kids are to know all about everything, so you can all three work together to take care of her—that all three of you are to be treated exactly the same—and she promised it will be that way." He had enunciated each word and watched me intently as he spoke, imploring me to understand.

And I did. My father was by nature a fair and just man, as well as unassuming, unaffected, and unpretentious. It was not in him to be deliberately scheming or conniving. He was telling me he had not willingly compromised those values where I was concerned; it had not always been his choice to act as he had during family dissension, but he had held back, not knowing what else to do. I realize that as a parent, perhaps he had felt as trapped by fear and ignorance as had I as a parent. He had protected me, protected and pacified my mother, and pacified in-laws as much as he could.

He was also promising me I need not fear I would be disinherited as my brothers wanted; he was saying—promising me—that no one, not myself or my children, would be cheated in anyway. He was assuring me he was still concerned about my welfare. (I recalled the times I had found garden vegetables on my doorstep and how he had cosigned the loan for my car following my divorce.) These were the best ways he knew to make amends and let me know I was as important to him as my brothers. I reached out to touch his hand, to reassure him that I no longer needed to press my point—that it was okay. He didn't owe me an apology about anything. "Believe me," I said, "I really do understand. Thank you."

Having both had our say, we sat quietly and made a couple of attempts at small talk. Then I had an idea. "How would you like to talk to Becky?" I asked. "I can call from here and have it charged to my home number." He was delighted. My daughter has a way of sparkling at people, especially at this grandfather whom she adored, and he always had a special rapport with her. He seemed to be comfortable with her in the way I want to think he would liked to have been with me.

Watching him laugh and chatter on the phone with my daughter, it occurred to me that maybe God gives some people the gift of long life because they live it so well; maybe others live on and on because they are being given every chance to repent and make amends. It must be horrible to grow very old, sick, and alone, and still be filled with suspicion, self-pity, malice, or a vindictive heart, and to die without peace of mind and a clear conscience.

If I added together the ages of both my parents and myself, it would come to over 200 life-years in which we each had been given a choice—free will—to live life in enjoyment and thanksgiving for each and every family member, or to spend that time in unresolved, unconfronted, misdirected, and disabling fears, re-sentments, self-pity, and jealousy over real or imagined injustices. What a waste to not reach out for the former. My father, as best he could, had taken advantage of the opportunity to make amends before it was too late. My father was—very much—a gentleman.

"I'm leaving now," I said, interrupting a chuckle over some-thing Becky had said. "Talk as long as you want." He grinned at me and waved. It was the last time I saw him alive. With that experience—when my father reached out to me that way—I could sit back and reflect.

I realized that Bill's suicide, my childhood, my first marriage, and the current family situation all had a big factor in common. They all contained some form of unresolved abandonment; all were deliberate withdrawals from my life by someone I loved, and whom I wanted to love me. It's no wonder I missed Bill so much and felt such despair and anger for so long following his death. Bill had been the substitute for an entire family. Several years my senior, I had found in Bill the parental, nurturing traits of affirma-tion, encouragement, and acceptance of myself as I was. But also with him I experienced the laughter, games, and bantering com-panionship of siblings, without every comment being taken as a personal insult. I could fuss over him as I no longer could over my kids—and he liked my being a girl.

In addition to fun, he gave me loyalty—not just lip service—but real loyalty, the kind where I knew he would come to my defense. I'd always envied that in other families. With Bill, I expe-rienced the ability to trust that this loyalty would always be there, regardless of his drinking. I knew he wouldn't lie about me or make fun of me.

During the good times with Bill, I felt as if I'd finally found trust and comfort, only to lose it in just a few short years. How-ever, there was another reason I had worked so hard to save the marriage. One of the most valuable insights to come from that time of reflection was to realize I was not a weak, needy person who was asking for, or wanting, abuse all those years, but rather, I was strong enough to be willing to work for and toward all relationships I valued, regardless of resistance and untruths.

I am not an attractive woman. I am short, plump, and plain. But I have been an easy target for two insecure men who were controlled by their addictions and needed someone to control. I had been trained from birth to please, to give in to others and to never complain or defend my own rights.

Because of those traits, both men were able to take a great deal from me; yet both also gave me a great deal. T. J. exploited those traits and pushed me to the edge with sexual demands, and the cutting jabs, snide put-downs, and criticism that destroy love and respect so completely.

I had known T. J. since childhood, dated him at age seventeen, married him before he went to Korea, and had expected to stay married. And good things happened: building a home, starting a family, memorable holidays and vacations, camping, scouts, Indian Guides, dancing lessons, and the list goes on. Because of all that, the children and I deserved better than to be selfishly discarded as we were.

Bill, however, probably saved my life in spite of being so emotionally needy himself and violent when drunk. He never abused me sexually or plotted (at least when sober) to undermine my self-image or relationships with my children or parents. He comforted me when my heart ached for the pain and loss my children were suffering, supported me when I was alone and frightened, and we could laugh together.

With Bill, I experienced true love, and belief and acceptance in myself. When he took his life, he left me with no choice but to find mine and make it worthwhile. With T. J., I shared a precious part of my life's history, and on some level, despite our years of divorce, I always remained married to him. T. J. was my husband; Bill was the love of my life.

Grieving over the loss of Bill was easy in some respects compared to grieving over the older loss of acceptance. It helped to know I was resolving more than one issue in my life. Bill's death had unleashed this other, hidden heartache that may never have had the opportunity to heal otherwise. Together, the two grieving processes were tough, but they had to be experienced in order to break the bondage.

Generations of family dysfunction had finally driven one of us to the limit. I could no longer be part of the game of judging one another with assumptions and insinuations, and then denying having done it. I had to break free—to confront the shame and the shamers head on—and Bill's suicide had given me the insight and incentive to do so. I realized that if I had not been forced to deal with my childhood and first marriage, I would probably not have developed the insight and compassion to begin the ministry of Ray of Hope. In that sense, I could thank God for my past—not for the pain but for what I had become and could now do because of it.

The entire experience was the catalyst for an incredible soul-searching experience. I spent a great deal of time searching for triggering factors, underlying causes, and the meaning of priorities. Gradually, I realized I was beginning to perceive things differently—that relationships are too fragile to jeopardize, and time too precious to waste with petty judgments. I learned not to blame people for what they didn't know or couldn't do. In my great need, I'd been looking to my earthly family for the total, unconditional love and acceptance only my heavenly father, as I perceived him, could give.

I was finally—albeit slowly—getting my expectations and priorities straight concerning others, myself, and God. I had been to hell and back, and I knew where heaven was. Hell was living in the presence of hate, of destructive feelings and forces; heaven with living in the presence of love, forgiveness, and healing. In order for forgiveness to come full circle, I had to give love fully, even if it was not given in return. When I felt as free with my family as I did away from them—when I no longer felt as if I had to walk on eggs around them—then I was free of being the underdog.

I learned a great deal about myself. I discovered strengths and resources I didn't know I had and maybe would not have developed otherwise. I had not realized the extent of my mental toughness. Now, I figure I have calluses on the brain. God help the doctor if I ever need brain surgery, or he'll never get through the scar tissue. But that's okay. It means something has pushed me beyond insurmountable odds which could have destroyed another. A lot of my toughness was born in anger (another issue on my list of things to be resolved).

Anger is interesting. A friend once said, "People told me to get angry. So I did, and it just made me mad all the time. I got so sick of the misery I couldn't stand myself." There's a Sanskrit wisdom that says the anger of a good person lasts an instant, that of a meddler for two hours, that of a base man for a day and a night, and that of a great sinner until death. In Ephesians, the Scripture says to be angry but not to sin. The feeling of anger is normal; the way it's dealt with can hurt oneself or another. That can be sin.

Undirected, misdirected, or denied anger can turn into a ball of energy that burns us up inside, until we are just a shell filled with ashes. Then, when insight and an idea are at hand, we can do nothing, because we are only ashes. Perhaps this is the meaning behind the idea that hate hurts the hater more than it does the hated. I believe that strong denial of anger (or guilt or hatred or whatever) is often evidence of its existence. Better to mobilize all that energy. Summon it, harness it, and direct it toward correcting an injustice; make is useful in a positive way.

Things were settled with my mother when I took a six-year leave of absence from ROH to be her guardian. Crippled with arthritis and suffering from dementia (*not* Alzheimer's), she lost her ability to make judgment decisions but not her memory. While sorting through boxes of papers and photos, as she loved to do, I came to know her as someone other than my mother. We journeyed through her life as a lonely little girl, a typical teenager in love with life, and a new bride in love with my father.

As I listened, I realized that although my birth had been unwelcome and difficult at the time (I had a twin who died during the seventh month), Mom had not resented me as much as I had believed, especially when I grew older. She said she never worried about losing me in the same way she feared losing her sons to their wives. She had given in to Jude's demands because she'd learned that Jude would slap her if she didn't. Too late, Mom realized that catering to Jude's bullying had not prevented the loss of her youngest son anyhow, and she gave up hoping for the relationship to mend. It was, after all, what Irving and Jude wanted.

During the time I cared for her, we saw a neurologist, who tested for the degree of dementia. He told me that she had possibly suffered some slight brain damage in the frontal or temporal lobe areas as a result of the high fever and coma accompanying the small pox during her early infancy. He said this could account for some of her behavior over the years such as the frustrated emotional outbursts, the inability to develop insight, and being so easily influenced. I believe she must have been often falsely accused of some things she could not help.

Mom maintained a strong bond with Norman, her oldest son, and with good reason. He accepted her without condemnation and was always there when she needed him. She wanted to be good to the son who was good to her, and I can understand that.

In caring for my mother, I decided that every time I felt angry or remembered a hurt from the past, I would counterbalance it with a kind act in the present. It turned out to be an incredible healing time for both of us.

When Mom was hospitalized with a broken hip, Norman held her hand and prayed for her the evening before she died. Flowers from my daughter and granddaughter were on the bedstand. She died the following morning just four minutes after I arrived—she had waited for *me* to be there with her. My memory closet is at rest.

Following Bill's death, I had lost that exuberant innocence when life is everything—when death is only a fantasy and you're sure you really are immortal. I had encountered mortality head-on, in a sobering but realistic way causing me to question the sanctity of life. I had lost the will to fight for the sheer fun of it. I wanted that exuberance back, not to fight for the fun of it—but to fight for the right of it.

With action, the anger dissipated. Resolving guilt wasn't much different. I was just so sick and tired of having it, and that helped. I knew, however, that guilt also had to be transformed into

something else. Someone once said that his sense of guilt intensified his pain but eventually became his deliverance. In that
sense, guilt can be used to bring about a change.

Thank God for good guilt; it leads to growth. When people
have the capacity for guilt, it means they also have the ability to
feel empathy, compassion, love, and respect for self and others.
With proper channeling of guilt, we can promote healing and
growth; with denial of any guilt at all (i.e., "Now, don't feel
guilty"), we risk the danger of creating a ruthless people without
conscience. It's important to make a distinction. The same is true
concerning shame. Shame is feeling bad about who we are; guilt is
feeling bad about what we do.

It's the wrong perception and wrong use of guilt, such as
using it to shame someone, that destroys. When I blamed myself
for Bill's suicide, I was overwhelmed with a guilt and denial I
could not rise above. When I realized I could take responsibility
for any of my actions—intentional or unintentional—even though
Bill may have allowed them to influence his decision, I experienced a new release. Many different things and people may have
influenced Bill's actions, but no one thing or person was to blame.
Being responsible and taking blame are not the same thing. I think
that's what some people are really trying to say to survivors when,
in an effort to offer comfort, they say the suicided person "had a
choice."

Just as it had not been possible to build my first marriage on
self-abasement and apology, nor the second one on someone else's
strengths, neither could I build a future for myself without stripping away all that fogged my mind and spirit. I had heard it takes
an extraordinary person to incorporate the limits of pain and rise
above it. I wanted to be extraordinary if I could.

Surely, my children felt as rejected, betrayed, and abandoned
by the divorce as I did from what I perceived as parental and
family disapproval and Bill's suicide, but in their lives as well as
mine, the adverse circumstances gave them a strength to be proud
of. They each possess a sense of self which is not affected by
anything they perceive as bribery, flattery, guilt trips, or coercion
from anyone, including family, and I respect that, even if it sepa-

rates us at times. They are self-sufficient, tolerant, open-minded survivors, not whiners, complainers, or manipulators. True, they got there through adversity and necessity rather than informed guidance, but they got there, scar tissue and all.

I believe we do not exist to the fullest unless we know ourselves. Some people cope by seeking insight; some cope by avoiding it, but without insight, we rob ourselves of honesty. If we are not honest with ourselves, the lies we tell ourselves will go with us into death. I want all my family and children to be free of that. So I continue to involve myself—if only through prayer.

The primary question—what I wanted most for myself—was easy to answer. I wanted that quality of spirit which comes with knowing I have both given to life and taken from it graciously. I wanted the peace of mind which comes with knowing I have a destiny, knowing the things I must do are more important than I am. This destiny is the continuum I leave to my children. It's a cord, a center, something they will carry on, even if they don't realize it.

I knew I had that peace of mind and spirit when I realized something had melted the icy casing within. My earlier resolve never again to allow myself to love anyone so much that I could be hurt so much was gone; I was willing to be vulnerable again. I knew I was a new person, operating on a different level of consciousness; I wanted to reach out and hug heaven.

Ray of Hope's ministry is a gift from God—to others through me. This new sense of self-worth was Bill's gift to me and it reflects his faith in me when he said, "Walk tall and hold your head high, little lady. You're a Ross now."

2

❖

In Their Own Words

The question "Why did they do it?" seems to elude all of us in the final analysis. We tell ourselves that the real answer died with the victim. But, I wonder, did it really?

— A Survivor

Note: The following stories and comments from other survivors could not be more heartfelt or eloquent than when told in their own words.

My Husband

My husband, a psychiatrist, overdosed on an antidepressant drug after writing his own prescription. Although he helped heal the minds of others, he was unable to heal himself; he had attempted suicide several times. As a result, I lived in constant fear, overwhelmed and frustrated by my own helplessness. Two years before his death, I began this journal, where I poured out my feelings of anger, self-pity, love, confusion, and pain. Excerpts from the journal show the transitions that took place as I struggled to survive.

September 1977

My heart stopped when I heard an announcement on the radio that a young man had been killed in a car accident this afternoon. My husband didn't go to work this morning, and all day I've been waiting for the call that says he's in the hospital again or even dead. Whenever he's home alone, I worry about what he's going to do. It's not an easy way to live. I don't know how to handle it except to keep trying to live as normally as possible. I've almost accepted the fact that it will happen someday, but it doesn't make it any easier to face. I may not look it to other people, but I think I'm going crazy.

October 1977

How do I feel about all of this? And why am I staying? All I feel when I'm with him is anger and fear. I don't want to go home at night. I dread weekends. I'm exhausted, and all I want to do is sleep. I can't even cry any more. I scream inside. But I can't leave. I don't know how much more I can take. I take it by blocking it all out. All he gives me these days is pain. I'm constantly waiting for the call that says he's killed himself. I expect to find him dead at home.

November 1978

It seems strange to me. Why do we tiptoe so carefully around each other's feelings, steering clear of each other's emotions? Why do we keep this glass wall between us? Are we both so fragile we can't face each other without fear that one of us will break? Are you afraid of me? I'm afraid of you. I'm afraid of being swallowed alive by you, and yet no one has ever meant as much to me as you do.

March 1979

He did it. I wasn't there. I found him.

May 1979

The pain is so great sometimes, it is actually physical. Other times, I feel nothing but numbness. I always thought suicide wasn't the answer for me, but now, at times, I see it as reasonable. I hurt so badly, I don't think I can stand it. I wonder why I should have to.

May 1979

It bothers me that he was alone when he died. I wish he had let me be there. I wish I had held his hand and talked to him before I called the police. I want to erase that lost, empty look on his face, and make myself believe he achieved what he was looking for. I want to tell him I understand, that I know how much he suffered, and I understand his need to end that suffering. As time goes by, I understand it even more.

June 1979

Mornings are so difficult. I'm more vulnerable then.

July 1979

The last weeks have been frantic with going places, drinking, partying until all hours, being with people, and forgetting. I know this won't last. It's just something I need right now.

November 1979

At times like these I sit and cry, wondering why this had to happen to me. What did I do to deserve this? And I ask him, "Why did you do this to me?" Why did he have to go away and leave me to face this messed-up world by myself? We belong together. Can I make it alone?

August 1980

Maybe after all this time, I'm letting go. Everybody else thinks I already have, except for a few people who know better. It's a very long, extremely painful process. In some ways, I don't want to let go. But I guess my mind and body, nature, God, whatever, view survival differently.

June 1981

My husband seemed to be pursued by demons I could never comprehend. He did not feel "unworthy" or "bad," but rather, that he was a misfit without a niche in this world. He was afraid others would take something from him. He was angry and frustrated by this power, real or imagined, that others had over him. His depressions were painful and frightening to watch but his occasional, almost manic, highs were exhilarating and drew people around him. He played a great part in shaping my adult life, and was a man whom I loved and respected. Therefore, one thing I must consider is that his choice was rational and proper for him in his thinking.

July 1981

His suicide was the ultimate rejection of me and my efforts to help him. There's also the element of my contribution to his death. I am human. I often was angry when he needed sympathy; cold when he needed my love. I built barriers to protect myself from the pain he caused me. When I could no longer cope, and needed my own private space, I turned away from him. Now I have to deal with that guilt, and learn to accept my own human frailties.

August 1981

I'm angry. What gave him the right to hurt all of us who loved him so much? I feel cheated and abused. He made his dreams mine and then snatched them away. How dare he?

October 1981

All goes well in my life. I'm buying a house, getting A's in school, and will attend graduate school. I have as many dates as a young, single woman could want. Friends ask me to join in their fun, or just talk. My life seems to have a good balance of fun, work, future plans, even security. So what is missing? I recently took part in a friend's wedding. I want that. I want it back, that special relationship—to love and be loved. That's simple enough, isn't it?

May 1984

As of last week, I'm no longer a graduate student! I'm fairly amazed at myself! Five years ago, I said I was going to buy a house and go back for my Master's degree. I did both!

December 1984

I've been rereading this old journal and it's time for another addition. It's worth noting that most of these writings were done at my lowest. I still remember how I felt when I was writing, and how much better I felt afterwards. Since my husband died, I've worked, gone to graduate school, and developed deep, loving friendships. Next week, I will start a job in another state. While reading the old journal, I was struck how often, both before and after my husband's death, I doubted my sanity and wished my life would end. Now, I want to live for as long as I can. And I'm sane (well, mostly!). I still get depressed, frightened, and frustrated.

There will be more bad times. I will lose people and wish I had told them, "I love you." People will hurt me; I will hurt them and feel guilty. I will feel all of those petty emotions of anger, jealousy, envy, and more, and regret them. I will feel more insecurity and loneliness. But I also know, even if I don't believe it sometimes, that I will survive. It's good to know that.

—C. S.

My Mom

On a bright Monday morning, I followed my sister, Peg, into the garage, but upon entering the garage, I stopped. Something was wrong. Then I realized I was staring at a vacuum cleaner hose stretching from the exhaust pipe of the car to a window. My mother lay inside, bundled in her red corduroy coat. She looked as if she were sleeping. I shouted and began pulling at the door. It wouldn't open. My sister rushed over and yanked the hose from the window. The door opened. In all the noise and confusion, my mother never stirred.

I was ten when my mother committed suicide. Many years have passed, and although I vividly recall the events leading up to the discovery of her body, much of what happened in the ensuing hours and days seems lost or obscure. I remember meeting my father in the hall on his way to meet the ambulance. We hugged each other, wordless. Later that morning, I overheard him being interviewed by a state trooper, and was astonished to hear that my mother had received psychiatric care several years earlier. The trooper then asked if my mother had done or said anything the previous night to indicate she planned to commit suicide. I remember only that she had seemed unusually happy and serene.

My mother was an attractive, energetic woman in her midforties, and was passionately devoted to her family. Like many women of her generation, she defined her accomplishments according to her duties as mother, wife, and homemaker. My own recollections of her are based more on youthful impressions than understanding, but from relatives and my sister, I've learned that the last years of my mother's life were increasingly marked by change and stress.

During the previous five years, she'd had two surgeries and believed she was developing cancer. My father had been promoted to head a new division for his company, and the pressures of his new job made him withdrawn and demanding. Finally, with each passing day, my mother saw her children growing up and away from her.

Although embarrassed by her lack of education, she joined an elite community service. Elected to vice-president after a short time, it was an indication that her talents compared well with those of college-educated women. As she became more assertive, she got into arguments with my father. She also discovered that her relationships with women on the board were changing. Some of them resented her, and my mother complained that she was being betrayed by her friends. Less than a year after winning the vice-presidency, she decided to resign.

She died the night before she was to deliver her resignation speech. That same evening, a family argument had upset her, but later, however, she seemed calm. Peg's last memory of mother alive, is of her sitting in the family room watching TV and holding her "worry stone" in her hand.

Words cannot convey the shock, the disbelief, the numb emptiness caused by my mother's suicide. As weeks passed, my family adjusted and our lives took on a more normal rhythm; but we had undergone a far-reaching change. Our father remarried a year later, we moved away, and he has never mentioned her name since.

Many relatives and friends offered solace for my family the next few weeks, but within months, my mother's name was dropped from all family conversation. Recently, one relative, who had been particularly close to my mother, said this was the first time in seventeen years he had spoken of her to another family member.

Years later, Peg and I discovered that we still retraced the events of that night to see if there was some way we could have prevented her suicide; as if we had failed in some vital, unspoken responsibility. We also extended this responsibility to other family members. "I blamed myself and everybody else for not being there when Mom needed us," Peg said.

Peg's guilt was heavier because of the relief she felt. "For several months," she said, "Mom had been confiding in me, and I guess I felt that she put a burden on me that I really didn't want. I got tired of being a sounding board."

Peg also recalls the reaction of her co-workers. "About halfway through the first day, a woman told me that everyone had been very nervous about seeing me again. She said that I seemed the same as ever and thanked me because it made them feel a lot better."

Back in school, I recall a classmate telling me that her mother had seen me in the parking lot the day before, and identified me as "the boy who caused his mother to kill herself."

To this day, even casual questions about my family cause an ongoing debate in me over how much I should tell. I could be evasive, but somehow I resent the feeling that I should hide part of my past. Then, too, I loved my mother and was proud of her, and to refrain from talking about her seems like an act of betrayal. But explaining to a stranger, or even a friend, that my mother died of suicide has social consequences; the very least of them is an embarrassing silence.

For me, the one most enduring part of this legacy stems from a single question: Why? I doubt that I will ever fully understand why my mother chose to kill herself. I ask the question more from concern for my own future than curiosity about my past. Simply, I wonder whether I carry a seed of her despair.

I chose to write my story because I hoped that by talking about my mother, I might learn more about her and how she influenced my life. It seemed like a long shot, but it helped. I have a better understanding now of how tortured my mother really was, and how difficult it must have been for her to leave us. After all these years, the sting of my mother's death is still sharp. But because of what I know now, it hurts a little less.

—D. R.

My Sis

We were pulling our Ford Clubwagon into the farm lane when we saw the long black hearse parked by a shed. We knew that this time, her fourth suicide attempt, my only sister, my best friend, was dead. The newspaper reported that her body was recovered from the family-farm pond—her death ruled a suicide.

At her funeral I played the organ, the last gift I thought I could give her. Father said it was the hardest funeral he'd officiated in all his years of priesthood. A loving and creative lector suggested that the Prayers of the Faithful be from her husband, from each of her children, and her brother and sister.

I had always put my sis on a pedestal as being the strong one. She started out married life in a second-story apartment, with a hot plate and no running water. Eight of her ten children survived. Once, following a farm accident, when she nearly had to have her leg amputated, I was at her side almost every day, because I was a nursing student at the time. She said she didn't know how she'd have made it if I hadn't been there. I always thought if something happened to me, she'd be the one I'd trust to help with our two Fragile-X sons.

Before her suicide, she had undergone almost four months of treatment at a psychiatric unit with the usual locked doors, drug and talk therapy, and shock treatments. Why, oh why, hadn't I forced her—or at least been much more persuasive—in getting her to a therapist eighteen months earlier? I think she preferred death to the psych ward. When I read through my diary, I realize that hints were there all along.

- "She talked of ending it all."
- "Doesn't know if she can take depression any more."
- "She looks awful—so worried about her."

I knew mornings were her worst time of day; so I had given her money for long-distance calls, or told her to call me anytime, collect. Six months after her death, I still couldn't look at her picture. After months of therapy I still got angry with myself because I wasn't getting better faster. Why not? Everyone's life has tragedy. Darl's life had many.

I attended a spiritual retreat, met a nun who has a healing ministry, visited a counselor priest in Davenport, listen to *Healing the Family Tree* tapes, have read several books. My days off from work are structured to the hour to keep myself busy. Organ playing is therapeutic. My parish priest is not afraid to give me a hug. My husband, children, several cousins, and one niece in particular, have been supportive. Friends have invited me to call or talk anytime.

God? He's been both near and far away. I shout questions at him, and then later, an answer comes in the words of a song, or from a friend, or even a TV program.

While in high school, my sis had secretly given up a baby girl for adoption. When that girl later searched for, and found, her birth family, it unintentionally resulted in confusion. I pray constantly for family forgiveness and reconciliation.

In addition to counseling, I have found two ways to beat depression: help others (I get that through my profession), and keep my mind busy. It has worked in the past, but I'm older. Maybe one course at a time and try for a Master's. Just can't bear to look down the corridor of years without you, Sis. Thirty-five-plus years of breakfast together almost every Sunday between masses, a time to sum up the week and support each other. Thank God, I had you for fifty-eight years.

—Verabeth Bricker, Victor, Iowa

* * * * *

Note: Verabeth lives on a farm with her husband, three of their six children (two grown sons have Fragile-X syndrome), and numerous animals. At age sixty-seven, she received her M.A. in nursing and is working toward a second M.A. Some of the family estrangements are slowly dissolving.

My Lover

Over the years, I had plenty of warnings of what was to be Cliff's fate. We loved each other, but Cliff was unhappy most of the time and often talked of suicide. I remember feeling very alone during the last two years of our relationship, because nothing—not medication or psychiatric care—seemed to help him for very long. He withdrew from me, and more and more into workaholic behavior, even though it offered little or no emotional support. He saw life as increasingly unfair after several important career advances were denied him.

People often ask me if Cliff had AIDS. He did not. We were both monogamous, and neither of us had any HIV infection. I believed he had every reason to live, and that's why I need, and attend, a support group.

I first felt relief for Cliff when I learned of his death, almost five years after our separation, then complete numbness. I couldn't cry at all for the first two weeks; couldn't stop crying for the next four months. My siblings have always been supportive, as have Cliff's parents—more so than my own parents—who still cannot confront the fact that I am gay.

When people ask me how to help someone who has lost a loved one to suicide, I advise, "Let all feelings come to the surface. In feeling EVERYTHING—*love, hate, betrayal, loyalty, grief, forgiveness*—I believe one can ultimately "let" the deceased one go.

—*Larry Kaplan*

My Beautiful Daughter

On June 3, 1993, my thirty-six-year-old daughter, Susan Buhl Tulley, took her life. Although suffering from a deep depression, she never shared those feelings. Not living in the area at the time, I was unaware of the seriousness of her condition. Married, and the mother of two beautiful children, her death came as a complete shock to all who knew and loved her.

Hospitalized on Memorial Day weekend, she saw very little of her doctors, so remained in the hospital for observation until the holiday ended, when a more thorough diagnosis would be made. On Tuesday, the psychiatrist and attending female physician worked with her regarding her depressed state. Susan had no history of depression. Bright, talented, and outgoing, her childhood was happy, although her father and I had divorced when she was twelve. We learned during her sessions, that this was still very painful to her, even after twenty-five years. She and her husband were also experiencing some marital challenges, and this was very alarming to her. She kept a bright smile on her face, but inside, her heart was breaking.

On June 2, following two days of therapy, it was decided she could be released from the hospital the next day and be seen as an outpatient. On Thursday, June 3, her husband, doctor, and chaplain spent one hour with her. Susan seemed in good spirits, knowing she would go home for the weekend and return on Monday as an outpatient. She would be put on medication, her progress monitored.

After the meeting on June 3, her husband left the hospital to pick up their son from school. Susan returned to the psych ward, where they told her she could go for a walk around the hospital, because she was doing so much better. She went for that walk—which consisted of leaving the hospital, walking out into the neighborhood, and going into a stranger's garage. She poured gasoline on her clothes, set herself on fire, and died.

On that day, my life as I knew it ended also! For many days following this tragic event I prayed my own life would end. I really don't remember all that happened. I do know there was a terrible storm the day of her funeral, and over 1,200 people attended. Someone said that the angels must have cried, since it was the worst rainstorm in forty years.

Two weeks after her death, I realized I needed help if I was to survive. I saw a counselor weekly for the next year, and also drove 180 miles every week to attend a survivors of suicide meeting. It was very helpful to be with other survivors. Soon after the eight weeks of sessions ended, I met Karon Pfile from a local funeral chapel, who wanted to start a survivor group in our area. Together, we held a meeting for the public, and over seventy people attended. From that time on, we met bimonthly and later had the good fortune to meet Betsy Ross and learn about Ray of Hope chapters. We are now an active Ray of Hope group.

My grief process has been long and very difficult. It is my personal feeling that suicide must be talked about. Support groups were unheard of until the 1970s; today they provide great comfort and help. Society has made few strides in teaching people how to relate to survivors. Suicide is not a natural part of life; therefore, we aren't prepared for the continuing trauma that accompanies it.

There is the saying, "Never a tear belines the eye, that time and patience does not dry." Perhaps this is true, but as a survivor of a suicide death, I know my healing journey will continue throughout my lifetime. The death of a child is always difficult, but when by suicide, understanding is sometimes much farther out of reach. I will continue to learn new ways to resolve my pain and hope that each new day brings me deeper insights of what happened to my beautiful daughter.

—Carole Buhl

My Mother, Husband, and Grandfather

Suicide has touched my life three times in five years. On January 5, 1988, my mother took her life by carbon monoxide poisoning. My mother was my best friend—her death was a TOTAL shock to me. But I believed I could get through my grief alone, so for five months I "managed" to live day by day, hour by hour, and sometimes, minute by minute. With no survivor support group in Lincoln at that time, even that was not an option for me. Finally, my body, mind, and soul let me know that I was dying on the inside and could not go on without help. I started seeing a counselor at a mental health clinic, but no one there had ever dealt with suicide death, so I felt more like the teacher than a client. Instead of getting help, I continued to suppress all those feelings, until they came back to haunt me three years later.

On June 19, 1991, my husband of nineteen years took his life by carbon monoxide poisoning. He was forty-two years old, an alcoholic, and drug dependent. I was left a widow, with a daughter, age eighteen, and a son, thirteen. His suicide completely changed my life. It was after his death that I found Ray of Hope. All I could do at the first meeting was cry. Every time I tried to talk, nothing came out but tears. I was also seeing a Christian counselor in Lincoln once a week, just to keep my head above water. However, once again, even though this counselor was MUCH more informed than the first one, he still commented that he was learning from me. At Ray of Hope I felt comfortable, able to really talk, and have people identify with what I was saying. Little did I know then how much more important that group would become to me.

Less than a year after my husband's suicide, my grandfather shot my grandmother in the back, killing her, then stuck the gun in his mouth and shot himself. These were my mother's parents; he was eighty-six, she was eighty-five. They had both been in failing health, and a rest home was no option in my grandfather's mind, so I think he decided he would help their deaths along. I couldn't believe this was happening for the third time. I was so distraught that I returned to counseling and continued to attend Ray of Hope.

This year, my daughter will graduate from college, and my son is a high school senior. I have remarried and plan on living a long, happy life with my husband. My children and I have come a long way over the years, but we could not have done it without unceasing support and understanding from family, friends, and community. We have never been rejected or accused, and have never blamed one another. It's love and acceptance that has saved us, and I am so thankful for the people at my Ray of Hope support group. I learn from them at every meeting and continue to heal every time I'm able to share with them.

—*Wendy Workman*

Other Voices

The "loss" and "missing" are just as bad as when my son died. The "time that heals" only means I don't think about him as much as I did at first. I understand why he left, but he never knew how much he was loved. So sad. I feel like I always walk in the shadows. "A merry heart doeth good like a medicine: but a broken spirit drieth the bones" (Proverbs 17:22). My spirit inside is broken, but I put on my "merry mask" to get through the days. It's all I can do.

—*S. D.*

* * * * *

My father killed himself two years ago. My mom and I have good days, but the pain is always there. She cries so much. I try not to say anything to her about it, because I don't want to make her cry more. But I hurt, too. It's sure hard to know what to do.

—*Mike*

* * * * *

I lost my oldest sister to suicide two years ago. I thought I'd forget, but it hurts more as time goes by. I wish she could have known how much I loved her. I wish I had told her. Maybe she wouldn't have done it.

—Nicky

* * * * *

When my daughter killed herself, I took it in stride. Six months later, I could take it in stride. One year later, I still took it in stride. Now, two years later, I can't take it.

—Frank

* * * * *

She was my childhood playmate, my best friend. I knew she was sensitive ... she talked a lot about death. She said no one would care or miss her, except me. Her parents always laughed at her when she said she was going to do it. They would say, "Go ahead" or "You're a coward. You won't do it." But she did. It was I who knew something was wrong. I knocked, and there was no answer, so I broke into her apartment and found her. Now her parents say it was my fault because I was a bad influence. I miss her so much and wish her family and I could be friends. I could tell them such neat things about her. Why don't they want to know?

—Ginny

* * * * *

The last thing my daughter-in-law did in her life was tell me that she was going to kill herself. The last thing I did was to let her. I didn't believe her. How can I forget that?

—Vi

* * * * *

After two years of agonizing over my husband's suicide, I still have only negative thoughts. Because he was a prominent citizen, we kept the circumstances secret. Now I have no one to whom I can honestly expose my feelings. My children cut me off completely when I try to talk about their father. We used to be so close, but now I feel estranged and alone. I need their support and love more now than I ever have, or will. They are breaking my heart. I don't want to go on without my husband and children. I think he may have been right in what he did. Is my solution to be the same? Suicide?

—*Iva*

(*Note*: Shortly after writing this note, Iva, age eighty, killed herself.)

* * * * *

It's been three years since my wife killed herself. She was schizophrenic. Friends have been supportive as I try to raise our three little girls by myself, but my wife's relatives are a different matter. They try to convince the girls it was all my fault. When I was hospitalized several months after her death, they tried to gain custody of my children. At first, I made sure my kids visited my wife's relatives, but now I'm afraid to let them contact them, because I don't know what might happen. The girls don't understand and get upset with me. They miss their grandparents. What am I to do? Why does this hell have to be?

—*John*

* * * * *

My twin brother killed himself four years ago. None of us has been the same since. The devastation we experienced has been unbelievable. My mother and father were very proud and social people. Now, Mom stays home, and Dad is always gone. They don't talk to each other. She talks to me, though, and I try to tell her to seek help, but she says she'll be okay. I don't think so. I worry about her, but I don't know what to do. I don't like to say it but I think my parents are ruining my life.

—*K. M.*

* * * * *

My husband shot himself in front of us while I held our three-year-old in my arms. My son has nightmares and wakes up screaming. I'm afraid it will affect his entire life. My husband meant to hurt me, but he has hurt our child more. Sometimes I hate him.

—*Lynn*

* * * * *

I knew for a long time before my husband's suicide that he would someday do it. He was a brilliant professional man but often lost work because of frequent depression, followed by long periods of heavy medication. Neither of us believes in life after death, salvation, sin, or that sort of thing, so I do not worry about forgiveness or being reunited. He did what he had to do. It's over, it's all blackness; he's gone, it's not my fault, and that's it.

—*S. D.*

* * * * *

On January 3, 1981, my beloved son Danny killed himself, just one week before his twenty-fifth birthday. I was deeply shocked and ashamed. My greatest need was to talk about him and find a reason for his untimely death, but I was alone in my grief, because friends seemed to be uncomfortable with me. After checking around, I discovered Ray of Hope, inc., where I could share my grief with people who had experienced the same emotions. I was not alone anymore. After about a year and a half, I was able not only to talk about my feelings, but also to be a good listener and help others overcome some of their emotional scars. Six years after my son's death, I can handle my emotions and have control over my life. I'm not ashamed to say, "My son died by suicide." I still love him. Thank you Ray of Hope, for saving my life and helping me to be normal again.

—*C. T.*

My Brother

It would be a November I'd never forget. The year of the suicide of my older brother, James; a year when innocence decayed and my childhood foreclosed. I became a victim of his pain and a survivor of his choice. James was my mentor. I carry memories of him holding my five-year-old hand while crossing the street, and his involvement with my education such as algebra tutoring and philosophy discussions. He was beautiful, humorous, and intelligent; everything I wanted to be. James could always make me smile; warmth and love pulsated from his soul. James was my hero.

His death sent shock waves through my existence and ravaged my threads of life: love, happiness, and trust; things James taught me to admire. The devastation of his death has stained my life with guilt, anger, grief, and depression. James died a month shy of my sixteenth birthday. He missed my high school graduation, my first year in college, and my engagement to be married. Just as he will be absent for my wedding, my first-born child, and years of holidays. Precious occasions are now underlined with sorrow and thoughts of "what should have been" and longing for his presence. Rage sets in from the feeling of being singled out and emotionally caged. He not only ended his own life but a large part of mine as well.

Returning to high school was a challenge. Everyone knew of James's death, and I quickly became known as "the girl whose brother killed himself." I received an avalanche of support for the first two weeks and then it ended. People pointed and whispered as I walked by in the hallways. Friends were always trying to update themselves with the latest version of the incident. People would either stare at me or treat me as though I was nonexistent. Everyone expected me to be right back in the game, completely over the death of my only brother. People would ask me how I was; yet they didn't want to hear the truth. I was miserable, and no one cared. Emotionally I was a wreck, and physically drained, yet I played the character everyone expected me to be, a happy normal high school girl. Coming home from school I would collapse and cry. Stress was high and my energy depleted. My grades plummeted, and I didn't care. I was tired and beaten. I miss the youth that James's actions robbed me of.

My health was strained and illness set in immediately: respiratory infections, flus, strep throat, and something similar to mono. Nightmares disrupted my sleep. Picturing how James died enters my head the moment I lay down and often is the thought I wake up to. Two years later, I still don't sleep well. Some nights are long, making those days even more untolerable. Closure is far from taking place.

My greatest pain is the suffering of my family. The unforgivable guilt my mother feels, and the way my father dismisses holidays, birthdays, and almost every other enjoyable event as just another passing day. Or how my older sister has hardened and closed herself off from the rest of us. I wish I could wipe away their pain and the feeling of being incomplete as a family. James had no right to hurt them or me this way.

I realized that I needed to talk with other people who were dealing with the same issues. I could not bare the isolation I felt any longer, and so I joined the organization Ray of Hope, founded by Betsy Ross. The comfort and support I received was wonderful. It allowed me the opportunity to talk about my brother without anyone feeling uncomfortable, and the group listened. Without the love I have received there, I doubt I would be so far along in my grieving process today. The group has been a lifeline for me.

During my senior year I gave lectures for the abnormal psychology class and organized a panel presentation about the importance of suicide awareness and prevention. Of the 1300 students that attend City High School, over 800 attended the presentation. I have also had the privilege to attend and participate in two conferences, and recently was a presenter at the national conference of AAS. in Memphis, Tennessee. Speaking about my situation helps me to understand where I am in my grieving process and also gives me the opportunity to help others who might share similar feelings. I feel it is necessary to have someone represent my eighteen-year-old age group, and so, I am a crusader for suicide awareness. I can make something positive from my brother's death.

James is gone, and I am learning to live without him, but he left his poetry to give me a glimpse of how he was feeling. His poetry is a great comfort for me. It is a window to his heart that I love to open. And so I leave you with the words he left me.

—*Ruby Bollinger*

The Forever Dream

As the hourglass empties, my life flashes its last image.
I cross the flowing sands on deaths made bridge;
Able to support me as long as I am alone.
With each step, closer I become to the unknown.

The bridge is made by memories I tried to forget.
In my death walk the bridge I try not to upset.
The bridge is long, but has a very quick ending;
Hypnotizing me from the messages life is sending.
After each step the past can no longer be found;
Continuing my walk, proving my life ready to impound.
Each step a chapter in the book I write:
Each step a candle of remembrance I light.
Finally, I've come to where no more steps can I take;
Welcoming me to my dream, I am no longer awake.

II

Growing through Grief

Save Me from Drowning

Imagine you're standing on a river bank and, just within arm's reach, a wader steps into a deep, dark hole and begins to sink into the water. He thrashes about and calls for help. What would you do?

Would you look down and say, "So you think you're drowning, do you? Well, don't look at me. You have to learn to help yourself sometime," or "Well, if that's what you want to do, go ahead. Drown."

Would you say, "Oh, you're drowning are you? Well, you probably brought it on yourself. You asked for it," or, would you casually remark to others, "So-and-so over there is drowning but he just wants attention, so ignore him."

Would you say any of the above, or would you reach out a hand to pull that person to safety, offer comfort, and call for assistance? Indeed, you would give that person the attention he or she needs in order to survive.

The person who has fallen into a deep, dark hole of despair and confusion leading to suicide, or a deep, dark hole of sorrow and confusion following a suicide, is in just as much danger of drowning in unresolved emotion. Yet it's so easy to ignore these outstretched hands and cries for help, or to complicate things by responding with a thoughtless or insensitive remark.

That drowning person doesn't want a list of instructions on how not to drown. He/she simply wants to be saved, as do the suicidal. The survivor wants to be comforted. All want love and acceptance.

3

❖

After-Suicide Grief

As soon as a suicide occurs, the surviving group has lost an inalienable right to live an unstigmatized life.

EDWIN SHNEIDMAN
Founder, American Association of Suicidology

Several years ago, my father was hospitalized with a heart attack. After each of us had been in to see him, my family gathered in the hallway outside his room. A nurse then ushered us into a small, comfortable waiting room, and the doctor arrived a few minutes later. He knelt beside my mother, took her hand, and gently told her that her husband, and our father, was gone. He answered our questions and discreetly left the room.

We were given time to cry and hold each other before we were allowed to see my father again. A curtain separated the cubicle from the rest of the unit, staff members were out of sight, and equipment had been removed. No longer the mask of pain we'd seen earlier, my father's face was relaxed, serene, and peaceful. We could touch or kiss him—again, in respectful privacy.

At home, neighbors greeted us with condolences, food, and offers of assistance. Someone had already called our pastor. We were allowed to grieve. This cushion of family and community protection and understanding softened our dreadful shock, pain, and sadness. Throughout those days, everyone knew what to do, as though we had rehearsed the scene. Together we made funeral arrangements. Each of us contributed, each had a part. Knowing our role was comforting.

At about the same time, in another state, a widow (Mrs. A.) was opening her front door after returning from a bridge game. She had left the door unlocked, because her recently divorced son was now living with her and was working around the house that day. When she entered the dim hallway, she discovered that the huge sliding doors to the living room were closed. She had always left them open, so the sunlight from the bay windows could also light up the hall and stairway. Puzzled, Mrs. A. moved through the equally dim parlor to the dining room, opening yet another set of doors that she had not closed. Finally, she stood before the door of the sunporch, which her son was remodeling into a den. Suddenly, she knew what she would find.

A double-barreled shotgun lay by his body. Blood and pieces of hair and flesh covered the sun-splashed walls. One eye hung next to what had been her son's ear. She screamed. And screamed.

Later, police cars and flashing lights drew attention to her home. A policeman asked personal questions. She wasn't sure he believed her. Reporters arrived and took photos of her son's uncovered, disfigured body. Strangers and neighbors were standing on flower beds in order to peer through the sunporch windows. Others walked in the front door and wandered through her home. Long after her son's body was gone, a crowd lingered outside, whispering and pointing.

Having run out of screams, Mrs. A. simply sat alone and wondered why all the doors had been closed. Relatives asked one another, "What do we do now? How do we handle this? I don't know," each answered after a while.

"I guess it's best to leave her alone and not bother her," someone finally observed, breaking the embarrassed silence. Two women headed for the sunporch to clean it up. "Better make arrangements," said one of the men, picking up the phone. "Let's get this over with as quickly and quietly as possible."

* * * * *

Mrs. B. and her three young children, chatting and laughing about the movie they had just seen so "Daddy can have some peace and quiet" had just returned home.

"Mom, come quick," yelled her ten-year-old son. Dropping her purse, she ran. Her son was staring into the laundry room. She stopped at the door. The other children gathered around her. Stupefied, they gazed up at the body hanging from the ceiling. "Mom, what are you going to do?" one child asked.

Mrs. B. stood rooted to the spot. She couldn't think. Finally, she stammered, "I don't know. We can't do anything right now. Daddy's dead. I guess we might as well go to bed. I'll think of what to do later."

Dazed and numb with shock, she put the children to bed, put on her nightgown and lay down. After a moment, she got up. She went back to the utility room door and stood there until dawn before remembering she should call someone.

For weeks, Mrs. B. sat in a hospital room, seldom moving, silent. Relatives cared for the children. When she finally returned home, her neighbors shunned the woman who had gone to bed when her husband killed himself. Except for one. One neighbor asked her if it was true that a man has an orgasm when he hangs himself. Mrs. B. and her children moved out of their family home.

A Grief Comparison

Circumstances surrounding the "normal" or "natural" death of my father were quite different than those experienced by survivors such as Mrs. A. and Mrs. B. We had the comforting support of hospital personnel; they were alone. Our father's body was clean and in repose; the bodies Mrs. A. and Mrs. B. confronted were messy and disfigured. Our shock response was tempered; theirs was heightened. Our family was given gentle answers in response to our questions; Mrs. A. and Mrs. B. were subjected to personal and/or embarrassing questions. We were given community support; they were isolated. The hospital staff respected our privacy to be alone together and also in the room with my father; Mrs. A.'s privacy was rudely invaded. Our family was given respect and reassurance; Mrs. A. and Mrs. B. were either the objects of gossip or openly ignored. People were not at a loss with words to comfort my family; there was nothing to say to Mrs. A.

and Mrs. B. There was concern for our comfort as the bereaved family; the focus of attention for Mrs. A. and Mrs. B. was the act of suicide. Our roles as grievers were defined; the roles for Mrs. A. and Mrs. B. were not. Our family was brought together; their families were pulled apart.

Death by suicide is different from many other forms of death. From the beginning, survivors may be suspected of foul play while authorities determine whether the death was a suicide, an accident, or murder. Police officers, coroners, news media, and insurance investigators haunt family members with questions and implications. The family's privacy is invaded and violated rather than respected and protected. Curiosity and speculation replace sympathy and understanding.

In the case of a nonsuicide death, people know how to respond and react. After suicide, survivors have no guidelines for dealing with the nature of this death. Unable to give in to the natural and accepted reactions of shock and loss, they may form defenses in those first few hours that adversely affect their entire grief and resolution process. In addition, survivors are often considered in some way responsible for the suicide.

In order to understand the unique characteristics of grief after suicide, consider first the natural and healthy grief process following the death of a loved one. The first reaction to death is shock and disbelief. As awareness of the loss increases, pining and sorrow set in. Some symptoms of grief are sleeplessness, confusion, forgetfulness, deep sighing, loss of appetite, and/or uncontrollable crying. Intense grief can be physically painful. It hurts. One experiences headaches, muscle aches, stomach pain, and so on. It's also hard work, uses time, and can lower one's resistance.

It is normal to search for the deceased, to affirm his/her absence, or to be preoccupied with photos, belongings, and memories. To some degree, survivors may identify with the deceased by taking on traits of the lost one, for example, by continuing his/her work.

The bereaved may feel bitter, angry, cheated, may worry about the future, wonder how to bear life without this loved one, and feel regret or guilt over things said or unsaid, done or undone. Believing they are different, or a burden to others, they may withdraw socially, and at the same time feel angry at being left alone.

Everyone's way of grieving is different and may be affected by many individual variables, such as personality, habits, attitudes, past and present experiences, the circumstances of the death, the age and gender of both the deceased and the survivor, one's role in the family system, and the dependency and depth of the relationship. Past losses and present stresses such as finances, physical and/or mental health, medications, and social, cultural, religious, and ethnic backgrounds influence our actions and attitudes.

Months after the death, the bereaved slowly begin to function normally again. The length of this grief process depends greatly upon the success of the survivors' grief work. In the last stage of the grief-recovery process, the bereaved again begin to focus on the future. They make plans and can enjoy life, even though sadness and the sense of loss return from time to time.

Posttraumatic Stress

We all know that any death from natural causes is traumatizing for survivors. However, professionals have long realized that the unique dilemma of suicide survivors places them in greater need for counseling than many other grieving groups. Often associated with suicide, in addition to the usual grieving process, is the experience of Posttraumatic Stress Disorder (PTSD). Literature that discusses PTSD may be found at length in diagnostic manuals, libraries, Veterans Administration literature, and numerous trauma centers.

This widespread disorder, which results from severe traumatic experiences, is not new. It was described as "shell shock" during World War I and "battle fatigue" in World War II. Since the Vietnam War, PTSD has been studied in depth by the medical community. According to the *Diagnostic and Statistical Manual of Mental Disorders* (Third Edition), posttraumatic stress can occur in relation to a variety of tragedies and/or stressful situations such as rape, fire, abduction of a child, loss of health, witnessing the death of someone else, or encountering a life-threatening situation.[1] Some of the key words or phrases in relation to these events are *sudden, violent, severe, unknown threat, death* and/or *life-threatening, psychologically damaging* and *helplessness*. Stress response stages following the crisis itself may include outcry, denial, the intrusive stage, working through, and completion.

During the outcry stage, survivors feel overwhelmed and exhausted. Their concept of time may slow down or speed up. Excessive crying or screaming is common. In extreme cases, a person's system simply shuts down. In the denial stage, people may use any means they can to avoid dealing with the event, such as refusing to discuss or think about it, avoiding any situation or activity that would remind them of the event, depression, excessive sleeping, or excessive "busyness." Some people may develop phobias, experience feelings of impending death, or may lose interest in their families, their sex lives, and even life itself.

The intrusive stage is signified by survivor guilt—preoccupation with what one should or shouldn't have done, accompanied by outbursts of anger and feelings of guilt because they are still alive. A survivor may have flashbacks (reliving the event) so intense that the person returns to the denial stage or simply blacks out the event, unable to recall what happened. There may be constant attempts to understand and integrate one's own role and actions in relation to the event. Without proper "working through," a person in this stage may develop maladaptive symptoms such as psychosomatic problems, physical breakdown of the body, isolating oneself, behaving oddly, and not relating to other people. Without treatment, these symptoms may become excessive, prolonged, and intense.

Counseling for persons suffering PTSD should assist them in retaining their sense of self-worth without stripping away realistic, helpful mechanisms. A primary goal is to promote new growth and maturation.

I believe the experience of aftersuicide survivors compares in many ways with the combat soldier, who must always be aware of and on guard against a surprise attack by an unseen enemy and be prepared to protect himself and his buddies from sudden death.

In a similar way, many survivors have lived for months or years with the dreadful suspense of finding the body of the suicidal person or of actually seeing the suicide happen. Coupled with the threat of suicide might have been threats against others, resulting in fear and anxiety for one's own life, the children, or parents, in addition to the suicidal person. Like the combat soldier, they have been prepared to act on an emergency at a moment's notice. The majority of their time and energy has been concentrated on the survival of themselves or someone else. This "state of alertness" has interfered with and overridden all the normal actions of living. Like the veteran, they are already battle weary.

When the suicide actually occurs, the survivor may witness a sudden, violent death, much as a soldier may see his buddy destroyed in front of his eyes. And it can happen despite all the precautions so carefully taken by the survivor. The result is survivor's guilt: blaming oneself for being left alive and for failing to save the other; questioning one's motives, abilities, responsibility and involvement; flashbacks, reliving, and even relief. Just as the event itself was sudden and violent, so do the states of outcry, denial, intrusion, and working through have sudden violent elements.

After-Suicide Grief

In the following list of characteristics unique to suicide survivors, you may recognize some as symptoms of grief, some as symptoms of posttraumatic stress, and some as a combination of both processes. This list is compiled from a combination of my own studies and observations, and from an article by Albert C. Cain, "Survivors of Suicide: Current Findings and Future Directions."[2] These points are simply a description of the possible destructive aspects of after-suicide grief and not a suggestion that all survivors experience all these symptoms. Solutions, suggestions, and guidelines for resolving these issues and for helping one another recover are found throughout the following chapters.

Shock and Denial

Suicide survivors experience shock not only because the death has occurred but also because it is unnatural and unexpected. There is no chance for anticipating grief as with terminal illness. We expect people to die from old age, illness, accidents, even acts of war, but not by their own hand. "She should not have died that way!" is the cry afterward. At first, survivors may try to deal with this shock by denial and repression. Some of the ways in which people react are confused memory, anxiety, feelings of dread and horror, contradictions, fantasy, and even deliberate lies. Some survivors refuse to discuss the death at all or may engage in half-truths about the event. Others refuse to believe a suicide has occurred, insisting that it was an accident, or accusing the police of hiding facts.

In her book, *Living Through Personal Crisis*, Ann Kaiser Stearns states:

> The person who resists grieving successfully wards off intense pain. Still, a nagging ache will likely take its place. Denied feelings of grief will be expressed in hidden ways. A low-grade crisis can then endure for many years: moodiness, irritability, restlessness, nervousness, abuse of alcohol or other drugs, conflicts in relations with others, physical ailments, accident proneness, reckless spending, or general dissatisfaction and disappointment with life. Grief doesn't go away just because it is ignored.[3]

Searching for Meaning

Survivors experience a desperate need to find a reason for the suicide. When death results from illness or an accident, even though it may have been untimely or tragic, we know the cause. But with suicide—even when a note is found—it is difficult to pinpoint the reason. There is always a nagging question about the degree of one's own involvement. Why didn't I know? Why didn't I listen to him/her? Why wasn't I there? What should I have done differently?

Some people shut out all talk or analysis of the event, whereas others replay the event over and over, searching for an answer to the question "Why?" Cain points out that many survivors struggle alone over the perplexity of it and "the fit of the experience itself into the larger order of life."[4] This floundering search is an important part of coming to an understanding of the experience before one can properly begin to cope with the loss and progress through the grief work. Survivors need to remove the aura of shame and restore a sense of dignity to the deceased's memory, as well as repair their own shattered self-esteem.

Incomplete Mourning

Compound this search with denial, guilt, shame, anger, concealment, evasion, withdrawal of social and family support, subtle accusations, stigma and taboo, lack of reassurance, and the absence of a chance to share one's grief with others, and resolution can be severely crippled, if not altogether destroyed. "Survivors may become subject to the destructive effects and results of unresolved mourning often characterized by prolonged depression and self-destruction," according to Cain.[5]

Depression and Self-Destruction

In his work with survivors, Cain found these forces characterized by self-hatred, apathy, withdrawal, sadness, despair, rage, and a myriad of self-neglectful behaviors. This self-destructiveness stems from unmet yearnings and unresolved grief. Implied disapproval and lack of empathy may "drag survivors deeper into a depression from which some may never recover, or into a pattern of continued self-destructive acts including suicidal behavior," states Cain.[6]

Memories

Many survivors are haunted by vivid recollections of finding the body or of scenes of violence mingled with confusion and/or conflict prior to the death. Perhaps they had spent agonizing hours of waiting in a hospital emergency room on the chance the victim might be saved. Many resent what they perceive as intimidating, cold, or accusing attitudes of investigating officers and medical or emergency teams. These memories are relived and replayed in the survivors' conscious and unconscious minds.

Anger

Survivors struggle with anger in a number of ways, such as (1) anger with themselves for not having prevented the death, and thereby having played a part in bringing about their own misery; (2) anger at the suicide victim for deliberately leaving them alone and burdening them with feelings of guilt, isolation, and desertion; (3) anger at others because of the social branding and sometimes outright ostracism. With nonsuicide deaths, anger may be directed toward God or circumstances; with suicide, it is also directed toward the victims and oneself. The nonsuicide survivor feels angry over the death; the suicide survivor feels angry at being made to look responsible for the death. Survivors feel angry for not being given a chance to intervene, for being forced to face both old and new problems alone, and for having to change and rebuild lifestyles. Finding a way to deal with this very intense anger can be quite perplexing. Although it is real and justified, it just hangs there.

Identification

Survivors go through a time of identifying themselves with the victim. They may believe that they know "exactly" what the deceased felt or thought just prior to death. This identification may go as far as imitation of the act. Some feel they can atone for their neglect of the victim by copying the suicidal behavior. This identification may be greatly intensified if there were conflicts or disturbed relationships prior to the death, or if the survivors depended upon the deceased for their own sense of identity.

Importance of Anniversaries

Suicide family survivors place great emphasis on suicide-death anniversaries. They either dread or anticipate the date as a day of mourning. Especially crucial are anniversaries for each of the first six months, one year, eighteen months, and for some, the second year. Studies have shown that people strongly identifying with the deceased may choose an anniversary for their own death.

Withdrawal

Mingled with doubt and distrust is a need to be with people. There is a hunger to be welcomed—included—but conversation and activities simply take too much energy. Cain explains that, fearful of closeness, survivors may withdraw, thereby playing out "object separation, i.e., the repetitive need to reenact separations; to drive loved ones away by replaying the experiences of estrangement and reunion."[7] David Crenshaw, Clinical Director at the Astor Home for Children, calls this process in troubled children "trauma replay." He explains that there is a "powerful need for traumatized children to reproduce their original traumatic experience in current relationships in a belated attempt to resolve these past traumas."[8]

This backfires on survivors by repeating the loss with yet others and results in more isolation and feelings of worthlessness. Many survivors lose emotional and social support when it is most needed. Continued isolation and/or implicit accusation may lead some survivors to feel they are somehow permanently scarred.

The Legacy

In the foreword to *Survivors of Suicide* (edited by Albert Cain), Edwin Shneidman, suicidologist and founder of the American Association of Suicidology, says,

> I believe that the person who commits suicide puts his psychological skeleton in the survivor's emotional closet—he sentences the survivor to deal with many negative feelings and, more, to become obsessed with thoughts regarding his own actual or possible role in having precipitated the suicidal act or having failed to abort it. It can be a heavy load.[9]

This heavy load is called the *legacy of suicide*. My dictionary says that a legacy is something handed down to the next generation—not *up* to parents, or *over* to siblings—but down, which implies that children are the primary recipients. Indeed, a great deal of study, research, and publications is centered on the legacy of suicide as it applies to children, who, according to these studies (and common sense) are at greatest increased risk for suicide. Although I believe this is most certainly true, I also believe that with suicide, the legacy explodes all over everyone: children, yes, but siblings as well. Spouses, parents, friends, community—all inherit some part of that legacy.

Shame, Blame, Guilt, and Relief

Many survivors say they feel emotionally naked, unable to justify the idea that "someone preferred death to living with me." They may feel that others are making the same judgment, and sometimes, they are. This may leave the survivors with a damaged self-image. An acute sense of worthlessness often compounds the feeling of abandonment, since the other person chose to leave.

Again, blame enters the picture. Survivors search for something or someone to blame. The victim? Friends? Family? One another? Themselves? Health or finances? Conflicting thoughts whirl in their heads. "Why didn't I know?" "I did know." "I could have prevented it, but I didn't. Why?" "I didn't know he was so down, but I should have," wailed one survivor. "I feel such *major* guilt because he did ask for help and I didn't take him seriously. My God, how do I live with that?" This is a terrible burden for survivors to bear.

The feeling that others should acknowledge and share in the blame may occur within some families as members attempt to select "who was the most at fault" in order to pass on the burden of blame. Some people, knowing they were not at fault, despite accusation, nevertheless feel guilty, because they don't feel guilty.

More often, however, parents, children, and spouse feel directly responsible. Guilt then, may compound itself, and often, what are actually feelings of regret or shame may be interpreted as guilt. In natural death, guilt tends to diminish with time as survivors reassure themselves they did all they could. However, with suicide, guilt may increase the first few months, or even years, before it begins to diminish.

At the news of the suicide, some people feel great relief that the stress and anxiety of the previous weeks, months, or years has ended. This may be true, for example, if a husband abused his wife, or if someone has threatened suicide so many times that the family is glad the ordeal is over. But their relief may in turn intensify guilt feelings, resulting in a tendency to strongly deny and repress honest feelings not only of relief, but also of guilt, anger, sadness, and even the grief process itself. In this mind-set, it is often easier to pretend that nothing is wrong—that everyone is or will be all right—to convince oneself that death was not by suicide, or even to act as if that person never existed.

It has been said that we are a death-denying society, and I agree. I believe we are preoccupied with the grisly morbidity of death. We sensationalize the experience of death. We romanticize and glorify the *idea* of death—but we deny the *reality* of death.

4

◆

Helping Yourself Survive

We examine our life, our past, our attitudes and actions; we search ourselves for whatever we did wrong—but also, and ultimately, we must search for what we did right.

ELEANORA "BETSY" ROSS

In order to help yourself, learn as much as possible about the causes of suicide. Libraries, crisis centers, mental health centers, and funeral directors can provide you with resources. Generally, this literature assures survivors that although most suicide victims would have preferred to live, they believed somehow that they could not. To those beset with problems, a sense of failure or rejection, death may have been seen as the solution to a problem or a promise of peace—the absence of pain. Information on the reasons for suicide will help you better understand what happened and why. Also, inform yourself about what you may expect to experience during your grief-recovery process.

Realize that it may take a long time to recover. Although you will never forget, or ever again be the same person, you can still find life meaningful. Your need to search for meaning is not only justified but also necessary. Sometimes the mental and verbal replaying of events helps to make sense. This is not a morbid dwelling on grisly details, but an action which examines and interprets the situation, thereby giving insight.

Claim your right to grieve. Experiencing the pain of grief is somewhat akin to childbirth labor. You can't put it off, give it away, change your mind, go around it, or hire it out to someone else. Rather, you know you must suffer through the pain in order to gain relief and obtain the joy beyond. With each grieving episode, the pain becomes less intense, of shorter duration, and less frequent. To lose your right to grieve is to suffer yet another loss.

Some people feel a need to display photos of the deceased or to sit quietly in the deceased's room. You may feel drawn to revisit favorite vacation spots, restaurants, and so on. You are searching for that person, trying to recapture a sense of his/her presence. Searching for the deceased is normal—it affirms his/her physical absence. Once your need to search is satisfied, you may discover you still have a relationship with the deceased, although on a different level. C. S. Lewis wrote about this experience following his wife's death, in his book, *A Grief Observed* (1957). Simply in the act of finally releasing grief, you may somehow find an essence of your loved one.

Grief and Tears

Do not be afraid to express grief and emotions. Grief is emotional. It is the natural reaction to a significant loss. Find a time and place where you can cry. It also helps to talk about the loss, recall it, and perhaps write about it. Believe that in due time, the painful "reliving" will give way to a satisfying "recalling." One survivor described it as "my happy–sad memories."

You may want to plan a "cry day." Pull the shades, lock the door, unplug the phone, and cry or yell to your heart's content. Don't fool yourself into thinking that you should not cry, or that tears are evidence of weakness or an emotional breakdown. Tears are a law of nature and can be turning points, where pain is released and one's attention can be turned toward expressions of hope, caring, and healing.

We were discussing the value of tears at a support group meeting when Beth, who had been crying all evening, said between sniffs, "I wasn't expecting to be doing this. Usually, I refuse to have a good cry without my Puffs." At the next meeting, I put out a box of her favorite tissues.

Tell people when you need to talk or cry. Ask them to be understanding, to mention your loved one's name, to recall events and his/her characteristics. Let people know that you need time to grieve and their supportive comfort while you do so.

Unfortunately, society has provided us with few guidelines for dealing with after-suicide bereavement. Even though you are the one in need, you may have to teach others how to help you and what to say. If you sense someone is uncomfortable with you, ask, "You don't know how to deal with me, do you?" I believe it is a sign of strength to ask for help when you need it. There is value in being able to receive as well as to give.

Choosing a Listener

Be careful when choosing confidants. Some people cannot relate to your grief, some do not know how to listen, others don't want to. Plan to find yourself more than one listener, because we listen twice as fast as the average person can talk. Some people can also listen better than they can "do" for you, while others are better "doers." Don't mix them up. Ask which they would rather do or be.

Be aware of those who appear to sympathize, but who are actually feeling a morbid curiosity of their own. They only want to hear the bloody details. You may encounter people who try to feed on your pain. When Bill died, there was a person in my life who wanted to see me suffer. Knowing that, I would not cry in front of her.

Susan had a similar experience. "While I was complaining about how my father's suicide had hurt me, I had this great friend who supported me. But when I forgave my father and began to laugh and to look at the future again, she got real mad at me. She liked me better when I was miserable." Susan's complaining had fed her friend's neurosis. When she began healing, her friend felt betrayed. Susan had mistaken her friend's anger as empathy for her own experience.

Survivors are especially vulnerable when the pain is fresh. Although your need to talk is acute, trust your instincts. Don't hesitate to challenge someone who invades your privacy. Counter it with a remark like "May I ask you personal questions as well?" or "I resent it when you say that to me." As Bill would have advised, "Choose someone you can ride the river with."

Watch out for the hope mongers. They will have all the answers without hearing what you really say. Don't exhaust yourself trying to point out or explain a reality they'll never comprehend. Well intentioned, they always have a well-meant store of "Well now's." I once drew a picture of my favorite hope monger on a cardboard box, covered it with printed "Well now's," "Well, you know's," and "Yes, but's," and kicked it to kingdom come in my garage. You can always make something work for you.

We can't live without hope, but it has its place or we lose it. Hope is not the same thing as dogged-blind denial or pie-in-the-sky naivete but, rather, is based on a balanced view of realistic expectations and common sense.

Depression

Beware of doctors who are quick to label your grief as chronic depression. Although depression may be part of grief, depression and grief are not the same, nor are chemical depression and a sad or depressed mood swing the same. Know the difference in yourself. True, some normal grief symptoms, such as confusion, fatigue, loss of appetite, loss of motivation, and sadness, may resemble symptoms of chronic depression or other conditions. However, normal grief is not an illness which automatically requires mind-controlling medication. Some medication can trick you into feeling okay when you really aren't, and cause you to miss out—or not remember—important times and feelings. Remember that grief may be expected to deplete your mind and body of energy, perhaps for several months. Better vitamins than drug dependence.

Rather than scolding yourself for being depressed, think of depression as a turning point, where your body sort of goes into neutral so that your mind and emotions can make important decisions. It's during depression that you decide either to give up, or to survive, while your body gathers the strength to carry out your decision. Depression can have some positive benefits. It makes you rest and gives you time to think about the good times as well as the bad. It can be a time to heal and to grow. Remember that many of the most creative people in the world's history have struggled through terrible depressions only to create or contribute something quite valuable as a result. Don't let depression make you depressed.

Symptoms Serve a Purpose

Just as depression serves a purpose, so does shock, because it allows part of the body to continue functioning while protecting the part (mind or emotions) that is stunned. Expressing anger can relieve emotions which, if pent up, could harm one's health. Guilt encourages us to search our most inner self; fatigue is a reminder to give the immune system a rest; searching helps to affirm reality; identification helps us to understand the deceased's mind-set. Even denial, which is so often discouraged as harmful, may be the only way some people can function at times. These symptoms and many others are a part of accepting, understanding, and re-building.

Control

One side effect of prolonged grief can be that it gives the bereaved person control over others. One mother still sobs uncon-trollably or takes to her bed many years later, whenever her son's name is mentioned, or when she sees some object that belonged to him. It is understood by the family that no one ever says or does anything contrary to her wishes for fear of "setting her off." She uses her unresolved grief to manipulate her family and others, and resists any professional treatment because she is afraid of losing this power.

Another survivor threw a temper tantrum at a support group meeting when other members refused to agree that her grief was "worse" than anyone else's. She then blamed her behavior on her uncontrollable grief of the past many years. When that excuse failed, she became ill. Grief, debilitating as it is, should not be used as an excuse for rude, selfish behavior or a contest for attention. No one should be made to feel that they are not as important—or their pain not as valid—as someone else's, just because their loss was that of a different relationship. It is ridiculous to fuss over who hurts the most. Each and every survivor hurts their own individual most.

Don't allow yourself to become so dependent upon grief that you are afraid to lose it or refuse to give it up. On the other hand, if you do choose to hang onto prolonged grief, you can use it to make yourself as miserable as you want. It's a good way to get attention, get your own way, get lots of pity, and get left alone.

Anger

Anger usually surfaces when shock wears off and acceptance begins. This anger is natural and justified. The person did leave you with old and new burdens to handle alone. It happened, and you are angry about it. But take care not to lash out at innocent people or the family pet. Anger becomes dangerous when we let it take control of our thoughts and actions. There is a difference between being angry and expressing anger. Find a way to express anger constructively. Yell at society, ignorance, and apathy all you want. One mother stomped on her son's grave. It didn't hurt him a bit, but it sure helped her.

It's not uncommon to feel anger—even rage—at odd times. Addie told of how she first expressed rage at her husband, who was sitting in a chair in the kitchen with his back to her. When she walked around in front of him, she could see that he had shot himself. "I stood there and looked at him and got so mad that he could do this to us. So I slugged him. Just slugged him as hard as I could. I hit him so hard he fell off the chair. Can you imagine trying to explain that to the police?"

Not all survivors feel anger. One mother said, "How can I be angry? He didn't kill himself to spite me. He felt hopeless and believed he was doing the only thing he could. Since he couldn't make it in life, he could make it in death. I believe he knew how much his depression worried and upset the family, and he really believed we'd all be better off without him. All I feel is loneliness and sadness." Another said, "I can't get angry at my daughter, but I'm very angry about what happened."

Guilt

Understand your guilt feelings. Do not be afraid to face them. Admit and explore them in order to resolve them. Just as you cannot cement over a volcano and expect it to stop boiling, you cannot make guilt disappear by denying it. It continues to churn inside and retards healing. Do not be afraid to say, "I feel so guilty," even though you know you aren't. It is not the validity of guilt which is important at this time, but how you feel and your ability to express yourself without feeling threatened. The more you confront guilt, the less its hold over you.

Some people hold onto guilt because it serves a purpose. Unconsciously, they may be trying to gain control over their circumstances. "I couldn't prevent the suicide, but I can control how I feel, and by golly, I'm going to feel guilty." Others use guilt as an excuse for not changing, or for not doing something about their situation. A perpetually guilt-ridden person can ward off any accusation or expectations from others. Guilt can also be a way of gaining approval. "See how good I am. I'm feeling guilty." Do not allow guilt to become a self-defeating habit.

Most people are willing to let go of guilt once they have suffered enough. But why wait years for that to happen? Face your guilt feelings, painful as they may be, early in your grieving process. Perhaps they are valid to some extent. If so, admit them to God, or to others, if it helps you. Don't underestimate the therapeutic power of simple confession of wrongdoing, mistakes, or misjudgments. Simply state the facts without justifying or blaming yourself or others. This takes courage. It is risky, but you can change yourself, others, and your relationships with others. Use guilt as a turning point for growth.

On the other hand, if you know you need not feel guilty, do not allow others to assume or convince you that you should. Our society often sends double messages. You will hear some people say, "You shouldn't feel guilty," while others will assume, "You sure must feel guilty." Don not pay much attention to either comment.

Remember that feeling guilty or thinking that you let someone down indicates that you felt a responsibility for that person, and that's good. There has to have been a personal commitment and an ability to feel compassion or you wouldn't experience the guilt. Find comfort in the fact that you loved him/her. In some families that love isn't there.

Consider very carefully the difference between guilt and shame. Shaming is a process that starts early in childhood. We believe parents when they express disapproval of us and internalize that shame until we become our own parent, shaming and punishing ourselves. If shame is there, eating away at your soul, you will react much more acutely to guilt feelings and may even confuse the two. If your parents have shamed you, and you then shame yourself, and then someone close to you suicides, you're in deep trouble. The message, "Shame on you—you made me kill myself," will be taken literally by you, and you're now fighting both shame and guilt. That's heavy, and you may need therapy to help separate and settle the two issues. Guilt results from something we have done. Shame arises from what we think we are.

I believe that some people who are so terribly devastated after a suicide are those who already live in a world of internalized or externalized shame. If you think that shame is a factor in your grief process, you might want to buy some good books on both guilt and shame. You will find books listed in the resource guide on the subject of shame and how to become released from it.

Guilt is easier to resolve; usually, we can make restitution. But shame involves deep spiritual and/or emotional healing to be resolved. Use this grief experience as an opportunity to clear up both issues. Think about the difference between guilt and regret. You may have some claim to guilt if you took a certain action while fully aware of possible adverse consequences. Regret means feeling bad about a situation over which you had no direct control.

Action

Use actions rather than thinking to resolve some of your feelings. Visit places you enjoyed together, or do things you had planned to do together. John and Emma bought a camper for a trip they had planned for years. Before they could leave, Emma became terminally ill and took her own life rather than endure severe pain. Several months after her death, John took the trip just as they had planned, alone. He visited the places they both had wanted to see and "talked to her" as he drove just as if she were sitting beside him. "I did it for both of us," he said. "Maybe it doesn't make sense to anyone else, but I feel like we had our trip together." John took care of unfinished business rather than punish himself with regrets and remorse.

Keep a journal, write poetry, or write letters to your loved one. Edith could manage her busy days but not that special time each evening, when she and her husband had shared a private cup of coffee and conversation. "I tried to do something else during that hour, but I was always drawn back to our special time, thinking about things I wanted to discuss with Ken. Finally, I decided to keep that hour as it had been rather than to avoid it. So, I settled down as usual with my cup and talked to the chair where

Ken always sat. I answered myself the way I thought he would have." This ritual helped Edith to let go of Ken and to accept his absence.

Rituals

A Native American ritual applies this principle. Suppose the father died. The first day following his death, the table is set as if he were there. His plate is filled with food; his chair is pulled out, but no one sits in it. Family conversation excludes the deceased, but everything else is the same. At the following meal, his plate is left empty, then his chair is pushed up to the table so that "no one can sit in it." Gradually, utensils are removed. And so it goes, until, within a few days, someone else uses his chair, eats from his plate, and joins in the conversation. This process, it is believed, gradually allows both the deceased spirit and the survivors to accept reality. The spirit can come to realize that it is no longer a part of its old world, and it is free to move on into another realm. The actions and time involved can help a family adjust to the change.

Make use of rituals on anniversaries. Although you may dread anniversaries, your apprehension may be worse than the actual day. You may want to plan a family gathering or a memorial service, or set aside the day to look at photos and mementos.

Constructing a memory history is something a family can do together to keep a person's memory alive. For example, a young mother worried that her small children would never know what their father was really like, and a woman who was nearing the age at which her mother suicided wondered obsessively about what sort of person her mother had been at that age.

At Ray of Hope we suggest to people that they build what we call a Living Memory History which is much more than a collection of photos, mementos, videos, and family stories. You can phone, write, or visit a variety of people who might be willing to reminisce about your loved one. The list may include childhood friends and their parents, neighbors, teachers, high school and college classmates and faculty, scout leaders, coworkers and employers, club and lodge acquaintances, and so on. Anyone who interacted with your loved one at any time in his or her life may have a story or insight to share in writing or on tape, and each one will have seen your loved one from a uniquely different perspective.

More Tips for Healing Work

You will often hear or read (even in this book) the exhausting term "grief work." People say, "Grieving is hard work," and it is. But consider this: Every physical injury hurts while its beginning to heal. Think of your emotional pain as *healing* work rather than *grief* work. Your pain is evidence that your body and mind are helping you to heal. This pain is healing pain—healing grief—*healing work*.

1. Learn about the grief process and its phases in order to better understand yourself and your moods, and do not gauge your feelings by what others say. Although grief patterns have similarities, individual patterns may vary. Different aspects of reality will hit you at different times, so avoid unrealistic expectations of yourself. It's normal to feel out of control at times.

2. Join a group of survivors as soon as possible. They understand and will listen. Those who attend groups early are less likely still to be grieving years later.

3. See a professional counselor if you think it will help. But remember, there is a difference between grief guidance, counseling, and psychiatry (which focuses on diagnosis and medication for disorders). Maybe all you need is grief guidance.

4. Be with people if you want to. Spend time alone when you want.

5. Don't tell people you are all right if you aren't. You can be honest without going into details. Resist pressure to wear a smile until you feel like it.

6. Don't automatically assume that everyone is blaming you.

7. Talk to your loved one through imaginary conversations.

Recall special things, explain how you feel now, and explore your future. Say good-bye even if you have to say it more than once.

8. Don't clear out your loved one's things too soon. You may feel quite differently about them a year or five years from now.

9. Change things if you want to: hairstyle, furniture, wardrobe. But don't be in a hurry to make major decisions about moving, changing jobs, and so on. If you consider moving, make sure you will still have a support system in the new community, or the move itself will just become another stress factor.

10. Your body is trying to recover, so guard your health. It takes energy to grieve and to heal. Resistance is low and you are susceptible to illness during bereavement, so exercise, eat well, and get plenty of rest, even though you may not feel like it. Expect sleeplessness at times, so avoid alcohol, food, or caffeine that may add to sleep problems.

11. Use this time of renewal to get in touch with yourself. Discover your strengths. It helps overcome the fear of being alone.

12. If widowed, make the most of independence. Making decisions alone may not be easy or enjoyable, but they have to be made, and you are not answerable for them to anyone but yourself. There is satisfaction in knowing you can do it; it helps you to feel less helpless.

13. Take time to do things you like to do and want to do, with no excuses.

14. Think in terms of what "I will do," "can do," or "want to do," not what "I should do." Should do's can wear you out. When they come from others, ignore them.

15. Start referring to some of your belongings as "mine" rather than ours/his/hers.

16. Consult your lawyer, banker, and other professionals on legal and financial matters. Don't rely on family and friends too much, even if it is easier.

17. You are quite vulnerable during grief or depression. Do not let an unscrupulous church or charity representative take unfair advantage of your time, guilt, or finances.

18. Give thanks each day for your health and well-being, your family and friends, and the precious memories you and

others share of your loved one. You may not *feel* thankful—may not even want to feel thankful—but, sometimes, saying "thanks" out loud can make a difference. Give it a try—more than once.

19. Find a church where you feel comfortable. Many congregations now sponsor grief groups and singles groups for all ages.

20. Do consider the comfort, inspiration, and guidance, and spiritual healing to be found in prayer, or in the Bible, Koran, or Talmud. Some of these writings contain many examples of people who overcame tremendous losses.

21. Forgive. Forgive yourself, the deceased, and others. Never underestimate the power of forgiveness. It is the greatest gift you can give yourself. Not forgiving is a weighty burden.

22. Examine carefully the things you think and say to yourself. You may have experienced criticism or stressful events during childhood that are still influencing you. Sometimes we think and act according to what we've been told by someone else rather than what we've learned for ourselves. Sort out your beliefs and feelings, and question their validity.

23. You may be grieving over losses other than just this death. Sometimes a traumatic event triggers unresolved losses of years past.

24. Make some lists:

What's good in my life?	What causes me stress?
How do I belittle myself?	What relieves my stress?
Things I enjoy doing.	The best times in my life.
Things I don't enjoy doing.	Three good things about
The most important things in	someone I can't stand.
my life?	What have I accomplished?
The least important things in	What do I like about myself?
my life?	Am getting?
What do I need but am not	Who I love/loves me.
getting?	What relieves my stress?
Positive strokes I have	The funniest times of my life.
received.	

25. Question what you do and how you feel: What is this grief/depression doing to or for me? Do I really want to change

how I feel? Do I deserve punishment? Why? Why not? Am I making amends? How? Do I need to? What are the payoffs for prolonged grief? Attention? Ongoing sympathy? If I were not depressed, what would I be doing? What are my expectations for myself? What has this done to or for my sense of self-worth? What really matters? Does not matter? What is my belief system? Do I limit or handicap myself? Claim that important sense of pride in who you are.

26. Don't be too hard on yourself. Expect a certain amount of physical distress, daydreaming, and panic over an uncertain future.

27. Don't be too hard on others. They can't fill all your needs.

28. Don't make it difficult for those who sincerely want to help you. Some people can still understand the feeling of loss and grief, even if not your actual experience.

29. Understand that some family members' own pain may be too great for them to be of help to you. Sometimes, your pain may threaten their ability to respond.

30. Remember that people who love you don't want you to hurt.

31. Pay attention to your gut instinct.

32. If you know you can't do something, don't try. If you don't want to do it, don't.

33. Remember that if there had been no love, there would be no sadness. We pay a price for love, but it's worth it.

34. Remember that to say, "I am responsible for my actions" is not the same as to say "I am to blame." Taking responsibility is to empower yourself. Wallowing in blame or shame is emotionally crippling. Countless factors working together brought about the event. No *one* person or thing is to blame.

35. Allow yourself an occasional pity party. You deserve it; you have been abandoned, rejected, and hurt. Who can feel sorry for you better than you?

36. Consider that current problems may also affect your grieving pattern.

37. Do seek out counselors with knowledge of both grief guidance and PTSD.

38. Although "the business" or "busyness" can help keep pain at bay, don't let either one become a substitute for grief.

39. Sometimes the burden of grief itself is as miserable as the loss itself.

40. Protect your purse and charge cards. Shopping may be a tempting way to get out of the house or focus on something other than your pain, but it can get out of hand. I believe that shopping may also be a way of affirming to oneself that "I *will* live—I *will* have a future." Know the difference.

41. Learn to recognize defense mechanisms so that you can tell when you are using them, such as excuses, rationalizations, projection, denial, withdrawal, overactivity. Listen carefully to yourself to see if you are being realistic. Examine your own attitudes and actions objectively. Don't allow grief or self-pity to become deep inner needs of a way of life.

42. Remember that you may forget things, make mistakes, and sometimes move as slow as molasses in January. Plan ahead. Make lots of lists and a master list of your lists.

43. Invitations can be a problem. You want to accept them, but then you change your mind, are too tired, or forget them altogether. Forestall hurt feelings by explaining this to people at the time. Ask them to call you just prior to the engagement and to not take it personally if you change your mind.

44. Expect to remember conversations and situations where you think you could have said or done something differently. Consider, as well, that the suicided person may have lived longer because of your love and concern.

45. When your mood is dark, seek out light: sunlight, lamplight, light-colored clothing.

46. If you live alone, bring life into your home: green plants, cut flowers, and/or pet persons (dog, cat, bird) who may be lonely too.

47. Write letters. Letters of love, apology, explanations— whatever you need to say. If you decide to write an angry letter to someone who is still around, you might tuck it away for a time— or toss it. Don't be hasty.

48. Remember, humor is a part of life, so don't be afraid to laugh. Sometimes, laughter can be as healing as tears.

49. Do not become obsessed with the "right" or "wrong" of

the event. You need to be able to say that something was right or wrong, but do not become preoccupied with looking for fault or blaming people until you hurt yourself and others even more. Assure yourself, "I may be changed, but I am not destroyed."

Direct your energies toward learning, growing, and finding a new and richer meaning in the lives of others and yourself. Your loved one was worth your tears and sadness, but you can honor his or her memory by refusing to let that death be for nothing, and turn your grief process into a growth experience.

5

Helping Survivors Survive

*In order to meet the need, we must first understand; in order to
understand, we must first become informed; in order to become
informed, we must care, and caring is what it is all about.*

ELEANORA "BETSY" ROSS

Keep in mind that *death* is what happened to the person who died;
suicide is what is happening to those who are left alive. This is, in
part, because society perceives death by suicide as a personal
insult. Helping these injured survivors survive is no easy task. It is
sometimes difficult to be patient. Often, without intending to, we
react against the confused person rather than the crisis situation,
thereby making matters worse.

Many people have contacted me for suggestions on how to
help a survivor they are concerned about. Family and friends also
struggle with questions, frustrations, and feelings of helplessness.
"What shall I do or not do?" they ask. "What can I say to help ease
the pain for this person I love?" The next two chapters attempt to
help you with this problem. Most of the suggestions come from
survivors themselves. "Begin," they say, "by being sincere." Next,
learn what you can about the causes of suicide and the grief
process of survivors.

Searching for Why

Survivors have a strong need to search for meaning. They are trying to understand something they can't understand. Recognize and understand that their search is justified and necessary. This need to gain insights into what may or may not have contributed to the death must be explored as much as possible before they can fully accept the loss and get down to the business of healing work.

I believe the reason survivors search so relentlessly for a reason is because we always perceive the death to have been preventable, no matter what. Despite a history of depression, attempts, or threats, we perceive the suicide as preventable. Even if the person said, "I don't want to live/I'm not happy/I don't belong/I am a burden," and, even when we can honestly say, "They are at peace now/They couldn't handle life," we still believe also that things could have changed. Death from terminal illness is inevitable, we say, but not suicide. And we are right. That's why suicide is so hard to live with.

This searching (and/or denial) process may be seen when survivors place photos about, treasure certain items, leave the deceased's room untouched, or keep personal belongings and clothing. That is all right. These things should not be disposed of too quickly. Many a painful reminder may become a treasured memento. It may be better to put some things away at first and then, months later, sort through them and make decisions. It takes time to completely comprehend and accept a loved one's physical absence. Advise patience, and be patient yourself.

This searching is normal. Help survivors accomplish it by being willing to listen to their story over and over. The most sincere compliment we can give anyone is to pay attention. Take time to be sensitive to the inner need. It makes no difference how often they tell the story, or how much it varies. It is in the involvement of replaying of events—struggling to understand and accept within their own frame of reference—that survivor's find a fixed sense of what happened, before they can even begin to consider the future.

Rebuilding

Not only are survivors working to rebuild their own self-image, they also need to develop a positive image of the suicide victim. They need to believe that their loved one made a rational decision. This process may take many months, but it is an important and maturing part of the recovery.

Suicide survivors carry a triple burden: accepting loss by death, believing death was self-inflicted, and reshaping a new lifestyle. Research on survivors indicates that some suffer intense psychological and physical reactions during grief, because suicide deaths usually are more sudden, have a greater impact on survivors, and allow no time for preparatory grief. Anger at the suicided person and fear of following in his or her footsteps can produce a frightening bondage between the survivor and the deceased. Survivors *need* to rely on family and community, and may feel abandoned if that need fails to be met.

When social response to survivors of suicide is influenced by stigma, survivors tend to withdraw. Make a special effort to encourage others in the family and community to offer comfort and support. This will allow survivors to use others as support for building a new lifestyle. It will also help them to discover, develop, and reinforce coping strengths they already possess.

Although a mother's grief is doubtless devastating in a very special way, a father's grief should never be considered less sincere or painful just because he doesn't show emotion as openly as she does. "Most people gave attention to my wife after our child suicided," said one father. "They never seemed to notice I was busy with notification and arrangements. Even my wife remarked that I was filling my role as caregiver and provider. Things didn't really hit me until after I returned to work. My son who died was my best friend, and I had looked forward to doing things together and to someday being a grandpa. All that future is lost forever, and sometimes the pain is too gut-wrenching for me to even speak of it. If I did, I'd fall apart and men aren't supposed to do that."

Our society teaches men that to show emotion is an indication of weakness. As a result, it's understandable that if men feel repressed when trying to work through grief, they would also have trouble sharing their feelings with family and friends. I once read a prayer written by a man who was aware of this problem. He wrote, "Oh, God, please help me communicate my deepest needs and feelings to my family so we may become whole together." Never assume that one person's grief is "worse" than another's simply because the relationship is different.

Recovering

Shock, denial, and sorrow may last longer following death by suicide. Let survivors heal and recover at their own pace, whether it takes two years, four years, or more. Each person's timing is different. Each must follow his/her own inner messages. Don't tell people how you would grieve if it were you. They know how and when they need to grieve. Be patient. It's their grief. Take care not to imply that survivors are mentally or emotionally unstable just because they are grieving, or because they aren't grieving your way.

Expressions of denial, anger, and guilt may be much stronger in survivors of suicide. Let them talk freely about their anger and guilt. Don't argue about who is or isn't really guilty, or how much guilt one should or shouldn't feel. It is important to consider only "How guilty do you feel you are? Let's talk about it. Tell me how you feel." Survivors know how they feel. Perhaps it is out of proportion, but they must see that for themselves rather than be told. Most people will begin to sort things into a different perspective after they have had a chance to bring those concerns out in the open and examine them through discussion with caring others.

Severely depressed persons often sleep a lot, and that sleep can be a form of practicing for death or for a restoration of life. Don't tell survivors to "snap out of it" when they are obviously depressed, and be sure you know the difference between clinical depression and a temporary depressed mood. Depression can be frightening to both the depressed person and anyone else involved. But consider the possibility that depression can be a time of transition as well. With that thought in mind, we can grow or be productive during transition from grief to resolution.

Most important, give survivors permission to feel bad. They should not be made to feel guilty for feeling bad. Insisting that survivors should "do something," or refusing to acknowledge their feelings, may be perceived as an attack on their courage to say, "I feel bad." This can be emotionally paralyzing. For example, Suzanne was describing the frustration she encountered during a suicidal depression following her friend's suicide. "My family just wouldn't hear what I was saying. When I told my sister that I was so weak I couldn't even put toothpaste on my brush, she said, 'Oh yes, you can.' Every time they said I could when I knew I couldn't, they doubled my burden. You know, it's like they just put another bullet in my gun. I had reached for rescue, and my rescuers became my persecutors."

It is very easy to unknowingly invalidate or squelch someone's efforts even though your intentions are the very best. For example, if someone should tell you, "I'm falling apart," your response might be to ask, "In what way?" rather than to immediately counter with "Oh, no, you're not." Other examples include the following:

If They Say:	You Don't Say:	Do Say:
"I feel so guilty."	"No, you're not."	"What do you think you did?"
"I feel like killing myself too."	"No, you don't."	"Tell me about it."

Usually, your responses are meant to discourage negative thinking. But what if it's not negative thinking? What if it is a realistic expression? Perhaps your response is inadvertently negative in the sense that you have invalidated the other person's feelings and squelched a courageous attempt at honest expression. Don't diminish his/her feelings or words. Instead say, "Explain what you mean."

These responses pop up a lot when the subject is guilt. It is a touchy subject most of us want to avoid. But listen carefully.

Perhaps that person is not just wanting to wallow in guilt. Maybe he/she is trying to say something more but doesn't know how. Consider the possibility that the person has become aware of the effect of his/her actions and influence upon others. Perhaps that person is owning accountability for some sort of action or influence. This is a risky, but exciting, step toward maturity. It takes a lot of courage to say, "I am accountable for this or that"— especially after a suicide. That does not mean they are responsible for the suicide itself. Respect a survivor's courage, and give it permission to emerge.

On the other hand, remember that some people think asking for help or advice indicates a weakness on their part. They may indirectly seek your advice, then seem to resent it when you respond. In this case, you are in trouble no matter what you say. Try to avoid giving advice when it isn't directly asked for. Instead, you might ask, "Would you like to hear what I think or what so-and-so did in a similar situation?"

Don't say, "Call me if you need help," and let it go at that. They won't call you. Instead, do something specific. Ask if you can baby-sit the kids for a while. Go fix breakfast, make beds, take out the garbage, mow the yard, walk the dog, help answer mail, pull weeds, or wash the car. The list is endless.

I once showed up on a friend's doorstep with cleaning supplies in hand and announced, "I am a gift from heaven. I do windows and toilets." She burst into laughter and said, "Would you believe it, that's just the two things I have been worrying about and can't get done." One survivor said, "I can't cry on the shoulder of a phone." Better to just be there to offer a hug or a shoulder.

Don't be hurt or put off if your invitations appear to be met with evasions or lack of enthusiasm. Since Bill's death, I've been told by various people that for the first couple of years, I never followed through on invitations I had accepted. Apparently, I was so preoccupied at the time that I probably couldn't move from my chair, or I simply forgot. But I do remember the times my friend Joyce came in and said, "We are going shopping (or to a movie)

and we want you to come along. I'm here to help you get ready."
Usually, with that sort of urging, I'd go and enjoy myself.

Death anniversaries are very important to suicide survivors.
Contact survivors each month on the date of death for at least six
months, and again on the first and second anniversaries. Do not
hesitate to mention to bereaved persons that you know an anniversary is approaching. They will be grateful that you didn't
forget. Remember the deceased's birthday, mention his/her name
from time to time, and recall little things. It may provoke tears, but
they will be thankful, healing tears.

A survivor's health may be at risk. Resistance is down, and
previous health conditions may worsen or new ones develop.
Grief work itself makes the person feel like a blob of pain. If some
pains persist or become increasingly worse over time, you may
encourage the person to seek a medical checkup. Remember, also,
that spiritual healing of the soul is as important as physical, mental, and emotional healing.

Do not be afraid to ask survivors if they have suicidal
thoughts. They may welcome the opportunity to discuss the topic
and will appreciate your concern. You won't be "putting something into someone's head" if it wasn't there already. If a person is
thinking about suicide, you can guide him/her to professional
care and perhaps save a life. When someone confides in you, "I
feel like killing myself," curb the impulse to sound off on your
feelings about the act of suicide. They are telling you more than
that. They are telling you that they also are experiencing fear and
fatigue, and a lack of achievement, pride, and dignity. They are
saying ten things at once and want you to hear the real message.

If a survivor is very disturbed, professional help should be
sought. But aside from that, the best you can offer is empathetic
understanding, acceptance, patience, and a listening ear. Allow
survivors to open their hearts. Don't be threatened by emotion.
People don't want advice as much as they need a nonjudgmental,
nonpatronizing atmosphere.

There are times, however, when listening may not be enough,
and professional help is needed. The following symptoms may be

evidence of delayed or unresolved grief or debilitating depression:

1. Changes in appetite, with marked weight gain or loss.
2. Marked changes in personality or behavior.
3. Insomnia or excessive sleeping.
4. Marked overactivity or extreme lethargy.
5. Prolonged and exaggerated feelings of hopelessness, shame, fear, low self-esteem.
6. Suicidal feelings and threats; giving away possessions.
7. Comments such as "I wish I was dead," and "No one cares about me."
8. Extreme isolation or extreme inability to be alone.
9. Alcohol and/or drug abuse.

La Rita Archibald, founder of Heartbeat, says, "I will always sorrow for the death of my son, but my healing is no longer hindered by the consuming obsession with the cause of death. At last, after many cruel, exhausting months, I am free to treasure the cherished memories of him and free to look toward the future with hope. I am free … to live again."

Helping a survivor of suicide reach for freedom can be perplexing, requiring much time, tact, and patience. But if you succeed, consider yourself eligible for sainthood. You may help someone find the ray of hope he/she needs to go on with life in spite of a terrible loss.

6

❖

A Time to Talk,
A Time to Listen

Words can hurt; words can ignite anger; words can destroy lives.
But words can heal; words can inspire and light fires of friendship
and hope.

JOYCE ANDREWS
1995 Friends Newsletter

Far too often, we are more worried about our ability to say the
right thing than we are about giving an understanding ear to a
mourner. We think we must offer advice or philosophical thoughts
to the bereaved, when a hug, a handshake, a deep look into the
eyes, our presence, or making contact is what counts most. But we
can't avoid talking altogether, so what can we say?

According to Dr. Abraham Schmitt, author of *The Art of Listening with Love*, listening to others in a loving, attentive way can
transform people and relationships, and help the speaker to feel
better understood. He means listen to their words rather than
your thoughts.

Most of the material in this chapter is taken from an ongoing
Ray of Hope study of after-suicide bereavement. The questionnaire asks survivors to list (1) the things that were said and done
that caused them the greatest stress, and (2) to suggest things a
concerned helper can do and say. Included are additional comments
some of the survivors made about the points they listed. Take time

to examine your motives when you offer your help. If they are less than pure, your offer of help will generate more resentment than gratitude in the long run. Motives that are actually self-serving or self-centered can sneak up on us. Be especially aware of the following pitfalls and examine your motives by asking yourself these questions:

* Do I resent his/her plea for attention? Why? Is my own need for attention so great that I am jealous of someone else who needs—or gets—attention?
* Am I more concerned with seeing this person's pain relieved, or am I making this conversation a power struggle because I need to be in control?
* Can I avoid my own guilt feelings by blaming someone or something else?
* Am I judging or labeling the person rather than understanding his/her reactions as part of the grief process?
* Am I saying this because I think it's the right thing to say, or is it what I truly think?

Don't:

* Condemn
* Patronize—"Well, now ..."
* Judge
* Argue
* Blame
* Advise
* Criticize
* Ignore
* Laugh or jest
* Put off
* Compare—such as, "So-and-so didn't carry on like you do."
* Overtalk—know when enough is enough.
* Put down—such as, "That's nothing. It happened to others."
* Overspout platitudes—(as helpful as a box of rocks).

* Compete—Are you actually more interested in proving you have suffered more?
* Heap on guilt—I feel guilty enough. Don't add to my burden.
* Try to convince me that my loved one "had a choice." I may not believe that, and I don't want to argue about it right now.
* Moralize—such as, "Think of what you are doing to your family." I am thinking about what I'm doing to my family. Are they thinking about what they are doing to me?
* Pressure—such as, "Now, put a smile on your face." Don't ask me to lie and pretend about how I feel just so you'll feel better.
* Make assumptions—check things out with me first.
* Remind me of obligations to others. That may be part of my depression. I am aware of my inadequacies in meeting my responsibilities. Harping on it will only increase my sense of helplessness and make me resent you.
* Dare or encourage me if I threaten suicide, on the mistaken notion that you will bluff me out of it. What I hear is that you just don't understand, or you are deliberately insensitive to what is really my cry for help.
* Label me—that reveals more about you than it does about me. It tells me that you judge people without getting to know the circumstances.
* Preach—I may appreciate spiritual guidance, but don't shove it down my throat! And please don't sermonize on the evils of suicide.
* Get defensive—we're talking about why my loved one took his/her own life, not your reasons for why you wouldn't do it.
* Don't complain about your spouse, parent, or children to me when I've just lost my spouse, parent, or child.

Do:

* Really care enough to listen. You can't fake caring and concern.
* Tell me you care and are available should I need you. Then *be* available.
* Allow me to cry—maybe even share my tears.

* Respect my privacy if I decline an intense conversation. Sometimes, it's too exhausting to talk. Sometimes, I want to avoid the embarrassment of losing control in front of others, so please accept my silence.
* Offer to pray or meditate with me. Share my spiritual healing times.
* Write a line or two in the card you send.
* Be patient and understanding when I repeat myself. Allow me to dwell on it from time to time.
* Come to my home with a hug for me and my children. Encourage others to come and visit me. You can help them overcome their discomfort that way.
* Be trustworthy. Don't offer to listen if you aren't going to. And ask yourself why you want to listen. Don't use my misery to satisfy your own morbid curiosity. I will sense that something is wrong and may later resent having confided in you. Then, both of us will have lost.
* Give both me and my loved one the benefit of the doubt.

Be Cautious about Saying:

* "Don't worry, you can have more children." (Insensitive, because it minimizes my loss.)
* "But you still have other children." (I have other fingers too, but I don't want to lose one of them.)
* "Maybe you'll get married again." (Insensitive, because it minimizes my loss.)
* "You just have to forget he/she ever existed." (That's ridiculous and cruelly insensitive.)
* "He/she died over a year ago. You should be over it by now." (Wrong. Better update your information about the grieving process.)
* "Anyone who commits suicide is weak or a coward." (And who are you to judge? Actually, it may take a lot of courage, determination, and strength to kill oneself.)

* "Life goes on." (Maybe so, but mine doesn't feel like it right now, and I don't care.)
* "He or she had a choice." (Intellectually I can say that, but inside, it's not like that because there were indications after the fact, and I want to deal with them.)
* "Well, it was God's will, you know." (Oh? Did God tell you that? How can that sort of pain and desperation be God's will?)
* "People who kill themselves are insane," or "They were crazy, you know." (Actually, a very small percentage of suicides are mentally ill.)
* "They are in hell now—all people who commit suicide are demon-possessed." (How do you know? Do you have an inside connection with Hell? Also, this was a terrible thing to say to me. It added to my hurt.)
* "I know how you feel." (Oh no, you don't know how I feel. You only think you know how you would feel.)
* "Oh my, you must feel so guilty!" (Please don't automatically assume that I should automatically feel guilty.)
* "You're strong, you'll be just fine." (Are you *really* saying you won't be here to help me?)
* "You've got to get on with your life." (What are you talking about? This is my life.)
* "You'll get over it." (No, I don't know that I'll get over it, and neither do you. In fact, at this point, I don't want to get over it.)
* "It will take time." (I know it will take a long time, but I don't want to think ahead like that, because it discounts what I am going through now.)
* "So-and-so wouldn't want you to carry on like that." (Why not? And how do you know? Wasn't "so-and-so" worth it?)
* "Grief will make you a better person." (You don't say! Well, maybe someone else should die, and then I can be an even better person.)
* (To others) "Well, I'd really like to help him/her, but I'm afraid that he/she won't listen to me." (Make sure that isn't a cop-out for your indifference, or an attempt to impress others with your concern.)

* (To others) "She/he keeps trying to bring up the subject, but I don't want her/him to get upset, so I ignore it." (That doesn't make sense. Maybe it's you who is afraid of being upset. Also, do you really believe that I have no thoughts in my head other than the ones you put there?)
* "Don't think about it." (I have to think about it. It happened.)
* "Don't talk about it." (Why not? Don't ask me to pretend nothing is wrong.)
* "You have to talk about it." (No, I don't. There are times when it is just too overwhelming to talk. Sometimes, it isn't any of your business.)
* "Be brave! Don't cry!" (Why not? Tears are a natural expression of grief, loneliness, and longing, a tribute to the one I miss. There is nothing shameful or unacceptable in my tears, or, do you mean that my tears bother you?)
* "Well, now, time heals all, you know." (That may be true, but it doesn't stop me from hurting now.)
* Don't add to my burden with a lot of "If onlys." (I'm doing that enough already.)
* "Snap out of it." (I want to, but I can't. Stress has weakened my body. Give it time to repair itself.)

Do Say:

* "I can't begin to imagine how you feel, but I'm here."
* "I remember 'this' or 'that' about _____." (Single out some special quality of the deceased, and comment on it.)
* "I don't have an answer."
* "You have a right to feel as you do."
* "You feel alone now, but some of us have been where you are. When you are ready, we may be of help."
* "There is no right or wrong way to grieve. Take your time."
* "You may not believe it now, but time will help in some ways."
* "Life can be unfair; this is unfair."
* "You're on my mind. I know you're surviving, but how are you?"

* "I'm glad you are showing anger, because it lets me know how you really feel."
* "Tell me how you feel."
* "I don't know what to say to you. Help me."
* "I feel so helpless. Do you?"
* "I have so many questions. Do you?"
* "Would you rather not talk about it?" or "Do you want to talk about it?"
* "I wish I knew what you are thinking."
* "What are you remembering?"
* "It's okay if you are at a loss for words when you are with me."
* "Of course, you don't always know what to say."
* "It isn't easy, is it?"
* "Would you like to discuss how you plan to deal with this?"
* "You must be very confused. Do you want to talk about it?"
* "I'm confused. May I talk about it?"
* "If you care to tell me what you want or need, maybe we can work together to find some answers."

Suggestions from Ray of Hope
Support Group Members

"Give us approval for trying to resolve our feelings rather than encouraging us to deny what we feel is or was our responsibility. This is growth—let us do it." *Jan*

"Just let me be where I am. I can only be into today." *Carol*

"Sometimes when people ask me how I'm doing, I'll say, 'I'm not doing well at all.' You'd be surprised how many will answer, 'Oh, that's good.'" *Barbara*

"It's never too late to send a card. It's been three months, and I still look for them in the mailbox." *Mike*

"When I got cards on my son's death day anniversary, I did not feel so alone." *Marty*

"So many people knew but never responded when my husband killed himself. I want to ask them did he mean so little that you can't even call or come over? Doesn't he deserve our grief?" *Barbara*

"It's very painful when people fail to offer support or condemn you for objecting to rejection." *Jean*

"You know what was great? We looked out one morning, and the neighbor was mowing our lawn." *David*

"People helped me that way too. Like little elves, they knew what to do and did it." *Pam*

"It helped me when people let go and cried. I felt in touch with those people." *Bob*

"People encouraged me to move—or visit them, or get out of the house. But I don't want to go away. There's a lot of me in that house. I want to be where I am." *Bert*

"I don't want to see myself as a victim, but in reality I am a victim. Part of this grief process is that of having been victimized." *Kate*

"I don't like it when people always ask me how my mom is doing. I say, 'She's okay,' but I want to say, 'Her life stinks, what did you expect?' or 'She's home alone, why don't you call her?' I guess they think they're doing their duty by asking us kids. But actually that's a way of avoiding her." *John*

"I want to be normal again. But I know it will be a new normal. I see a different me taking shape." *JoAnn*

"I want to be different—not necessarily better." *Joe*

"For a while I was so angry over her suicide that I wanted to kill someone—maybe even myself. Some days, I'd go around just looking for someone to fight with. At first, I didn't want to think or hear that anything positive would come of this. But as time passes, and I mellow, I do find myself seeing things that are positive. Maybe that's not so bad." *Jim*

"If you really want to know how to help us survivors, then why don't you (my friend or family member) go to a support group and learn what to say—how to help." *Lisa*

"Don't shut out friends of the person who suicided. I could tell the family of my friend such neat things about him if they would listen. Maybe it wouldn't hurt as much as they are afraid it would." *Joe*

"It's too bad that we are the victims and still have to educate the public." *Mary*

"My husband died. I disappeared. I am a suicide-survivor victim." *Beth*

"I feel like I goofed—big time. Like someone put something over on me and all the world sees it. I am embarrassed and humiliated." *Ray*

"People notice us in a different way. We feel as if we are the object of something—but what? We can only guess." *Rick*

"Don't call me codependent. It's not true. Codependent people stay with the situation and take the abuse or just complain. They don't put the troubled person in hospitals or go to counselors, or just leave. I tried all those things. I'm not codependent." *Anne*

"We know that we have no control over the situation when someone died a 'natural' death, and that helps in dealing with it. With suicide, however, survivors believe that we did have some control but messed up. The result is a personal affront. We feel as if we have been deceived, betrayed, duped. It's like running through the world naked. It makes news." *A Ray of Hope Group Comment*

"People are often quick to imply that if we had forced psychiatric care or hospitalization on our loved one, we'd have prevented the suicide. But what would you do? You take your child or anyone you love, whose psyche is sick, and frighten them with incarceration or remove them from the familiarity of home and family, isolate them, give them drugs, tie them up, befuddle their brain with shock treatments, and what can you expect? You've got to look at it from both sides." *A Ray of Hope Group Comment*

"Include us, please. Don't say, 'I'll see you at the meeting,' or 'Are you going to church?' or 'Are you getting out enough?' or 'You should try that new restaurant in town.' Instead, say, 'Join us,' or 'We'll pick you up.'" *Pam Tanous*

"A friend of mine got divorced, and we had a freedom party for her. She received gifts of sexy underwear and promises of being introduced to this or that eligible man. I've been widowed eight years, and I've never received that kind of support. Don't get me wrong, I'm all for her starting a new life. She's my friend, and I want good things for my friends. But I want good things for me, too. I want support for me, too." *Pam Tanous*

Widows, much more than widowers, at group meetings complained of being left out of social functions. Men reported they were invited out, taken care of. Women seem to be expected to find their own way, although they should be no more of a fifth wheel than is a man.

Suggestions from Support Group Leaders

"First of all, remember to give your leaders a pat on the head from time to time. We all need that, to be validated." *Pam Tanous*

"Remember that the focus for the survivor changes from dealing with the shock of the loved one's death to the shock of dealing with one's own life.

"With survivors of suicide, it is often not the crisis which exists in reality that should concern us. Rather, it is the crisis which their minds perceive as reality that's important.

"It helps survivors to understand that their grieving depression is different from clinical depression. The survivors' depression is situational—they know the reason why. Clinical depression affects a lot of people who attempt or complete suicide, but they often don't understand their depression." *Mike Millea, Counselor*

"Grief is not a mental disorder. Survivors are not 'sick,' but they do need attention and understanding, just as do those who are suicidal. In both cases, that cry for help is also a cry for life." *A Survivor/Leader*

"This condition wreaks havoc with a survivors' sense of self-worth. They need to be seen, heard, recognized, validated. That form of nourishment is needed as much as food. They also suffer from an assault to their self-image. That's not the same as having low self-esteem. Low self-esteem is basic—it goes way back—but this blow to the self-image is situational. In order to help, you need to be sensitive to the whole pattern." *Mike Millea*

"Suicide-survivor grief is characterized by its intensity and focus. Its persistence sets these survivors apart. I don't see how they can endure without people who love them. These grieving people just have so much to give—they are so sensitive to life and death." *Reverend Barger*

Many survivors suffer from PTSD in the sense that they have already battled for years with the fear and stress of suicide threats and/or attempts in the home. Some are exhausted from the "need to be there all the time just so something wouldn't happen."

Others have lived under constant threats from the suicidal person that he/she would withhold love and affection if the family didn't behave just as he/she expected. The entire scene can be a form of blackmail in which survivors experience years of guilt for "not meeting the needs" of a suicidal person long before that person completes suicide. The survivor then feels "I knew the worst would happen. I tried to prevent it and I failed. At the same time, I'm glad its over." This severe, before-and-after stress can cripple a survivor emotionally without proper guidance.

More Tips for Listening

It's very difficult to be objective in a conversation involving a person with whom you are emotionally involved. Some listening techniques used by counselors, however, can also be useful in nonprofessional situations. The following are examples:

* Schedule time when you are not tired and there are no distractions. Then you can listen intently and patiently.
* Hearing is passive; listening is responsive, so look at the speaker and nod, don't shrug, smirk, or slouch, and don't let your mind wander.
* Ask questions, but don't give them the third degree.
* Don't insist that the speaker get all details exact. That doesn't matter so much at this point. It's feelings that matter, so settle the feelings first. Facts can be dealt with later. Even then, different people will see the event different ways.

* Suspend your own feelings. Prejudgments can shut out vital or new messages.
* Ask yourself, "What is this person really telling me?" Am I missing anything? What do they really want from me? Avoid jumping to conclusions.
* Let the speaker know when you don't understand. Repeat what they have said, using feeling words to describe emotions, and interpreting what you hear. Double check.
* Let them know when you do understand.
* Focus on main issues, and avoid being sidetracked by details.
* Say, "I think I'm hearing you say thus and thus. Am I right?" Practice this until you can reflect back what has been shared. Confirm what has actually been said.
* Don't be surprised if you get an "I don't know," in answer to your questions. Often, they don't know. That's part of the problem.
* Watch body language: posture, eye contact, nervous laughter, tone of voice, hesitations, inflections. All these give clues to the person's reactions to you and to what they *aren't* saying.
* Realize that no matter how tactful you try to be, someone else may not see it that way.
* Understand that it is difficult for some people to share deep feelings. They may fear being hurt, rejected, or ridiculed. Some people have never experienced unconditional love from others and do not know how to accept it. They believe that talking will not help, that they are always misunderstood or tuned out by others, so why try? Some people may believe they have no worthwhile ideas to offer, and so withhold comments and personal feelings. Some people are just very shy, others very private.
* Be patient and understanding with these people. Their suffering may be compounded by their inability to communicate. You may have to take the lead more than once. If you feel you must say something, point out that, although tragic, suicide is not something shameful to be hidden away. Dealing with it openly can help restore the shattered lives of the survivors.

Bear in mind that a broken heart or broken spirit is not that different from a broken leg. We give a broken leg time to heal. We treat it gently; we withhold expectations and demands that it perform before it is able. We'd never say to the person who is lying on the street with a broken leg, "Well, if you won't help yourself, we can't help you, either," or "He just wants attention, so ignore him." That's like claiming that a crying baby just wants food, so ignore it, or that sick people just want medications, so ignore them.

It's all justified attention, whether it's food for the baby, medication for the ill, or warm, loving care and patience for the broken in heart or spirit. Often, it is the sharing of the brief reaction itself that helps bring out an acceptable understanding and emotional healing. By our presence, we affirm that the mourner is not alone. Just as joy shared is joy increased, grief shared is grief diminished.

7

Widowed by Suicide

It's as if there is something mysterious about us that not even our best friends will tell us.

A Surviving Widow

It has been said that when your parent dies, you lose your past; when your child dies, you lose your future; and when your mate dies, you lose your present. I believe that when any loved one dies, you lose something of all three.

All survivors of suicide share many similar feelings, but there are also differences depending on whether the survivor is a parent, child, sibling, friend, lover, or spouse. For example, siblings share about 90 percent of the same gene pool. No parent or child is as much like you as your sibling in this unique way. Siblings teach one another where to fit into the family, how to relate to adults, and so on; we practice living on our siblings. When we lose one, we lose our role identity in the family, school, community, and future.

A parent has a different tie. Parent and child each carry a part of the other within them. Parent and child can disagree bitterly but are bound by that innate desire to connect, no matter what. The breaking of that blood tie inflicts a physical wound. "I feel as though someone came up to me, ripped out my heart, and just left me standing here, a gaping wound," says one parent. "Part of me is gone and the sadness and anguish goes on and on."

With a spouse, people choose to invest time, emotions, love, and trust; by giving away a part of oneself to someone they don't know in the same way they know a blood tie. When broken by suicide, the response may more likely be rage along with sadness, because this relationship, unlike a blood tie, was more conditional—an investment—with expected returns.

"You led me on! I believed in you! I gave you my life, my time. I trusted you with my safety, my future, my children and you tricked me. You lied. You destroyed my ability to trust or love again. You violated me. I feel psychologically raped; foolish, rejected, deserted, abandoned, and I am outraged," they cry. "How dare you do this to me?"

When a spouse dies, the remaining spouse loses his or her companion, lover, peer, confidant, friend, and in many cases, financial support. One husband summed it up by saying, "She was the person with whom I shared my hopes, dreams, fears, and concerns. I expected us to grow old together. My wife was my past, present, and future."

When a spouse dies by *suicide*, the remaining spouse may feel different from other widows and widowers. His or her spouse died deliberately, not by accident, illness, or something he or she couldn't help. Some widows have called this the ultimate rejection. During the first Ray of Hope meetings in 1977, those of us widowed by suicide met separately to share our common concerns. *Most* of the following comments in this chapter are from, or about, women, because women are more inclined than men to attend support groups, and because twice as many men as women die by suicide.

One widower said, "I felt so sorry for a friend of ours when his son suicided, but now that I'm widowed by suicide, I envy him because he at least had his wife to talk with and share his grief—I feel so very much alone, and that loneliness just overwhelms me."

Overwhelmed is a word often used by spouses who have been widowed by suicide. They suddenly find themselves responsible for everything—parenting, running the home, running a business, earning the family income—in addition to grief. "I couldn't take time to grieve for over a year," says Pat. "I had to take care of his business, his employees, all his problems he left behind." Very often, the public, family, and friends never fully realize the demands made upon a wife and mother, or husband and father, when a mate suicides.

Nancy, the wife of a young farmer who shot himself when he realized he was losing the farm, said, "I've never had time to grieve. From the first, there was extra responsibilities on my shoulders and major decisions to make. I never grew up on a farm and couldn't operate one on my own. I had to hire people to do chores and finish the harvest, attend to creditors, continue my job in town so the children and I could eat, sort through thousands of items so a sale could be held before winter, find renters for the farm, find a house and move into town before Jenny started school, and on and on. My husband's family accuses me of not caring and not missing him, because they always see me busy and not grieving. They are retired and have time to themselves. I've never been left alone or free of demands and decisions for nearly a year now, and I don't know what's going to happen to me when I am really able to think about my loss and his suicide. I worry about that."

Some wives lose the sole source of family income and may even be deprived of their husbands' death benefits. The suicide of a husband or father can impact the standard of living in a way that does not occur when the suicide is a different family member, such as a child or sibling.

In suicide situations, I discovered that attitudes sometimes exhibited toward wives are different from those exhibited toward husbands. Frequently, the wife is blamed, no matter what happened. If her husband committed suicide, it's her fault. If she killed herself, it's also her fault.

A woman who completes suicide is often described as unstable, unable to cope, or "the nervous type." The implication is that she has a character defect, and that her problems stem from her own internal weakness. In other words, she killed herself not so much because circumstances drove her to it, but because, as a woman, she was too weak to handle them. A man in her situation, it is implied, would not have succumbed.

On the other hand, society sometimes tends to justify the husband's action by attributing it to external causes. Comments such as "He was under a lot of pressure, you know," or "He wasn't himself," or "With his family and his business falling apart, how could he help it?" indicate that people are inclined to blame other people and things rather than the man himself. This idea prevails despite the popular idea that to die by suicide indicates weakness or mental illness, and despite statistics, which show that twice as many men as women kill themselves.

Some widows also believed, more often than did widowers, that parents, in-laws, and even their children hold them responsible for the suicide. Sadly, their perception may be right. Many times, a mother has reported that one of her children told her, "It's your fault Dad killed himself." In some cases, these children had previously defended their mother against the father's abuse, then changed their attitude after his death, leaving their mother hurt and puzzled.

When children change their attitudes after a father's death, they may not necessarily mean to hurt their mother. Perhaps they feel guilty over negative thoughts and interactions with their father before his suicide. Maybe they were afraid or ashamed of him. Now, they are trying to compensate to make themselves feel better. Seventeen-year-old Doug, who counseled with me privately, said, "I didn't know my dad was so unhappy. I thought he was mean on purpose, and I hated him sometimes. Now I'm sorry and I can't tell him. By defending him when someone criticizes him, I feel like I'm making up for it. I can't tell Mom that, because she thinks I'm blaming her if I defend him."

Many of the surviving men I talked with have stated that children, other family members, and in-laws as well, are supportive of them rather than critical. In fact, although children and other people may have hostile feelings toward the surviving man, they often seem less willing to confront men than women about those feelings.

Society *in general* appears to be intimidated about confronting a man regarding his attitude or behavior but is most aggressive when confronting a woman under the same circumstances. But society, on an *individual* level, can be cruelly confrontational to surviving husbands. "How could she do this? Couldn't you have stopped her?" they are asked. The implication is that a good man who was taking care of his wife would not have let this happen. He's a failure as a man.

There are also some differences, as well as many similarities, in how spouses handle their grief. Generally speaking, women want to learn how to handle their grief through therapy, reading, support groups, prayer, and the like, whereas men seem to just want to get rid of it. One group member's father moved away after his wife's suicide, remarried quickly, and never mentioned her name again. Although this sort of denial seems to be more common among men, that is not always the case. Many more men are attending support group meetings. One surviving husband also reported to me that men do indeed find solace at the neighborhood bar; the focus is not that of a drunken good time, but that here is a place where they can let down their guard, cry openly, and not feel embarrassed.

Guilt is another issue where I sometimes see differences. Surviving women *talk more* about feeling guilty than do men. This is not to imply that husbands don't feel just as guilty; perhaps women simply can vocalize it easier. Society also seems to expect women to feel guilty.

Marie, who for years struggled with intense guilt feelings, had finally worked her way through them after the first few group meetings. Elated, she looked forward to sharing her new freedom with family and friends. A few weeks alter, she returned to the meetings, shaking her head. "I can't believe it," she said. "Some people are actually upset because I changed so much. They want me to feel guilty. Now, I feel guilty because I don't feel guilty."

The widow's low self-image also adversely affects her ability to recover from grief. Traditionally, a woman's identity is centered around family and marriage; a man's is not. Studies indicate that more women kill themselves following the loss of relationships, whereas more men complete suicide following a business or career failure. Because of this, the suicide of a wife may not be a personal blow to the husband's self-esteem in quite the same way as his suicide is to hers. This is not to imply that he does not miss her or struggle with feelings of responsibility.

However, his seeming ability to recoup and to go on with his life may be enhanced because he has not lost his image as a man, especially if he receives continued acceptance among his peers and family. On the other hand, since fewer men seek out support groups, perhaps many are also reluctant to talk with friends and family, and as a result, are more inclined to keep feelings to themselves. Perhaps men would like or welcome the support but sometimes don't know how to seek it out, other than through a new relationship with another woman.

Many women in our groups have claimed that being the spouse of a suicided mate definitely affects her relationships with other men. Jean discovered that some men were actually afraid of her. When she explained her husband's death to an acquaintance, he responded with, "What's the matter with you? Weren't you good enough to keep him alive?" "How could he say that?" she cried. "I know many widows and widowers whose spouses died of complications from smoking, drinking, or a car accident, and no one accuses them of failing to keeping their husband or wife alive."

"I've thought about this," continues Jean, "and I believe the reason why some men feel threatened by a woman whose husband killed himself is because he sees her emotional strength as dangerous. If a man is afraid of being in touch with himself, he will fear that she might see through him and expose his secrets or weaknesses. The strong or insightful woman is avoided, because she will not be easily controlled or fooled by a man who is unsure of himself and needs to feel in control." Jan, another group member agreed, but added, "It's really sad, because with my new insight into myself and others, I am less judgmental and more loving. I'd be a better wife now, and a mature man would welcome my depth of understanding."

Many of the women believe that men tend to shy away from intimate relationships after learning how their husbands died. "I have good relationships for a while," says Lynn. "Men tell me that I have helped them. But they date—and marry—someone else."

"One man listened attentively to my story, gently probing for details, then said, 'I'm staying away from you. You're lethal.'" reported Amy. "Would he have said that to me if my husband had died in any other way?" she asked. "I think not. He just assumed I was to blame."

Far too often, people *assume* a marriage was in trouble before the suicide occurred. Unfortunately, it is often the case that a separation or divorce is involved, but not always. "My marriage was good," said one widow. "We were in love and our family was not in trouble. It's unfair and doubly hard when people automatically assume the worst."

Both men and women express concern about telling other people that their spouses killed themselves. Jim, a widower, says, "Sometimes, after I explain how she died, people just look at me, and I think I can hear them think, 'You stupid ass. Your wife killed herself.' Judging from comments that have been made to me, I realize that people have assumptions which reflect back onto me. It's as if they think I am a weirdo—that I can't carry on a relationships. The whole thing is so unfair, because my marriage was a lifetime commitment to me."

As a result, many widows and widowers of suicides are evasive about how their spouses died. "When I'm truthful about his suicide," says Nell, "men scrutinize me, then they don't come around. So, when I meet someone new, I say my husband died unexpectedly or of heart failure. The issue with me is that he died. When I mention suicide, their reaction changes and the issue becomes *how* he died."

"People don't ask how I'm doing or what I need; they just want to know all about him. Even months after he's dead, he's still the one who gets their attention. It's amazing how much hold over us the suicided person has long after their death," said another widow.

There seemed to be general agreement among all of us, widows and widowers alike, that the blow to our self-esteem and the time involved in adjustment definitely affected our attitudes toward intimate relationships and altered the way we look at life. According to comments at Ray of Hope support group meetings, wives or women seem to have to work harder, or at least differently, than do men or husbands in order to free themselves from pain, trauma, and social stigma. This does not imply that the men grieved less intensely or recovered better than the women, just differently. "I feel embarrassed and betrayed," said one widower, "but I don't feel guilty or that I let her down."

The widows in our group believed that they usually waited longer than widowers before trying to rebuild a social life with the opposite sex. Two to four years was not unusual for many women to wait, whereas most men started dating within a few months.

Most of the women in the group fell into one of four categories: those who withdrew from all close relationships, those who avoided relationships with all men, those who remarried very soon after their husband's death, and those who had relationships but refused to remarry. Many of the women described their new relationships as destructive but hesitated to end them.

One young woman said, "I don't fit into any of those categories. I went with every man I could as soon as I could. I was intimate with over fifty of them in two years. Steve's suicide was such a rejection of me that it just about killed my image of myself as a desirable woman. Maybe, I thought I was 'showing' him (or myself) that someone wanted me after all."

Comments from some of the women in long-standing but destructive relationships were as follows:

* "Now I doubt my ability to be a good wife or mother."
* "People think I'm the merry widow. It's my front—a facade. Inside, I'm afraid to let anyone know how much I hurt. When people say or assume things that hurt me, I just laugh it off. That's my way of protecting myself."
* "I'm really hard on this guy. I push him around. I think that if he leaves me, then I'll know it was because of me that Larry killed himself. Maybe I'm testing to see if I really am a dangerous person—if I pushed Larry into it. If this guy stays with me, then I guess I'm okay."
* "I think I take abuse in my present relationship because I'm trying to make up for what I didn't do for John."
* "Maybe no one will want to marry me now. Maybe this relationship, bad as it is, is all I'll ever have. I don't want to take a chance on being alone again."

* "The effect of my husband's suicide on me is permanent. Relationships all seem to fall apart. I feel rejected over something and withdraw. I now tend to choose relationships with no future or commitment. I guess I want no ties—to be able to get out whenever I can."
* Some women choose to be alone. "I will never allow myself to go through anything like this again," or "I will never again love someone so much that I could be hurt this much."

Many of us, I believe, shared this underlying attitude that we would avoid the pain of another loss at any cost. For some of the women, that meant withdrawing or isolating themselves from family as well. Lola, for example, lost her husband, son, and a daughter within ten years. A surviving daughter and son try to stay in touch. "I want to respond to them, but I can't," says Lola tearfully. "I can't take the chance. Being close means that I'll love them too much—I might want too much from them, and should I lose one of them also, I'll hurt much more than I can handle."

Another common attitude among both spouses is "I no longer have the patience or tolerance for nonsense, or for people who play games, so I just stay away from people I choose not to deal with. I no longer allow the criticism or approval of others to control my life."

I believe those of us who are widowed by suicide sometimes think we have to become strong to offset the hurt. The more sensitive we are, the more we feel the hurt. People who are less feeling appear to be stronger because they don't care. They can throw something off and go on—but the caring suffer more and may appear weaker, when they are actually stronger. Perhaps it's this strength that separates survivors—especially the women—from other people. It's so misleading, because other people then think we are so strong—we don't need anyone else—but we do. Having a strong character doesn't mean we are not vulnerable to pain and loneliness.

Not all survivor's stories are war stories. Jim, a widower, and Kay, a widow, met in one of our groups and were married a year later. In many cases, family ties are strengthened, as happened with my oldest son, Daryl, and myself.

Sometimes, family members need to process their grief with others outside the family before they can reunite with their family. This is an important point to consider if you are puzzled or worried about a family member who insists on distancing him/ herself. Give one another and yourself permission to take some distance if you need to. It may not be a personal thing, and not everyone will understand the need for distance, but some people have to do it, because it feels right at the time. Be patient.

Although these attitudes of both the spouse who is widowed by suicide and of society toward him or her are mutually debilitating, I believe they can be overcome. A suicided spouse should take care not to project fears of rejection, judgment, or abandonment onto others, thereby ruining the chance to love or be loved again. Many a spouse does heal from these terrible wounds to the psyche and goes on to take part in close, loving relationships and remarriage. As feelings about oneself as a worthwhile person develop and radiate outward, the world relaxes and responds in kind. But these people need patience, assistance, and understanding to get there.

8

❖

About the Children

Together, parent and child, you will try to build the temple of tomorrow's dream upon the grave of yesterday's bitterness.
                                    RABBI EARL GROLLMAN

Children, just like adults, need to grieve and deal with their feelings. Losing a family member through death is traumatic enough. Losing a parent or sibling by suicide compounds the agony. Since children may cry one minute and laugh or play the next, their suffering isn't always obvious. But it would be wrong to assume that they aren't deeply affected. Because they are too young to have developed coping skills, as have adults, it may be years before this processing really begins. In order to avoid this "numbing out," children desperately need the help of caring adults to go from denial through pain and depression to acceptance and hope. Yet, the special needs of children are often not recognized by caregivers or family members, and therefore are missed.

Their Legacy

Studies show that nine out of ten suicides occur in or near the home. Next to spouses, children are the second largest group of persons to witness a suicide or discover the body. That's because they are naturally in the home. Think about the effect that has on a young and impressionable mind. Even if children did not witness the death or discover the body, they may have arrived home soon afterward. During the commotion with police, ambulance, and so on, they often are overlooked, pushed aside, or removed from the scene. As a result, facts may become distorted in their minds, and we can't begin to think what they may imagine and believe.

In some cases, a child has been directly involved—asked to help in the act. For example, a child may have been instructed to push away a stool or help steady the gun. A mother who took an overdose of sleeping pills, told her six-year-old daughter, "When Daddy calls, tell him that Mommy is asleep and won't wake up." Now a woman in her twenties, the daughter still struggles with self-blame and anger at both parents. She feels duped—used—by both parents to participate in the death of her mother. She has vowed that she will never have children of her own. She is experiencing what suicidologists refer to as having inherited a legacy of suicide, which means her entire life has been affected, and she herself is at increased risk to suicide.

Another example is that of a young widow who tearfully reported that her seven-year-old son asked, "Mom, how will I grow up to be a man now that Daddy is gone?" She answered, "Oh, you'll be a man—a fine one—just like your daddy was." He responded, "Does that mean I'll shoot myself, too?" A teenager whose father suicided after killing another person, says, "I feel tainted—as if I have inherited bad blood." Many times, parents report the loss of more than one child to suicide, indicating that sibling loss, as well as parental loss, share in the legacy.

An inheritance is something handed down; a legacy is something that can be inherited. I an *not* saying here that suicide is genetically inherited, but that the idea can be seductive and behavior copied. Edwin Shneidman states in his foreword to *Survivors of Suicide*, edited by Albert C. Cain, that Cain's book "invites our keenest attention to *the* largest mental health casualty area related to suicide: the traumatically created widows and orphans—in short, the benighted victims of the suicidal act."[1] Many authorities cite the alarming statistic that survivors have a 300 percent increased risk of suicide. We should never underestimate the power of that legacy, especially as it affects the child or sibling of a suicide.

Children of a suicided parent also show a higher rate of behavioral, emotional, and self-destructive disturbance even into adulthood than those who have lost a parent through other forms of death, according to a review of suicide survivorship literature by Ness and Pfeffer (1990). Some adults who lost a parent by suicide during childhood seldom experience a day in which they don't recall the parent's death or fantasize their own suicide. Some fear they are destined to die by their own hand, according to a study of the emotional impact of parent suicide upon children by Albert Cain and Irene Fast.[2] Teenagers also may be so involved with the turmoil of just being a teen that grief symptoms and/or emotional problems may be delayed from three to five years.

I believe we dare not underestimate the losses endured by the children of a suicided parent. That's why widows and widowers of a suicided spouse, who realize they must consider more than just their own pain, need individual and specialized care. The additional responsibility of dealing with the effects of this event upon the next generation—and possibly the entire family—is a crushing load for any parent to shoulder alone.

Acknowledge Loss and Grief

The period after a suicide is a crucial time for avoiding a serious disintegration of the parent–child relationship and for creating a special bond through love and sharing. Most professionals believe children should be told the truth about suicide under the following conditions: (1) they should be told while the parent or family is in counseling or therapy; (2) the information should be given to the child gently and perhaps gradually; (3) counseling should be continued after the children have been told. However, the subject cannot always be confined to the counselor's office; it can come up anytime.

When it does, invite children to share feelings by saying something such as, "My heart aches sometimes. Does yours?" Or "I miss Daddy's smile so much. What do you miss the most? When do you think about him? What do you remember?"

Encourage discussions about death; use opportunities such as the death of a pet, a neighbor, or even the news. If you don't have an answer to a question, don't hesitate to admit, "I don't know," but be willing to say, "Let's talk about it," or "What do you think?" Listen carefully to questions. Don't answer more than is asked, because children may have difficulty verbalizing their thoughts and feelings. For example, they may ask, "Do you still love me, Mommy?" when they really want to know, "Will you leave me like Daddy did?" Questions about heaven and death may really mean "What's going to happen to me?" or "Who will take care of me?" Constantly reassure them of your love and continued presence; hold them, rock them, spend time with them, cry with them. Actions sometimes speak louder than words. Your actions tell the child how you are handling yourself and what you expect from the child.

For this reason, don't be afraid to cry or show grief in front of your children. Reverend John H. Hewett, author of *After Suicide*, says, "You will teach your child about suicide, whether you plan to or not. They will watch you and notice your responses. They learn from you how they should act in the aftermath. So, decide now to be a good teacher."[3] If you act as if nothing has changed, so will the child, even at the risk of creating great inner (and secret) insecurity.

If you avoid expressing grief or talking about the deceased, you are also sending a message that says you don't care about that person and don't miss him/her. Children may also misinterpret sadness, depression, or preoccupation as personal rejection ("Mom or Dad doesn't care about me") or as blame ("They blame me for my sister's death"). A child may suspect that you wish he or she had died instead of the other person. A child may feel that if you don't miss his brother or sister, you wouldn't miss him/her either, if they were dead. In a child's mind, that may mean that you don't really love any of them. Not knowing how to express this fear, your child may become withdrawn, rebellious, angry, or resentful. This misinterpretation is not limited to small children. Adolescents, teenagers, and even adult children may share this feeling.

If, on the other hand, you actually are secretly rejecting or blaming a child or sibling for the suicide, don't think that you are fooling him or her. Children know when you aren't honest. They know when they are being resented, but accusing them outright is an explosive situation as well. You have a lot of power in your hands when you reject or blame the child, power that can destroy the child, the family, or yourself if you aren't careful.

For example, one father came to a meeting and confessed, "I told our fourteen-year-old he was responsible for his mother's suicide. Six months later, he suicided also and left a note saying he didn't deserve to live. I killed him with my accusations. I know I did. He needed me, and I turned on him. How can I go on?" This situation requires professional help for all involved.

Honesty and consistency about what happened cannot be underestimated. Being lied to, even with the best of intentions, is demeaning. It's worse than knowing the truth. Misrepresentations and changing versions will create suspicion and confusion which lead to distrust and resentment. Even young children may know more about death than you realize. Tell the truth in simple words, without dwelling on the gory details. It is especially dangerous to lie to a child who was present or nearby during the event. Avoid saying, "Oh, you saw that on TV," or "You must have been dreaming." The child may not argue but may come to distrust both himself and you.

Euphemisms, half-truths, and evasions tend to increase anxieties and add confusion. The child already has enough self-doubt, anger, guilt, and fear. If you pretend that Grandpa has gone on a long trip, the child becomes confused and may refuse to trust you. Respect a child's emotions and intelligence.

Having said the above, consider your timing. Young children may see death only as death. They may not understand, or be interested in, different kinds of death. To a small child, the loss of a beloved grandfather is the same, whether it's by cancer, accident, or suicide. Deal with their loss and grief first; they will let you know when they become concerned with the complicated *how* of death.

Depending on age, children may not have learned how to tell you how they feel but will show their feelings at play. According to Glen Davidson, in his pamphlet *Death—What Do You Say to a Child?*, there are clues that can tell you far better than the child can explain how he/she is handling the situation, such as a return to infantile behavior, thumb-sucking, bed-wetting, nightmares, or a fear of going to sleep.[4] Other clues are fighting, temper tantrums, poor grades, excessive crying, or even relief, especially if the child had been afraid of the deceased person.

Reverend Hewett explains that small children may act out their grief in play, while older children may constantly chatter, be full of nervous energy, or develop stomachaches or flulike symptoms.[5] Some children may assume the responsibilities of the deceased family member by trying to become, for example, the "man of the family." Others may try to become artistic or athletic in an attempt to follow in the footsteps of a deceased sibling. They may also withdraw or become rebellious. Be patient with all these behaviors rather than punish; assure the child that although this behavior is of concern to both of you, it will pass.

Dealing with Loss and Grief

Guilt is a more common reaction among children than we often realize. For example, if a child has wished a parent or sibling dead during a disagreement and that person later dies, the child may feel directly responsible, believing that his/her thoughts were powerful enough to kill. "I hoped Daddy would die and he did." Because such "wishes" are more likely to occur in families characterized by conflict and quarreling, the children may already feel guilty about a lot of other things. They may blame themselves for being a burden to their parents, for causing strife in the family, or simply for being "bad." If they knew about an earlier suicide attempt or threat by a family member but kept it secret, they may blame themselves for not preventing the death. If they wished "he'd do it and get it over with," they may later be consumed with shame and self-blame.

Other emotions to recognize are anger and feelings of rejection. Children may feel angry at a dead sibling or parent for leaving them or for inflicting grief, anguish, and shame on the family. At the same time, since they may feel the need to be loyal to the deceased, they are torn inside. Helpless and despairing about their inability to change the situation, they may lash out against anyone for any real or imagined shortcoming.

For this reason, be careful not to point a finger at anyone. A child who has witnessed marital arguments may blame the surviving parent for influencing the other parent or for not preventing the death. They need to know that other factors were at work. Creating divided loyalties or instilling anger will only harm the child.

Another common emotion is fear. Young children may suddenly fear being alone or may panic in normal situations. They fear change and separation, because they don't know how to handle it.

I believe that even small children feel a great need to protect and care for their parents, and much of their behavior stems from this. For example, an older child may hesitate to discuss the subject because he/she doesn't want Mother to cry. When she does, the child feels guilty and helpless because of failing to keep Mother happy. In frustration, the child may lash out in anger at either the parent or someone or something else.

Sometimes a child will attack someone he/she perceives to be an offender and cry, "Don't hurt my Mommy." A child may try to protect the remaining parent at any cost. After all, it's dreadful to realize that you are tiny, dependent, and may lose the other parent as well. If the suicided parent often cried or yelled (for example) prior to the suicide, then crying or yelling is a bad sign in the child's eyes.

Some children may decide to protect the remaining parent by staying glued to Mom or Dad's side. You can't fault a child for wanting to protect you, but you can talk with him/her about it. Offer the child acceptable ways to vent anger and energy through physical activity: permission to yell and scream sometimes, a punching bag to hit, or hammer and nails to pound.

Avoid blaming God, advises Reverend Hewett. Don't tell the child that God needed her daddy in heaven or took her brother to be with Him. She will believe that God is responsible for the death of her parent or sibling and will find it impossible to believe in a loving heavenly Father.[6]

Most important is a loving attitude by the surviving parent and other family members. Handle the child's feelings delicately. Forcing a child to repress honest fears about loss can prevent him/her from learning to adapt to the changes in life that loss brings about and may create future emotional or behavior problems. Encouraging children to express thoughts, feelings, and fear will ease their sense of helplessness and responsibility.

You might say to a small child, "Sometimes, I miss Daddy so much that it makes me tired, and all I want to do is sleep. Sometimes I don't hear you when you talk. That doesn't mean I don't love you. Let me know how you feel, and let's be patient with each other."

Some ways children can express themselves other than in conversation are through the creative activity of art or poetry and helping with decisions. Encourage them to draw pictures, keep a journal, or write a poem or story. Many professionals emphasize the value of family memorial services at home, church, or grave site. Allow children to help with funeral decisions, be involved in the service if possible, and put a drawing or poem in the casket.

Together, make plans and carry them out: donate flowers, plant a tree, or share pictures and stories, and make a scrapbook. Allow them to help sort through the deceased's things. On an anniversary such as the birth date or death date might be a good time to put pictures or a note in a balloon and send it "to heaven." Children may enjoy helping put together the Living Memory History described in Chapter 4.

You can also include the child in memory activities or rituals. Give flowers to the church on anniversaries, or go to the cemetery and plant a bush. One family placed a birdhouse near the grave and go regularly to feed and check on its occupants. Explain yourself if you don't feel up to the usual holiday rituals, and try a new one. Reach out to others by volunteering at a homeless shelter, for example, or invite in people who are away from their homeland.

Some communities have support groups, camps, or special activities for children after the death of a parent, relative, friend, or sibling. Read books about loss and grief, and don't forget the funeral director or local hospice office as resources for printed material, films, and videos. The Centering Corporation listed in the resource section offers an excellent catalog of books, activities, and a camp to help children, adolescents, and teens with grief.

Let children see you confront your grief and share in your efforts to resolve it. Give them the affirmation of life they so desperately need to dispel their own morbid thoughts and death wishes before they get out of hand after the loss of a parent or sibling. This is postvention in the truest sense—preventing the legacy of suicide a generation in advance.

9

❖

About God

*For he shall give his angels charge over thee, to keep thee in all thy
ways. They shall bear thee up in their hands, lest thou dash thy foot
against a stone.*

PSALM 91:11,12

The subjects of God, sin, salvation, and forgiveness are very important to many survivors who have contacted Ray of Hope. Some
of them being to question their prior belief that nothing exists after
death, because it no longer provides comfort. They want more: a
spiritual concept that allows them to coexist on some level with
that person after all. A future beyond becomes meaningful. But
what if that realm is one of lost souls and condemnation? "Is my
loved one doomed to eternal damnation?" they ask. "Is suicide
truly an unforgivable sin?"

Some Church History

Actually, several suicides are recorded in the Bible, but none of
these cases mention eternal damnation. King Saul's suicide (I
Samuel 31:4) for example, was culturally acceptable at that time. It
was an honored custom (and practical) for a defeated ruler or
military leader (and his aide as well) to die by his own hand rather
than face humiliation or torture by the victorious enemy. Samson
(Judges 16:30), although he took (or sacrificed) his own life in the
Philistine temple, is considered a hero of faith (Hebrews 11:32–34).

Even Judas (Matthew 27:5) was not condemned for committing suicide, but for betraying Christ. Two other suicides are Abimelech (Judges 9:54) and Paul's jailor (Acts 16:27).[1]

One may argue that the commandment, "Thou shalt not kill" (Exodus 20:13), applies to suicide as well as murder or homicide. But this argument may not be entirely scriptural. According to Walther Zimmerli in his *Old Testament Theology in Outline*, the Hebrew word used for "kill" (*ratsach*) means to violently slay or murder, with premeditation, or as a wanton uncontrolled attack upon another.[2] It is not used in connection with suicide accounts in the Old Testament, which seems to reinforce a distinction between suicide and murder. With suicide, death was considered to have resulted from the dying person's desire or actions rather than death being forced upon him or her.

In *The City of God*, fifth-century church father Saint Augustine discusses suicide at length and determines that it should be considered a sin, because it violates the sacredness of human life, which is created in God's image, and because there is no chance for repentance (even though many people die in a supposed state of unrepentance, such as war, accidents, and the like).[3] He used the commandment against killing as a basis for his argument (and the church concurred), despite the fact that for the prior 500 years, this commandment had been interpreted as prohibiting the taking of someone else's life.

The resulting condemnation of suicide by ecclesiastical law was later explained and expanded upon by Thomas Aquinas in his *Summa Theologica*, and is the foundation for the mindset regarding suicide that has stayed with the church throughout most of recent history. Alvarez, in his book *The Savage God* (1973), presents an excellent historical background of Christian influence on modern attitudes toward suicide.

Saint Augustine assumed his position because he was caught in a religious and social dilemma. On the one hand, he wanted to preserve the canonization of saints who had died for their faith, and on the other, to find a way to stop the increasing number of suicides "in the name of religion." Life was so difficult for the early Christian that the reward of heavenly paradise attached to martyrdom was too much for many people to resist. Suicide became so common that Augustine called it the people's "daily sport." Augustine's intent with this position regarding suicide was to prevent the needless destruction of countless lives. As a result, Saint Augustine was probably the founder of the *first* suicide prevention program in history. And for centuries, in its way, it has worked.

Nor was it Augustine's intent to punish survivors. Punishment came about later, when rulers and kings decided that if suicide was a sin against God, then it was also a crime against the state. This idea was taken from the earlier Romans, who condoned suicide except when someone did it to avoid punishment for a crime. The Crown then determined that in return for the loss of those individuals' contributions to society, they should forfeit their property. The Crown was especially interested in case that property happened to be a castle, land, or other riches. Since the suicided person was dead, the only way to collect property was from survivors. Naturally, survivors took exception to this and did all they could to cover up or hide the mode of death when it was self-inflicted.

Earlier suicides were buried outside the church cemetery walls as a message that life was sacred, and self-destruction was an act against God and nature, not as punishment, and not because of any avenging evil spirits. Those ideas are a combination of both centuries' earlier pagan practices and a later mindset arising from fear, superstition, and, possibly, a host of guilty consciences.

Influence of Superstition

Suicides were not the first or only corpses subject to desecration. Suspected vampires had long been buried under a crossroads with an iron or wooden stake through the heart, so their spirits would either be too confused by overhead traffic—or pinned down—to get up and away. Suspected witches or warlocks (who might be anyone who was different, alone, or a loner, crippled, ugly, unpleasant, or disliked) as well as the murderer, the murdered, and any victim of an unusual or unexplained accident or mishap, could be dragged by the heels face down, let out through a window rather than through the door, sent downriver tied to a raft, burned, or drawn and quartered, all actions designed to confuse, confine, or control a feared, evil, or avenging spirit.

Although these and many other atrocities were committed against the body of a suicide, it was not by church law or decree that these atrocities occurred. They were carried out by people following customs, beliefs, and habits handed down through centuries of superstitious fear regarding angry, tortured, lost, or evil spirits.

The origin of superstitious beliefs and rituals, some of which can be traced to the Stone Age, and some of which can only be speculated upon, are based on such things as personal experience, perceived events, and folklore. Primitive peoples, bereft of education and modern scientific explanations, could only attribute weather changes, catastrophes, violent behaviors, and personal mishaps to powers unseen and unknown.

Opting not to be at the total mercy of irrational or supernatural forces, people devised ways to tap into that energy in order to detect, avert, counter, or ensure certain results. Omens, amulets, rituals, and so on, were believed to give mankind's natural world a magical power of its own.

The ritual of sacrifice, human or otherwise, was a way of giving something to appease unseen gods, so they would not come later via famine or flood, illness or accident, earthquake or storm, and take even more lives, crops, or goods. It is similar to paying taxes to the IRS in the spring in the hope they will not unexpectedly return and claim everything.

Primitive man also believed the human soul could enter or leave its body through body openings, such as the eyes (windows of the soul) or the mouth. Temporarily minus the soul, a body could be vulnerable to marauding spirits with evil intent. A sneeze might propel the soul out unexpectedly, but a countering

"Bless you" offered protection until the rightful soul could get back in. For a similar reason, it was risky to suddenly awaken a sound sleeper, whose soul might be out traveling while its body was sleeping.

Protection against evil spirits was vital, as they could wreak havoc of all sorts. They could, after entering an unprotected body, drive that person to commit crimes, murder, rape, and a host of mayhem. In particular, it seemed reasonable that only something unseen could *"drive* a person to suicide" or other violent behavior. Or the tortured spirit of an unwilling victim, executed felon, or suicide, might, if harboring a grudge, return to take revenge on its tormentors or killers. This could be especially so of a suicide, just in case he/she was *driven* to self-destruction by family or pressures other than an unseen spirit. Even then, survivors dealt with their own guilt and feelings of accountability as best they knew how.

Numerous practices were used to keep spirits in—or out—of bodies. The power of the cross created confusion, which led to crossing fingers to ward off evil influences. The circle of life, symbolized in wreaths, was thought to bind a spirit to the grave. If that failed, a grave marker would hold a spirit down, or harking back to stone worship, provide housing for spirits while at the same time preventing wild animals from digging up the remains.

The Graveyard Watcher, popular in Great Britain for a time, was a job given each newly deceased spirit (until the next burial) to keep some spirits inside the cemetery walls, keep some out, and summon others to take its place. A suicide or felon buried outside the cemetery could be a permanent watcher, much to the relief of other residential souls, and since the spirit could not leave its job as watcher—it had no time left to haunt survivors—much to the relief of survivors.

Prior to burial, weights or coins kept the eyes closed, so one's soul would not leave its body through the eyes. Some societies filled up or covered all body openings (routes of escape) "just in case." Although we still cover the deceased's body, close its eyes, use tombstones, and either blindfold or place a bag over the head of those we execute, the reasons now are purely practical and sophisticated. Right?

Changing Attitudes

Lest we judge, it should be noted that our ancestors, although they may have been ignorant of psychology or science, and lacked the guidance of Scripture (or supermarket tabloids), were not stupid. They used all their knowledge at hand to explain and manage unusual or frightening behavior. And attitudes changed with time. By the fourteenth century, calamities, such as plague, were no longer blamed on multiple, unseen gods or spirits but were figured to be caused by the sins and faults of mankind, thereby transferring the focus of blame onto one another. And there it has pretty well stayed for the most part.

However, over the years, many well-intentioned people have attempted to dispel stigmatizing myths and labels of sin or crime regarding suicide. An explanation that suicide results from mental illness also went awry, and "crazy" was added to the list. But understanding hearts have persisted with scholarly writings and psychological analyses which have—and are—changing attitudes. And now, thank God, current study attempts to explain suicide as having multidimensional causes and to explore and develop multidimensional treatment.

And as attitudes change, laws and guidelines change. During the 1870s and 1880s in England and Europe, the last of the laws (1) forbidding suicide, (2) allowing property seizure, and (3) forbidding churchyard burial, were abolished. At present, no governmental law or ecclesiastical doctrine forbids or condemns suicide, or enforces certain burial practices.

True, one still encounters church members and nonmembers who pronounce judgment, but they are speaking on behalf of their own attitudes and do not represent the religious institution as a whole. The tendency to blame the church for all the ills of society is equally responsible for the confusion among church leaders and members—and the unchurched—as well as unfair to the religious institution at large. Human decision is an individual ability and action, not something forced upon one by the church or religious beliefs.

Just as it was the people themselves of earlier societies and communities who carried out ancient practices, it is still the collective beliefs of family, community, church, and society which interpret or honor, or disregard prevailing attitudes and customs.

An interesting observation by Alvarez, and one worth pondering, suggests that often-admired permissive or tolerant attitudes toward suicide may actually be based on indifference to life and the state of one's soul, rather than out of caring and concern. In that historical time of permissive Hellenistic influence, it was Augustine and his peers who recognized that the sanctity of life is God's premise rather than mankind's.

Currently, there is general Judeo–Christian consensus in two areas. First, interpretation of church policy and guidelines is at the discretion of both leaders and laity, with social and community influences taken into account. Second, although God gives life, and people are the stewards of that life, there are always extenuating circumstances.

Rabbi Jeff Portman summed it up for me this way: "Jewish tradition includes the belief that since man is created in God's image, then the act of suicide is destroying God's image. This is a sacrilege, but not a condemnation of someone who was in great physical or mental anguish." A similar empathetic perspective is detailed in the 1994 *Catechism of the Catholic Church*. Father John Boyles said, "God came to save the lost, not condemn them."

Comfort in Scripture

I would also like to share the comfort I received from scripture and my pastor after Bill's suicide. When I wondered if I could still pray for Bill's soul, Pastor Paul reminded me that early Christians prayed for salvation of departed Christians who had killed themselves in order to avoid Roman torture and assassination. Those suicides were treated with the same respect and rituals as any other death, with none of the later stigma and desecration.

To answer my own question about Bill being in heaven—yes,

I believe so! My doubt and anxiety about Bill's state of grace at the time of his death were put to rest when Pastor Paul pointed out that I had no way of knowing what sort of spiritual confrontation took place in the split-second between the time Bill pulled the trigger and total blackness took over. In that realm, perhaps only an instant was needed for Bill to repent if, indeed, he even needed to. Bill often told me he believed that the way he died would not separate him from the love of God. There is scriptural foundation for his belief. In Romans 8:37–39, St. Paul writes that nothing, including death, will separate us from the love of God.

That promise includes the grief-stricken. Some people seem to think it is wrong for a "Christian" to grieve for any length of time. At a prayer meeting, a young widow was trying to explain her feelings. She was in the longing and pining stage, where symptoms are as much physical as emotional. Her entire body ached. One well-intentioned member, in an effort to help her, quoted one Bible passage after another.

Not being widowed herself, she had completely missed Amy's point and insisted that Amy should have more faith, read more Scripture. "But I do," Amy wailed, "and I still hurt." Of course, she hurt, and she would continue to hurt until the stage had run its course. The implication that she was unfaithful to God because she felt grief only compounded her pain with new guilt and fears. Sometimes, a physical need must be met before one can be spiritually responsive. When Amy was ready, her faith was the source of strength she'd always known it was. Having faith means being open to the healing of grief, not the absence of grief.

The Bible is filled with stories of people who mourned. Scripture gives explicit permission to grieve and provides promises of healing, examples of how to mourn, and suggestions for using the experience to help ourselves and others. A few are as follows:

Effects of grief: Psalm 69:1–3, 20.
David mourned Jonathan: II Samuel 1:17–27.
Resolving despair: Hebrews 5:7.
Resolving anger: Matthew 5:23–25, 18:15–17, Ephesians 4:26.
Resolving anxiety: Matthew 6:34, Philippians 4:6–9, I Peter 5:7.

Resolving guilt: Psalm 103, I John 1:9, Jeremiah 3:13.
Resolving loneliness: Isaiah 40:31, Philippians 4:13.

While I cannot accept the idea that Bill's choice to commit suicide was within God's divine will, I believe that my God, as I know Him, is both just and loving. "God's will," says Pastor David Aananson (Christ the King Lutheran Church, Iowa City, Iowa) "is that we have life, and have it abundantly." The Bible is also filled with stories of God's compassion for people with troubles. The "free will" with which God created His people means that persons are free to make choices about life and death. And although Scripture warns people to consider the consequences of decisions and actions, it does not condemn them for having the ability to make decisions.

Perhaps one might ponder the possible intent of the suicide victim. Consider the circumstances of a young woman who kills herself in order to avoid being raped and killed during the capture of her country. It would seem that the invaders' intent was to experience a thrill through raping and killing the girl. It would seem the girl's intent was to seek relief through killing herself.

For survivors who are concerned with questions of sin and judgment, a look at the victim's possible intent can be very comforting. For those who are concerned with pronouncing judgment, a look at the possible intent may be quite revealing. When tempted to judge suicide as a sin, perhaps we should consider that we all are sinners in one way or another, and all constantly in need of repentance and forgiveness.

"While many things are condemned by God's word," said Pastor Aananson, "all mankind is covered by God's grace. Although God condemns sin, He redeems the sinner. With suicide, perhaps it is *only* God who understands the circumstances, who knows the desperation of the moment—much more than even the one who suicides—who meets us in the toughest of times. The fact of the matter is that deeply committed religious people do kill themselves, but in the midst of death—even suicide—God has the final word, and his final word is forgiveness, love, and hope. Such is the power of God, and the message of the cross."

The Bible is not explicit about suicide, and perhaps that is for the best. If suicide were definitely condoned as an easy and acceptable way of coping with stress, many lives might be needlessly destroyed. On the other hand, if suicide were explicitly condemned as an unforgivable sin, it would conflict with the biblical image of a just and compassionate God.

If suicide is generally viewed as behavior which influences the time and method of one's own death, then all forms of self-destructive behavior fall into that category. If self-destructive actions were unforgivable, a large number of mankind could be automatically condemned, and where would that leave hope? It is the absence of hope that leads to despair and death. I believe the very silence of Scripture concerning suicide, and the *lack* of silence about God's grace, allows *for* hope to flourish—both for the victim and for the survivor.

10

❖

In the Aftermath

The visitation is the social release of the body. The funeral is the spiritual release of the body. The burial is the physical release of the body.

ED VINING
Past President
Illinois Funeral Directors Association

"Funeral directors are in a distinctively unique position regarding suicide survivors. They are virtually the only professionals to come into contact with nearly all suicide survivors. Their influence on the suicide survivor's grief resolution process can be invaluable, and unequaled by any psychologist, physician, counselor, clergyman or other caregiver." They also are in a position to counteract three important issues that contribute directly to survivor stigma and to delayed or unresolved grief. Counteracting those issues is easy once the funeral director and family are aware of them.

The Funeral

First, suicide is a form of death in which we argue over the right or wrong of it. It is the only form of death in which society makes moral and value judgments concerning both the deceased and the survivors, and where the survivors' own moral and value judgments influence decisions concerning the funeral. The debate begins immediately.

Should the service be public or private? Or none at all? Do we hold it in the funeral home rather than church or synagogue, and why? If suicide is a sin, who officiates, the clergy or a friend? Do we keep details from grandparents and/or children? How? What do we tell the newspapers, and what do we say to insurance people? What do we tell visitors who ask personal questions? What if he or she was mentally ill? Can suicide be inherited? Whose fault was it? Mine? Yours? Should we see the body before it is prepared for visitation? The basic concern is not so much that someone died, but that he/she died by suicide. We need to ask if some of the issues would be so important if the person had died in any other way.

The funeral director can discourage the family from rushing through the service too quickly. Sometimes, decisions for a hasty or closed funeral are based on shame, fear, and humiliation. Be sure these feelings don't overshadow judgment when making plans. A private or hurried service can do the very things survivors want to avoid—invite questions and draw attention to the mode of death. The more you hide, the more suspicious it looks. Listen when the funeral director explains the importance of the funeral ritual.

The second factor is that of acceptance of not only death but also death by suicide. Listen to people carefully; are they saying, "I can't believe he's dead?" or "I can't believe he killed himself?" There is a big difference there. Self-inflicted death is intentional and not the same as death by natural causes; therefore, its very nature makes it difficult to believe and accept. These survivors often need to accept the fact of suicide before they can even begin to deal with the reality of death. This is a double blow: not just death, but suicide.

An opportunity to see the body before it is prepared can help a family come to terms with self-inflicted death—"He really did do it himself." The idea of seeing a bullet wound may be unthinkable at first, but weeks or months later, when survivors still question if it actually was suicide as opposed to an accident, murder, or natural death, they may regret not having seen for themselves.

Time alone with the body also helps to overcome shock and begin saying good-bye.

Kay, a young woman who attended Ray of Hope meetings, had been away at college when her teenage sister shot herself. Everyone but Kay participated in rushing the girl to the emergency room and was there when she died. When Kay arrived home, her sister was ready for visitation. "I envied the family's being there when she did it—seeing all the blood and gore. They can accept that she shot herself. I can't. When I saw her, she looked asleep." Kay also mourned another loss. She explained how the experience created a sort of bond among the rest of the family. They shared a common experience. She did not; she was left out.

Funeral director Bruce Conley says,

> It is the simple permission to hold the lifeless body of a loved one, to speak the unspeakable words of anguish ... to share the guilt of a loved one's parting note—the simple permission to do these things and more, which brings a comfort that nothing else can give. So simple yet so profound in the midst of the crisis.[1]

The funeral director can advise the family members to at least seriously consider seeing the body before preparation. He can explain what they might expect to see, answer questions about autopsies, preparation for burial, and the like. He can point out that it might aid them with acceptance of the idea of self-inflicted death, thus eliminating some of the future denial and searching, and then give them time alone to make their decision. Some people definitely know that they do not want or need in any way to take part in this ritual, and that should be respected. However, the offer and explanation should still be presented by the funeral director to all the family. Sometimes, not knowing can be as bad as knowing.

On the other hand, those who witnessed the death or found the body may already have all the visual proof they need. We tend to remember what we have last seen, so, in some cases, viewing the body in the casket may help to soften the impact of an ugly memory.

Third, death by suicide seems to imply a weakness or failure on the part of someone—the family, the suicide victim, or both. Much of the survivors' grief work consists of repairing these damaged images. They work to repair the self-image of the suicided person to show that his/her actions were justified in some way. They also work to rebuild their own shattered sense of self-worth as a valuable and competent parent or spouse.

This is a large part of the suicide survivor's grief work, and the funeral director can do a great deal to start that rebuilding process as soon as possible. Sometimes suicide survivors tend to be apologetic or defensive when they should be proud of their loved one. The funeral director's goal is to replace the curiosity and embarrassment of visitors with memories of the persons as they were at their best.

Many funeral directors now encourage the family to arrange a sharing table the night before visitation, where family members may bring something uniquely precious to themselves—a photo, a personal article, or a memento. Perhaps someone has written a poem or a moving tribute. Encourage the family to share not only the sorrow of death but also memories of living.

Something a little different than a sharing table is an appreciation table. I attended the funeral of a fourteen-year-old boy whose younger sister tended a display of her brother's prized possessions and achievements. She showed visitors his artwork, poetry, model airplanes, and 4-H awards. His favorite toys were there, his baby shoes, his first book, his school pictures, and papers arranged to show his progress and accomplishments as he grew up. This was the family's way of saying, "Our brother/son was a valuable, worthy, talented person, and we are proud of him." People left that service with impressions of Chris as a person rather than "that boy who killed himself."

At their first meeting, the funeral director should encourage family members to write personal letters to the deceased about whatever is in their hearts and minds, then privately place them in the casket when or how they choose. Others may want to place a personal item or other token of affection or good-bye in the casket as well.

Children should be allowed to participate in funeral plans and rituals as much as possible so they don't come to resent feeling left out or unimportant. Respect their love for the deceased as well. Unfortunately, suicide tends to pull families apart, so the funeral director can use these actions of sharing and participation to help unite a family from the beginning.

The funeral director should be aware of the unique aspects of after-suicide grief and be willing to spend extra time in discussion with the family or call in a trained survivor to counsel about funeral plans, the dynamics of their grief, and offer lists of legal and financial aid, grief groups, counselors, and so on. Many funeral homes now offer their own aftercare services and libraries of tapes, books, and videos on all forms of death.

A woman who attended our ROH meetings mentioned that she had asked her family and friends to make cassette recordings of their memories and thoughts about her son in place of flowers or money. I was so intrigued with this idea that I made arrangements with my own funeral director to set aside one room with a recorder and tapes (when the time comes). The tapes will be for my children, who know very little about me.

Funeral director Ed Vining cautions that involvement of the funeral director is proper up to a point. He says that too much involvement makes the funeral director primarily a caregiver, whereas with no involvement, the funeral is just a business transaction. However, armed with adequate information and sensitivity, the funeral director is in a position to assist greatly in reducing the stress and damaging repercussions of this tragedy. With effective intervention, some issues do not grow into big issues.

The Investigation

All too soon, the shock of suicide wears off and survivors begin to ask questions they were unable to formulate or confront immediately following the death, such as, "How do the police know it was self-inflicted?" or "Why won't they tell me how they know that it was not an accident or murder?"

These questions may have been there in their minds immediately following the death, but natural responses and spontaneous grief in the case of suicide must be put on hold during the investigation, and that's dangerous for the survivors. Their need (and permission) to cry and receive comfort is ignored and postponed so the investigation can proceed. By then, it's too late for survivors to respond naturally, and a profound sense of shame and guilt is already at work.

In a May 1990 telephone interview with William Anderson, coroner in McLean County, Illinois, he said,

> I'm often confronted by survivors who have many of the questions and statements used in the booklet *After Suicide: A Unique Grief Process*—memories, guilt, shame, anger, incomplete mourning, the lengthy search for meaning, depression, denial, and repression reactions. I would sum it up with the following: Suicide survivors do not understand what we do as coroners.

Anderson explained that a complete autopsy is used to eliminate rather than prove a point, that is, did or did not have cancer, did or did not die from gunshot wound, did or did not die from brain tumor, did or did not have blood or urine alcohol, did or did not have carbon monoxide, did or did not have drug overdose and/or therapeutic levels of prescribed drugs, did or did not find bullet or bullets in the body, and did or did not have other trauma. The scene of investigation is usually conducted with a police agency (i.e., position of body, measurements, position of the weapon, etc.).

"The families usually demand *right now* to see the suicide note, and they have a right to. So they speculate or jump to conclusions," Mr. Anderson explained and added, "Suicide is a horse manure death for everyone to work on—family, fire department, coroner, police, news media, and so on. We often aren't prepared to handle the surviving family, and it is frustrating to not have answers."

Mr. Anderson also remarked,

> I believe the coroner must in some way detach himself from that frustration so that he or she can then conduct an independent, unbiased and proper autopsy investigation to determine the cause of death (homicide, accident, suicide, natural

or undetermined). At the same time, this should be done with a sense of compassion and diplomacy in regard to the surviving family members, and to their right to know what the police and coroner's investigation has shown. One of the most involved and perhaps most misunderstood duties of the coroner or medical examiner is that of determining if the death is accidental, suicide, homicide, or of natural causes.

In a letter following our personal interview, Mr. Anderson wrote:

Although exact duties may vary from state to state, a general outline of duties is as follows:

1. Investigate:
   a. The manner of death (homicide, suicide, undetermined, accident or natural).
   b. The cause of death (through the use of physical autopsy, psychological autopsy, medical records).
2. Identify:
   a. The body.
   b. The evidence.
   c. The facts.
3. Notify the next of kin.
4. Estimate the time of death.
5. Assimilate this information into investigative reports and autopsy reports.
6. Conduct inquests into manner and cause of death.
7. Serve as coordinator between the decedent's relatives, law enforcement agencies, public health agencies, hospitals, public institutions, and political bodies of government.

Anderson also explained how the position, condition, and location of the body itself is significant, and that items on or about the body, the condition of clothing, and the direction and nature of fluid drainage are important. These things tell us if the person died here or somewhere else, if there was a struggle, and if the scene or condition of the body was altered after death. According to the *Illinois Coroner's Handbook*, the following types of deaths are investigated:

1. Sudden or violent death (whether apparently suicidal, homicidal, or accidental), including but not lim-

ited to deaths apparently caused or contributed to by thermal, traumatic, chemical, electrical, or radiational injury, or complication of any of them, by drowning or suffocation, anesthetic deaths or therapeutic misadventures.

2. Maternal or fetal death due to abortion, or any death due to a sex crime or crime against nature.

3. Death where alcohol or drug addiction may have been a contributory cause.

4. Death where the circumstances are suspicious, obscure or mysterious, or where (in written opinion of the attending physician) the cause of death is not determined.

5. Death without medical attendance by a licensed physician.[3]

The coroner or medical examiner looks for such things as:

1. Wounds: bullet, blunt instrument, stabbing, cutting, etc.

2. Burns: thermal, chemical, electrical.

3. Crushing injuries: Injuries from machinery, moving or stationary. Vehicular (includes automobile, streetcar, bus, train, motorcycle, bicycle, etc.).

4. Injuries from an explosion.

5. Poisons taken orally, by injection, inhalation or absorption from body surfaces.[4]

He also looks for evidence such as any instrument or object that can be associated with the death. He takes measurements between the body and walls, windows, doors, and other fixed objects, and of any distances between where the body was found and where the wound and injury took place. He looks at auto skid marks, takes fingerprints, and obtains blood-alcohol analysis.

Witnesses and family members are asked for names, addresses, and phone numbers of where they were at the time of death, what they saw or found, and any other pertinent information, such as the deceased's vital statistics and medical history.

If they are conducting a psychological investigation, they may also ask questions about the victim's past reactions to stress and to family crisis. They will examine past behavior by asking family and friends if the victim suffered any recent loss or change in home, job, finances, or relationships. They may inquire about mood change, changes in activity, or talk about suicide or about going away. The investigators then determine from all this information whether the death actually was suicide, homicide made to look like suicide, or an accident, and so on.

Notification

The manner in which survivors receive this most tragic of news— in public, second hand, on the news, or even over the phone— may be a source of pain for years. Poorly handled notification may even compound the trauma, thus setting a tone that can help or hinder their recovery and sense of self-worth for life. The person giving notification should be sensitive to the families' expressions of helplessness or powerlessness, realizing that in extreme frustration, they may lash out at anyone or anything.

We cannot underestimate the value of proper education for first responders, the clergy, funeral directors, and other health professionals, and how that information, in turn, contributes to understanding support for suicide survivors and how they cope with this death.

II

◆

The Value of Support Groups

A support group consists of caring people who will let you talk until you are sick and tired of hearing yourself.

A GROUP MEMBER

People who come to suicide-survivor support group meetings are fighters. They are saying, "I won't let this destroy me."

In times of crisis or stress, the help and support from other people is invaluable. Historically, persons in need have been offered assistance by family, friends, neighbors, church, and community groups. Today, however, hundreds or thousands of miles may separate family members. Many people are so transitory that they hardly put down roots and get to know one another before they move on. Therefore, distance and other limitations such as demanding schedules, family activities, and so on, often keep even the most sympathetic friends or family members from helping one another. Support groups partially fill this gap.

The objective of support groups is to offer a variety of ways to help with grief healing (see appendix for information on obtaining a list of group locations):

1. *Meeting other survivors.* Support groups provide a chance to share with others who have had a similar experience. You can express yourself without having to provide background information in order to explain or justify your position. What a relief!

2. *Acceptance.* Some survivors fear rejection if they share their

true feelings with friends and family. In the group, you can loudly express anger, wallow in guilt, and say what you want. Members of the group understand and can offer support and empathy better or differently than friends and family members, who may want to help but feel uncomfortable trying to do so. It's a safe place for those who are experiencing the sting of the stigma.

3. *Someone listens.* You can talk freely in an accepting atmosphere about your thoughts and experiences, no matter how frightening or offensive they may seem. You may discover you are not so different or "going crazy" after all.

A newcomer to one of our meetings watched in open-mouthed silence as another member grasped for words, repeated herself, lost her train of thought, spilled her coffee, and tearfully apologized for her confusion. Finally, the new member said, "This sounds awful, but it sure helps me to see you like that. The other day, I took the butter from the refrigerator, put it into the microwave, then put my purse into the refrigerator. Then I sat on the floor and cried because I thought I was going crazy." Her story sparked a valuable and funny discussion on how disorganized thinking is a part of grief.

4. *Someone cares.* As members begin to feel a responsibility for one another, someone may confront you in a way that no family member would dare try. This interaction can force you to come face to face with your own decisions and actions. It can help you keep from giving in to the temptation to withdraw behind excuses and cop-outs. You may become angry at a fellow member who "calls" you on something, but you'll probably learn to accept credit for failures and successes more realistically.

The group can also guide you through potentially explosive situations. For example, survivors often identify themselves with the deceased in an extreme way. They put themselves so much into his or her shoes, so to speak, that the thoughts of the victim seem to become their own. This kind of thinking can be dangerous, because the reasons for committing suicide may then appear quite logical and even appealing. When members see this taking place, they may allow you to identify up to a point, because they know you need to do so, but they will pull you back before you get lost in it. They are well aware of the danger points now and will take no chances.

5. *Getting in touch with yourself.* Isolation and emotional stress can distort your thinking in many harmful ways. One mother was blaming herself because her daughter often cried and became depressed after discussing her grandfather's suicide. In reality, the mother was handling the situation well. At a meeting, the daughter told us, "I get mad at Mom sometimes when she talks about Grandpa. But if she didn't, I'd never work it out."

A father in the group insisted that he was not angry at his suicided son nor did he blame anyone. It was obvious, however, that he was seething with anger, which he soon transferred to the group. Undaunted, one woman demanded, "Then, just who the hell are you so mad at?" When he hedged, someone else repeated the question. Then, gently and without condemnation, the group helped him to put his feelings into perspective. It was a breakthrough for a proud man. He didn't have to lose face, and he benefited greatly from sharing his feelings.

6. *Finding role models.* Lack of a role model can contribute to uncertainty and a sense of isolation. Sometimes you just don't know how to act. Within the group, you meet others who have developed workable problem-solving strategies and are willing to share ideas. Although group members cannot make decisions for you, they will suggest alternatives and will be interested in the outcome.

7. *Rebuild self-esteem.* The group helps to enhance your self-esteem in at least two basic ways. Genuine acceptance of you and your problems helps give you a sense of worth, and as you participate in the group and help others, you feel needed. This sense of making a positive difference in someone else's life is especially important if you feel rejected by the suicided.

8. *Supplement therapy.* If you are already in some form of therapy, the group can be a valuable addition to your treatment. If you have never considered therapy, the group can make you aware of other mental health resources.

9. *The family.* In a group, you can move back and see your family system from a distance. You can see yourself and how you

interact with your family, without that defensiveness which often arises within a family group itself.

10. *Information resources.* Most groups offer printed information on aspects of grieving, living alone, finances, coping with children, and so on. Some have a selection of cassettes, videos, pamphlets, book lists, and newsletters, or can help you find such information.

11. *Reintegration into society.* Grief and stigma associated with suicide can cause survivors to withdraw, believing they are a burden on society. Although, in some cases, additional professional help may be needed to return an individual to the mainstream of life, the group helps them reestablish social interactions.

12. *Meeting survivors socially.* Many groups schedule social activities, especially during holidays, when members are most likely to feel lonely. Often, close relationships develop within the group, and members contact each other outside the meetings for support and friendship. Many become lifelong friends; some even find marriage partners.

13. *The most important thing for leaders to remember is that this may be more of a crisis situation than a chronic condition.* Many people may only come to one, two, or a few meetings. That's all right. They may know how to handle grief; they just need help with the crisis and you probably met that need, so don't be discouraged.

Group leaders should also take care that each member's grief is recognized and validated equally, regardless of his or her relationship to the deceased. I've seen members refuse to return to a group or heard of groups breaking up because someone believed, for one reason or another, that their grief experience was not as important as someone else's. Leaders, regardless of whether a group member is a parent, spouse, or whatever, should remember that each and every person there is also experiencing his or her own individual "worst" or they wouldn't be there. Support group meetings are not the place where any member should feel he or she has been put down over "whose loss is worst." Try to keep your group a haven of kindness and sensitivity, where everyone's tender feelings are safe from rebuff.

14. *Rituals.* Sharing in rituals is a way of remembering the

past, affirming the present, and believing in the future. We have a special one at ROH. Each year in May our group observes our "Strawberry Memory Day" meeting. Members supply an ample-sized bowl of strawberries, small containers of powdered and granulated sugar (empty butter tubs are perfect), and toothpicks. The meeting consists of sharing humorous, silly, or special stories about our loved ones. The focus is on happy times and nothing sad is discussed.

A close friend shared this ritual with me years ago after hearing about a family from New England who, regardless of where they had scattered after they were grown, each carried a bowl of strawberries and sugar to eat outside the first Sunday in May—regardless of weather—in remembrance of one another.

At ROH, we chose May also for this sharing ritual of food and memories because May is a month of beginnings and transitions such as graduations and weddings; of continuance seen in new flowers and gardens; and of honoring those we love (mothers) or those who have passed on.

15. *Reaching out to others.* Many survivors feel a great desire to pass along their release and renewed interest in life. Chances are, your heart will reach out to others in a new, sharper dimension. There are numerous ways to help, but you already have what can help the most: your experience and your healing. Share it.

16. *Renewal of hope.* Never underestimate what participation in a suicide-survivor support group can do for you. Rhonnie DiStefano is the founder and leader of the Brooklyn, New York, Ray of Hope Chapter, which also includes survivors of substance-abuse-related deaths (drugs and alcohol) in their group. Rhonnie says,

> I am constantly amazed at the transformation I see in so many survivors who attend our meetings. I've seen people come to meetings so devastated they can hardly walk. Nearly prostrate with grief, some can barely speak between sobs and screams, while others, numb with grief, just sit and stare, and I wonder how—or if—they will recover. But, we just try to love them back into believing that the human spirit has the strength to overcome.

Then, like a miracle, perhaps only a meeting or two later, I see changes taking place. They've regained composure and dignity, they express themselves without fear of stigma, and they are hopeful. They may even manage a small smile, although there's little left in their life to smile about. It's the message of Ray of Hope and our acceptance of one another that does it.

Most Ray of Hope groups have a greeter at the door and a table with sign-in notebook, handouts, and coffee or juice. Although support group formats vary from highly structured to informal, ROH combines both styles and often invites professional guest speakers. Our bylaws recommend that group leaders (or leader) consist of those with survivor experience and training in group leadership skills. Our primary meeting goals are to (1) instill trust among leaders and members, and (2) meet the most urgent needs of the moment.

Our guidelines ask leaders to tell the story of ROH's origin and explain our philosophy that painful grief can be turned into growth and healing, and that we encourage regular members to serve as inspirational role models for newcomers. We then, in turn, ask each person to state his/her first name; the name, relationship, and circumstances relating to the one who died; and ask each person to explain, as best he/she can, "Why are you here? What can our group do for you?" We end each meeting with a positive topic or activity so people will leave the meeting on an uplifting note.

"As we share our strength and experience with one another," says Rhonnie, "we realize that we are bringing about our own healing as well. We learn, also, that restoring hope and faith in oneself is necessary for healing our broken hearts and spirits. Spreading this message to survivors has brought healing in my own life since the loss of my twenty-two-year-old son in 1992. I am proud to be a part of this ministry, which extends so much help and hope to those so desperately in need."

III

Reflections

The Ship

I am standing on the shore as a great ship
gently glides from the harbor and sails toward the horizon.
She is beautiful. Sails billowing;
and shining bright as sunlight sparkling on distant waters.
She grows smaller and smaller, until at last,
her white sails shine as ribbons
out where sky and water mingle as one.
And as I watch, a voice behind me says,
"Well, she's gone." She's gone.
Gone?
"No," I say to myself.
No, she is not gone. Not really.
She is gone only in the sense that I can no longer see her.
In reality, she is the same as ever;
just as beautiful; just as shining.
And deep in my heart I know,
that on another shore
other voices are crying out,
"Look! Look everyone! Here she comes!"

SOURCE UNKNOWN

12

❖

Reflections about Suicide

There is such an incredible loneliness there; a separation from life that begins long before the dying begins.

ELEANORA "BETSY" ROSS

"Why do people kill themselves?" is the one big question that survivors ask themselves, others, and God in the months and years following suicide. And in the asking, we look for reasons and examine life, and although we know we didn't *force* them to pull the trigger, we still discuss the pros and cons, and the nuances of word meanings. We just want something to fit, whether inside-out, or backwards, or whatever—if it will just show us an answer.

Obviously, those who could best answer the "why" question are not here to do so. We can, however, study the setting and events leading up to both attempted and completed suicides. We can listen to the people who are thinking and feeling suicidal. We can use attempted suicides, completed suicides, and survivors' grief to gain some sort of insights into the "why" and also to reach out and help those touched by suicide.

If the first part of this book indicates that I am sympathetic with the plight of survivors, this part will appear to say the opposite, that my sympathies are with the suicided. Both are true. Although I don't pretend to have solutions for both those who suicide and those who grieve, I do want to share my thoughts and observations about *why* people kill themselves, and *who* kills themselves.

Frankly, I think there are as many reasons for suicide as there are people who do it. But, reasons there are. Have you ever heard a child say, "When I grow up, I'm going to kill myself"? Something has to happen along the way to bring that about. Many reasons or factors regarding suicide are cited by suicidologists, such as hopelessness, helplessness, isolation, loneliness, peer pressure, divorce, unrealistic expectations, domestic abuse, sexual abuse, job loss, depression, disease, loss of identity or self-esteem, loss of control, affective illnesses, alcohol/substance abuse, neglect, violence, incest, and life changes (such as adolescence, postnatal depression, menopause, and male midlife crisis).

In addition, age, gender, ethnic background, social traumas, health, and financial status are listed as contributing influences. Others categorize suicidal acts as rebirth, reunion, control over death, atonement, retaliation, punishment of self, or symbolic punishment of another.

Suicidologists also cite a number of common denominators that may influence the decision to suicide. Two of those denominators are feelings of *low self-esteem* and *helplessness*, but I'm not so sure they are as "common" as we often think.

Consider those who have rebelled against a situation of conflict or abuse, and have fought for the chance to develop their own individuality. An example might be the teenager who suicides because he believes he can't measure up to expectations and is not aware of alternatives to his dilemma. Suppose family conflict and arguments took place prior to the suicide. Would you say that his suicide was (1) rebellion or retaliation to a perceived injustice or situation over which he had no control, or (2) an act of giving up because of helplessness and low self-esteem?

Maybe it was both, but you've got to have some pride and self-esteem in order to rebel or fight. Sometimes people with low self-esteem don't fight back; they give in or give up. Another example of suicide as an expression of fighting back, or of rebellion, may be that of a person or group of people who choose to kill themselves rather than submit to torture or a perceived enemy. We're helpless when we *don't* have a choice, not when we *do*.

Another example is that of people who actually have very

high self-esteem but find that things over which they have no control interfere with the quality of life they want for themselves. These are the ones who may say, "I've had it. I won't live this way." That's not indicative of low self-esteem or helplessness. In the prior examples, these people may be saying, "I don't hate myself; I only hate what has happened."

Another common denominator is *isolation*. A. Alvarez, in *The Savage God: A Study of Suicide*, discusses the relationship between society and suicide as it relates to isolation and explains how society (the family and the community) ignores, ridicules, or rejects certain individuals for whatever reason (illness, race, old age, poverty, underachievement, being less than the accepted norm, and so forth) until the persons quit trying to help themselves and begin to withdraw. The more they withdraw, the more they are left alone, often becoming objects of disapproval.[1] These people may believe they are unable to stop the circle of mutual rejection as it closes in on them and wipes out alternatives, choices, and escape.

Consider the emotional bankruptcy and devastation that can arise from this sort of alienation. The words *loneliness* and *isolation*, as we commonly perceive them, are simply not strong enough to convey the depth of despair brought about by the feeling, or knowledge, of being ostracized, ignored, unwanted, unable to measure up, unable to belong, or disapproved of by all of society.

This loneliness may be enhanced—not alleviated—by family gatherings and social fellowship. These people may be the loners at the edge of the crowd, or not present at all. In their hearts, they know, with crushing reality, that they are not really an accepted part of the congenial sharing of life. This realization, or belief, can repeat itself, sometimes shattering through the consciousness like a summer thunderstorm, sometimes seeping into the soul like a Siberian chill.

Say, perchance, that unable to tolerate the terrible heartache (and here we *do* have hopelessness and low self-esteem), a person kills him/her self. They all—society, community, family, and the victim—made choices leading to that end—choices to ignore and ostracize, choices to withdraw, the choice to suicide.

An example is that of a twelve-year-old boy from Oslo, Norway, who was badly scarred from smallpox. As the kids tormented him and his parents ignored him, he became withdrawn and sullen. Other adults began accusing him of just about anything that went amiss in the community. In the note he left, he said he was hanging himself because he could no longer endure the rejection and "mobbing," (a term used to describe long-lasting teasing and harassment), both in school and at home. I believe this child was not only trying to escape pain but also was fleeing toward a place of safety. (Associated Press, 1983). It could be said that this is not a case of isolated, individual self-killing, but collective murder. It emphasizes the need for intervention, prevention, and postvention education and information throughout communities and in family settings, in order to promote understanding and healing.

Medical studies indicate that some people experience overwhelming suicidal urges which are influenced by chemical changes in the brain. A person's mood can be affected by internal workings over which he or she has little or no control, and which are further influenced by environment. These genetic or chemical influences can also cause clinical depression—the kind that sticks like glue. It persists—it squeezes the juice out of life. Churchill called it the little black dog that followed him. That's different from *situational* depression, which is usually brought about by some loss or series of events too overwhelming to handle.

Survivors need more information about these chemical changes and influences, whether genetic or drug related, for their own peace of mind. One mother said,

> If the reason for my son's suicide is something that was beyond his control or my control, then that takes a lot of the burden off my shoulders. It helps to know that maybe the part of his brain that controlled his behavior just didn't work any more. That's tragic—but it helps us to know that maybe he couldn't help himself, and I didn't drive him to it.

Her observation is an important one. So often we say, "They were depressed," without really knowing what that means. Learning about the different kinds of depression (i.e., Major Depressive Illness; Borderline Personality Disorder; Bipolar, Uni-

polar, and situational versus genetic depressions) and understanding the dynamics of depression can help relieve a survivor's
self-blame and guilt.

William Styron, Pulitzer-Prize-winning author, describes his
suicidal depression in his book, Darkness Visible, as a pain that is
"unrelenting," knowing that "no remedy will come," and says, "It
is the hopelessness even more than pain that crushes the soul."[2]
He believes that unresolved grief over the loss of his mother when
he was thirteen, and problems with alcohol in adulthood were
influencing factors toward the "shipwreck of his soul."[3] Styron
explains that ridding himself of "this torment was a paramount
need," and credits his recovery in great part to a special friend
(and others) who refused to give up on him.[4]

Depression is not a person's choice or evidence of any personality defect. Healing is possible; medications do help; love, patience, and support are invaluable. The reasons for any suicide are
multidetermined—biological, spiritual, psychological and social;
therefore, an understanding and treatment of the whole person is
needed.

Some people may not be influenced by any of the above
reasons but simply decide that now is the time to stop living.
There may be no deep, dark secrets; no low self-esteem; no feelings of helplessness; no desire for revenge or atonement; no desire
to be with one who has already passed on; no seething caldron of
anger, fear, guilt, or frustration, but just a calm, simple, compla-
cent decision: "Well, this is it. The time has come—not that I want
to die, but that I'm going to die."

I am moved to think that not all suicides are carried out in the
depths of pain and despair, but rather, have gone beyond the
despairing stage. Perhaps some have glimpsed peace of spirit and
are ready for death. Somehow they know—or believe—it is their
time to die.

Death pulls at us just as does life. At certain stages—old age,
terminal illness, when mortally wounded—we may be powerless
to resist the promise of relief and a place of safety, and so accept
that it is time to go. The point to ponder is something deeper than
a decision to suicide; perhaps it is a letting go of life rather than

choosing death. Some people may see suicide as a means of death no different than cancer, terminal illness, accident, or whatever.

One mother said, "My daughter did not commit suicide. She was killed by something called suicide. Cancer kills people. Heart attacks kill people. Illness and disease kill people. Wars kill people. Accidents kill people. Suicide kills people, and it killed my daughter."

You can say this mother is in denial, or you can say she has a point. Bill described his suicidal urges as an "insidious, swirling thing that wraps itself about my ankles, invades my body like an infection, and clamps a vise-like grip on my mind. It's like standing on a foot bridge and watching the mesmerizing pull of the moving water. I'm afraid that pull will sometimes be too strong for me to resist." Some people fight this monster or pull throughout life and struggle hard not to suicide because they don't want to hurt anyone. But it takes too much energy to stay alive and they may eventually see death as their only escape—or a way to defeat the enemy.

Oh, we promise suicidal people relief right around the next corner. So, they sigh and go around the next corner for us, and there it is again. "Am I to go around corners forever?" they ask. "No," some of them reply, and take action to end the chase. Perhaps they are just too *tired* to keep on living.

Nowadays, some people are choosing "death with dignity" over pain (as in some cases of cancer or AIDS), senility, or poverty. I believe that death may be seen as a safe haven by some people. The elderly, for example, comprise 30 percent of the suicide rate. Many of them have experienced or are facing an incredible list of losses: health, independence, finances, eyesight, isolation from family and loved ones, unrealized hopes and dreams, and home and familiar surroundings. Even the knowledge that one no longer has the ability to recover or restore all those losses is a major loss.

Some elderly find themselves at the mercy of a vindictive son, daughter, or in-law and are unable to escape the abuse. In both cases, these people may believe they are caught in an impossible situation with no options and choices. Their suicide may be not only a seeking of relief from pain but also a fleeing toward a place of safety. Often, suicide appears to be a well-thought-out action. However, some of those who think their decision is rational may not realize they are depressed, or are just plain fooling themselves. I believe most people really want to live, even when they think they don't.

Perhaps just as important a question as *why* people kill themselves, is the question, "*Who* kills him/her self?" This may not be as simple to determine as we think. Maybe the "who" has something to do with the "why." It gets complicated. To begin with, some experts describe three categories of suicide: intentional, unintentional, and subintentional. With intentional suicide, obviously, someone fully *intends* to die and does so.

With *unintentional* suicide, the persons do not *intend* to die. They want to live and resolve things. They are crying out for help and die by mistake. Something goes awry—a miscalculation of some sort.

Subintentional suicide includes those whose lifestyle or actions have a direct influence on the time and way in which they die. This includes all sorts of self-abusive and self-neglectful behaviors and could be just about anyone, which is why it is so futile to label, judge, and stigmatize either the suicided or the survivors. Alvarez quotes Daniel Stern, who says, "All of mankind [is] engaged in a massive conspiracy against their own lives that is their daily activity."[5]

Mrs. C. tells about her experiences in a psychiatric hospital following a drug overdose. Two days after admittance, she was asked to seat herself on a chair placed in the center of a small room, facing a table where four mental healthcare professionals were waiting. They asked her questions about her background, her feelings, her current depression, and her view of herself.

"I suppose there is medical support for this sort of questioning," says Mrs. C., "but I felt like my privacy was being invaded and my person exposed—like being emotionally raped. Finally, one of them asked me, 'Why did you want to hurt yourself?' That did it. I lost my temper. I sat there for a moment and looked at them. One was so obese she draped over the chair. The person beside her was chain-smoking. Another reeked of alcohol. It would have been funny if it hadn't been so sad. These people, who were abusing their own bodies, were asking me why I wanted to hurt myself.

"Then I said, 'I didn't take the pills because I wanted to hurt myself; I took them because I *didn't* want to hurt anymore. If I wanted to hurt myself, I'd do what you are doing. I'd smoke myself to death, drink myself to death, or eat myself to death. Like you, I'd live on in such a way that I'd destroy my lungs or liver or heart or whatever. And like you, I'd take a long time to do it— hurting myself all the way. I took pills because I'd rather die quickly, without pain, than to destroy my body slowly as you are yours."

Shortly thereafter, Mrs. C. was dismissed from the room— and the hospital. But she had made a good point. Many people do choose to live in such a way that they hurt themselves slowly and die in agony. In a way of speaking, that is subintentional suicide. "These are the people," says Alvarez, "who do everything to destroy themselves except admit that that is what they are after ... everything except take the final responsibility for their actions."[6]

However, society doesn't judge or condemn these people for their mode of death when they die. In fact, we praise and admire their courage for enduring pain, all the while ignoring the fact that they chose a lifestyle leading to this death. Do you see the ridiculous contradictions in our opinions and attitudes?

It would seem that society approves and applauds when we kill ourselves slowly and passes judgment when we do it quickly. Perhaps that's the only real difference between many suicide and nonsuicide deaths. One is slow, expected, and called natural death. The other is quick, unexpected, and is called suicide. One deliberate way of dying is socially acceptable; the other, deliberate, way is not.

There is yet another difference. Subintentional suicides die in such a way that we can all become involved in their suffering. We get to hear about the pain, visit hospitals, compare surgeries, fuss over the sufferer, send cards and gifts. We can rub shoulders with blood and pain, and satisfy our nurturing instincts at the same time.

Maybe society resents the obvious suicide because he/she deprives us from using it as a socially acceptable excuse to be symbolically involved with death and dying. When we are involved with someone who is slowly dying, we can check out death for ourselves. We can look at death without trying it on. We can be voyeurs of pain but not experiencers. Perhaps there is something very normal, very human in us that needs to do this from time to time.

Alvarez compares the many centuries of mankind's personal involvement with gruesome torture and death (such as public executions, gladiator shows, and hand-to-hand combat) with the modern preoccupation with violence. He points out that the historical public was amused, excited, and delighted, rather than shocked, with displays of blood and gore, much as we are entertained by violence in the media, which Alvarez describes as "a kind of pornography, at once exciting and unreal."[7]

Those earlier people were involved with death in a way that satisfied both natural curiosity and the natural instincts of the darker side of the heart. In today's society, most people die only at a distance: in hospitals, in fiction, on TV, and in the news. We are separated from participation in the natural event of bloody death—except for suicide. With suicide, we can forget TV and jump into the fray. We publicize the death, rub the survivor's nose in it, and glory in the aftermath. And therein lies the fascination— as if suicide were a substitute for the public execution or gladiator show. We can use the event of suicide to follow a natural inclination to examine death close up, but at what price? No wonder survivors suffer deep scars from the resulting exploitation and humiliation.

There is yet another similarity between public execution and suicide, and that is survivors' guilt. A primary reason for abolishing public execution was the intense complications of survivors' guilt. This is why hospital visits, contact with the sick and infirm, the ritual of mourning, and active participation in funeral preparations are so important. All these activities are positive involvement which help alleviate survivors' guilt. Even as civilized human beings, we still need to participate in one another's death experience as well as life experience, but in a meaningful, humane manner, rather than as proxy executioners.

In addition, those who die the "normal or natural" modes of death usually pass on with the loving, supportive care and attention of family and friends right up to the last minute. And that's the way to die, isn't it, sharing it with someone who is being there just for you, or holding your hand?

My sister-in-law, for example, was ready for death. She was very ill and wanted release. While hospitalized, there was time for the family to gather, to take part in the last moments of her life, to witness this great event and passage in her life. As a result, this involvement helped to ease death for her and make her passing more acceptable for the family. My sister-in-law wanted death at the end but didn't choose it; some suicides choose death but may not want it.

I also believe there is a difference between suicide and self-inflicted death. Suicide is deliberate, intentional, but not, to my way of thinking, ever an accident. Self-inflicted death, however, may not be deliberate or intentional. One can accidentally die by self-inflicted death and not have meant to "commit" suicide at all. I can understand why some people refuse to use the word *suicide*. They have examined the circumstances, and deep in their heart, are convinced that death was not the victim's intentional deep-seated desire. They believe it was a tragically mistaken or impulsive, self-inflicted death.

In a similar train of thought, there is also a difference between wanting to be *dead*, and wanting to *kill oneself*. For example, "I wish I were dead" usually means "I wish I were free of this situation," and that statement is a cry for help. On the other hand, "I want to kill myself" may mean "I wish I were free of *myself*," and, in that case, is a statement of intended action. The difference is in the focus. In wanting to be dead, the focus is on a state of being which is free of pain and violence and is directed *against a situation*. Wanting to kill oneself is focusing on an act of violence and is directed against the self. I think it must take great passion or great fury to kill oneself.

We are so quick to say the suicided person had a choice, that he or she chooses to die. I don't think it's that simple. I think people *decide* to kill themselves rather than *choosing* to die. Think about the difference. In order to make a choice, one must be aware of alternatives and free to choose one. If one does not know what other choices or options exist, and, as a result, believes he or she has no other choice, then suicide is not a free choice.

In *Family Therapy for Suicidal People,* Joseph Richman writes that in order to make a truly free choice, one must first have the necessities of life: home, health, happiness, acceptance, self-expression, career, and social features that provide a background for genuine choice. If someone believes he or she lacks one or more of these necessities and is being pushed or driven to suicide, what then happens to free choice?[8] How can anyone make a choice about anything without having first been influenced by someone or something? It's the *degree* of influence with which survivors wrestle.

I believe it's the living who put so much emphasis on the word *choice.* With the suicided, the emphasis may have been on *solution.* They did not view their decision as a choice, but as the *solution.* Perhaps I'm not questioning the use of the word *choice* as much as the implications behind its use.

I used to bristle when people argued with me that Bill had a choice. I would politely demur, "You might be right," when I wanted to retort angrily, "You don't know that. You didn't know him. How can you presume to read his mind? This 'choice' business is only your perception of reality, and maybe in your reality there are choices. I believe you should respect *his* sense of reality, and in his reality, there was not a choice. And in his perception of reality, yours doesn't matter. He acted on his reality, and you have no right to judge that! Just because your choice or view of reality is different from his doesn't mean it is the only right one."

I have since mellowed and am willing to concede that his decision was also, in a sense, his choice. I think my earlier defensiveness was influenced by my perception that all this talk about choice may be used as a generalized answer to everything, or a denial of any accountability. I also saw it as a put-down of Bill's emotional state, an implication that he wanted to die, although I knew that he did not. And it was an effective way to shut me up.

The subject of suicide has been greatly rehashed, debated, condoned, and denounced. Well-informed researchers have pondered, probed, and discussed the id, the ego, and the superego; the wish to kill, the wish to be killed, and the wish to die; the victim, rescuer, and persecutor; projection and introjection; sadism and masochism—all as they relate to suicide. (Indeed, one can become so carried away by study and research about suicide that one might consider it either for the sake of science or to escape the mountains of prose.) And yet, we still can't pick any one isolated act of suicide and satisfactorily explain all the variables. We can offer a selection of variables to choose from; that's the only beginning we have.

Even if all we ever have to answer the "why" are reflections and introspections, we still must continue to search for common denominators in order to establish guidelines that will help us prevent senseless self-destruction, however we may perceive it, choice or not, because, no matter how you look at it, it always comes back to the belief that suicide is one of the most preventable forms of death.

In summary, it's pretty difficult to determine who does, or does not, die by what we traditionally consider or define as suicide. It is far more preferable, I believe, to turn one's thoughts and energy away from judging either the deceased, or the survivors, to healing the wounds of both the suicidal through prevention and survivors through postvention.

Suicide may be one's choice; it may appear to be rational, it may seem to make sense, and it may be done in the best way possible, but there is still something sad and wrong about it. There is such an incredible loneliness there: a separation from life that begins long before the dying begins. It's so sad when someone believes that he or she must die alone like that. I believe that the passage from life to death should be a natural experience, shared with loved ones in attendance, just as is the birth passage into life.

Perhaps the final reason why grief after suicide is so difficult to resolve, is because we know that life should not have to be something from which anyone chooses to escape.

13

◆

Deadly Messages

*The more one thinks they are lowly and flawed as a human being,
the more one's choices diminish. One becomes bonded to violence.*

JOHN BRADSHAW
Psychologist and Author

Many situations in today's society both create and send messages
that some of us are expendable—unwanted, not needed, in the
way—or objects for ridicule, and that the rest of society would be
better off without these misfits.

Adults, teenagers, and children alike wonder who they are,
where they belong, and who cares. Some families, uninformed
and unequipped to deal with the overload of stress, turn on one
another with verbal, emotional, and mental abuse or neglect, and
physical or sexual abuse. Thus are created scapegoats and expendable persons—followed by an easing out of those who can be
sacrificed for the sake of harmony.

Complicating these situations are divorce, spousal and child
battering, drug abuse and/or alcoholism, depression, life changes
(such as adolescence, menopause, male midlife crisis), and it's no
wonder some people both target and want to eliminate the perceived cause of trouble; while others perceive life itself as a deadly
message of rejection, resulting in self-destructive behavior and, all
too often, suicide.

Joseph C. Sabbath, an instructor in psychiatry, writes at
length about the "concept of the expendable child to account for

one of the multiple factors contributing to [adolescent] suicided behavior."[1] He says, "Investigations ... have underscored the importance of the nature of interrelationships between parent and child. Giaser (1965) discusses emotionally detached parents and absent father as not being ... resources for love and support in times of stress. Gould (1965) ... writes "for many reasons the parent may wish the child did not exist ... or [they] would be happier without children. ... The child picks up these cues ... and may try to follow his [or her] parents unconscious or conscious wishes and attempt suicide if this is the only way to get [parents] approval and love,[2]

"Next time, cut deeper."	"Oh, go shoot yourself."
"Next time, take more pills."	"We don't reject you—it's all in
"Next time, take better aim."	your head."
"Why were you ever born?"	"Oh, we forgot about you."
"You make me sick."	"Don't listen to him/her. He/
"If it weren't for you ..."	she lies."
"I wish you were dead."	"Oh, just stop talking about it
	and do it."

Idle words? Words uttered in a moment of anger or teasing and not really meant to be taken seriously? Perhaps to some of us that would seem so, but to many others, the message is deadly serious; some clearly perceive it as a message telling them to die— that they are expendable, not wanted. What they hear may not always be all in their heads.

We like to perceive ourselves as a society that always has the best of motives at heart and does the best it can for one another. But it is just not always true. Any history book, any current news medium, shows us differently. We do kill deliberately. From the beginning of time, people have hated and killed others and, sometimes, themselves. Parents do abuse—and kill—their children, and consciously or unconsciously, don't always want their children. Some hate what they are doing and seek help in order to change, but there are those who seem to abuse deliberately, who know they will again, and do not appear to want to stop. The causes for that behavior are not the issue in this chapter. The issue here is the abusive use of scapegoating, the expendable child, and victimizing, as they relate to the message to die.

In his book, *Family Therapy for Suicidal People,* Joseph Richman describes the process of scapegoating, the reasons for it, the ways it is acted out, and counseling techniques for healing the problem or changing the situation.

In a process Richman calls "the 'quasi-courtroom procedure,' one member of the family is subjected to a series of charges of wrongdoing without the opportunity to defend himself and with no one to support or defend him."[3] As a therapist listens to these charges, a pattern emerges: "Those who are doing the scapegoating are [actually] fighting for their lives."[4] There is a "rigid, all-or-nothing quality" about scapegoating, ... where one is totally guilty, ... [and] the others are totally blameless.[5] (For additional reading, Vogel and Bell [1968] have traced the steps through which a child is inducted into the scapegoating role.)

The following examples show how the perceived "message to die" may be carried out by the person targeted. Names and events have been changed and altered to form a composite of cases. Any resemblance to any person or family is purely a coincidence.

*   *   *   *   *

A mother, whose twenty-year-old son had suicided, reluctantly attended a support group meeting with her daughter. As she left, she said, "I don't need your meetings or your sympathy. He was my third child, and from the moment I knew I was pregnant, I knew I never wanted him. I had two more babies after him, but it didn't change things. I still didn't love him or want him. Even when he was little, I'd tell him that I wished he would just go off and die. I don't understand why I felt that way, because I love my other children and grandchildren. He knew how I felt. He accused me of not loving him, but I always denied it and called him a liar or a troublemaker. And as he got older, he did get into a lot of trouble. I *regret* some of the things I said and did to him—it was wrong, but now that he's dead, I really don't feel any grief or guilt. Just relief. We're all better off now that he's dead. We really all wanted him gone."

238 ◆ Life After Suicide

Her attitude may sound shocking but is, in actuality, all too commonplace. However, she was bluntly honest.

* * * * *

Janie, a beautiful young woman who attended support group meetings following the suicide of her brother, struggled with strong feelings of hatred toward her father, whom she held responsible for her brother's death. The eighteen-year-old was often in tears when she discussed the situation at home, which included incestual attentions from her father, and often trembled when we spoke to her or touched her.

At the third meeting she announced, "I finally had the nerve to accuse my dad of what I think. I said to him, 'Well, Dad, you finally killed one of your children.' He just looked at me, laughed, and said, 'How about that. Maybe you'll be next.'" A couple of days later she left for college. Two weeks later, she hung herself in her dorm room.

* * * * *

Several years ago, a young man named Joe bought a revolver, wrapped it in bright paper, and placed if far back under the Christmas tree. He wrote on the card, "To all of you from me." When the gift exchange was completed, Joe drew out the package, unwrapped it, placed the gun to his temple and said, "I'm giving you all what you want most for Christmas. My death." He pulled the trigger and died.

This appears to be a terrible judgment to hand down to his family, but Joe left notes stating that he believed he had been driven to this point. Throughout childhood, Joe had been beaten by his parents and ridiculed by his brothers and sisters. He was often left out of family festivities, sent to his room, or locked out of the house, as one punishment or another. No matter what happened or went wrong, Joe seemed to be held responsible.

Joe's mother would sometimes call all the children but Joe to come into the house from where they were playing. After a while, wondering where they were, Joe would wander inside to find them finishing a meal. Joe's father would say, "You're late again. If you can't come to the table on time, you don't eat." Joe's mother would smile sweetly and say, "What's the matter, Joe? Aren't you hungry?" He wasn't, as his stomach was a painful knot of fear and sadness.

Joe's father had a routine of favorite lines about Joe whenever he had an audience.

"Oh, he'll always be worthless."

"I don't know where he came from, someone's garbage, more'n likely. Don't pay him any attention."

"He's sure not like one of us."

"I keep trying to lose him, but when I turn around, he's still there."

Joe knew his father was not joking. Neighbors knew the sound of blows and the sight of bruises on Joe's body were no joke either. But in those days, you minded your own business.

After Joe's death, the father ordered that every photo of Joe and his every possession was to be destroyed. "I don't ever want to hear his name mentioned," the father said. "As far as we are all concerned, he never lived—never deserved to live. He did what *he* wanted to do. So be it."

In the years that followed, one member of Joe's family died in a psychiatric hospital, another became alcoholic, one sibling ran away from home, another became involved in abusive relationships, and one is in jail. Each lives privately with his or her pain and memories, but no one ever mentions Joe. Someone, however, still keeps fresh flowers on his grave.

* * * * *

In a small midwestern town, a young man who liked to dress in western boots and hat was often the object of laughter and ridicule. A loner and an alcoholic, he finally announced to others (while in his favorite bar) that he was tired of being the butt of jokes and was going to hang himself. Amid more jeers and laughter, he left the bar and attempted to do just that, but the rope broke, and he survived. Back in the tavern, they said, "Hell, that Lee's so dumb he can't even kill himself right." Oh yes, he could—the rope never broke the next time. Suicide is not funny.

* * * * *

I believe it is possible that far too many suicides occur because some people believe (either rightly or wrongly) that they have received a message to die. Tragically, many have often perceived wrongly. Also tragically, many have been right. These messages may be the kind that forbids any notion of leaving the family fold, or they may completely exclude the offender. Richman believes that many suicidal persons probably receive more death messages than they send out, and says, "Suicide is itself a communication of unresolved problems and unfinished crises in all those touched by the act, not only in the suicidal individual."[6]

He also states, "At the time of the suicidal crisis, the potentially suicidal person has become the bad object for the entire family.... For this to occur the guilt, shame, sense of failure, and separation anxieties are all placed upon the suicidal individual, through the process of projective identification," which is accompanied by "the expressed or implied message that his or her demise is necessary, after which there would be no problems."[7]

If the person who has symbolized all the ills of the family actually dies, the family may, at first, feel that atonement has been accomplished. But they needed their scapegoat—how dare he/she do this! Too late, they realize that the suicided person represented both the good and bad of the family, so the death leaves the family feeling "as if part of themselves has died."[8] Now they are frustrated and angry. They did indeed kill part of themselves—the part they had projected onto the scapegoat.

Richman explains that (1) scapegoating is a means of dealing with overwhelming guilt on the part of the abusers; (2) the scapegoat is blamed for all problems, and the intensity or widespread nature of the scapegoating is an indicator of the family's desperation; (3) scapegoating is used to avoid confronting family problems or dysfunction; (4) through scapegoating, the family participates in the suicidal act, either directly or indirectly.[9]

John Bradshaw, in *Bradshaw On: The Family*, explains how dysfunctional parents reenact their own original pain onto their children. He says we must understand that "every persecutor was once a victim," or in a Biblical sense, "the sins of the fathers go on and on." He adds, "The abused child in the persecutor is angry and hurt" but is forbidden to express anger toward his own parent, so the anger is "either projected onto others or turned against the self."[10]

According to Bradshaw, the dysfunctional or abusing family is locked into a closed family system, where "shame is an organizing principle; that abuse and shame are inherited generationally, and acted out through the rigid roles and ego defenses."[11]

By no means is a closed family system always or necessarily outwardly brutal. They may appear and claim to be most loving and the closest of families. There may be a great show of concern over one another and lots of fuss over doing things together. That's wonderful if it allows for healthy rebellion and individualism. It's the family which perceives itself as close, when it's actually closed, that is dysfunctional.

A number of factors are common in the way the abusive or dysfunctional family communicates its deadly message to the scapegoat or expendable child. For example, *common themes in tone of voice* are scorn, contempt, impatience, disgust, sneering, patronizing, or condescension—usually accompanied by similar facial expressions. *Common themes in attitude* are condemnation, judgment, vindictiveness, blaming and shaming, punishing, and self-pity on the part of the abuser. For *common expressions*, see the beginning of this chapter. Other expressions toward the abused, if he or she confronts the family, may be of outright denial or rather sneaky reverse accusations, such as, "Oh, that's all in your head," "The neighbors all know we love you so why don't you?", "You ask for what you get," or "Oh, all you want is attention (or pity)," or "Everybody knows you lie."

A common self-image of those who abuse is an incredible belief and insistence on their own innocence. They never see themselves at fault but blame others or the world. They worry a great deal about what neighbors or other people think. They are afraid someone may discover the truth, so they work hard to retain an image of their own "goodness" and the scapegoat or expendable child's "badness." A typical comment in this case might be "We did everything for this kid—spoiled him or her rotten–and this is how he/she treat us." A therapist or someone else who defends the scapegoat might then hear, "Well, I see that so-and-so has got you fooled."

Common actions are the silent treatment or deliberately ignoring (the ultimate in rejection) the distress of the suicidal person; walking out, leaving, or turning away (which is tantamount to abandonment and symbolically represents one of the most profound and despairing forms of nonverbal communication); blocking out (refusing to hear or comprehend), such as, "I don't even listen when she tries to tell me what's wrong. I just let it go in one ear and out the other"; hanging up the phone on the person, and the failing or "forgetting" to pass messages of need or crisis on to a possible helper, rescuer, or comforter.

An example is Wanda, a woman who sought therapy to overcome strong feelings of rejection and thoughts of suicidal ideation. She reported that she had several hospitalizations for cancer, and each time she had notified her family. Each time they failed to visit, call, or send a card or flowers. When Wanda later confronted them, they claimed not to have known about it, or that "they forgot." They accused Wanda of being "selfish" and "contrary" for wanting family support during this crisis in her life. "Oh, you always want *something*," a niece said.

"The amount of covertness, indirectness, [blaming], and covering-up found [in abusive families] is truly striking," claims Richman. They are experts at excuses and justification, and the greater the need for a facade, the more the abusive family will create an effect of innocence and extreme insensitivity to the victim's pain or despair.[12]

Dominated by this theme of complete innocence and the denial of any guilt, they feel a great "sense of rightness of their [abusive] actions."[13] That would explain why some people continue to abuse, take great care to conceal their problems, and do not appear to regret their actions, instead of seeking ways to change their actions and attitude. Any rebellion against one's prescribed role in a closed dysfunctional family—especially to the member who is most insecure and fearful, and who has learned to control the family—would be a threat.

"A real or supposed fragility of a central figure in the family ... dominates the family atmosphere. The family rallies to protect this figure, but the means taken are maladaptive and the result is a further closing off of the family," Richman states, as he compares this person with a "queen bee who must be protected ... even at the sacrifice of lives."[14]

The controlling figure may be someone who is ill or emotionally unstable. The family goes along with this controlling figure because it's easier. Resistance to scapegoating, or defense of the victim, requires thought and courage. Who has the time or inclination to face the wrath of an abuser on behalf of the victim, especially if the abuser is bigger, stronger, hands out the money, or happens to own valuable property? It's an old story for parents to threaten to, or actually, cut off someone's inheritance as a form of control or punishment. Let's face it—greed is a solid controlling force in the hands of an abuser.

Triangling is also a factor in family scapegoating. This occurs when one member discusses the scapegoat (or suicidal person) with other family members. The victim knows the talk is going on behind his/her back, and also knows that anything he/she says will be repeated and discussed with others. The victim believes that he/she has no defense against being maligned by his/her own family, through labeling, innuendoes, and assumptions. If a myth or lie is voiced often enough, it becomes a reality in the mind of the listener and can destroy relationships and reputations.

Richman calls this a two-edged double-binding; "the suicidal person has almost literally no one to turn to and nowhere to go. He or she is alienated and isolated both outside the family and within it, and may be ostracized as a form of punishment in order to bring him [or her] back to the former role."[15] Scapegoating works only with those who desperately want what the family refuses to give. It does not work when the scapegoat refuses to cooperate.

And then there's guilt. If we blame the victim, we can avoid facing our own guilt. The executioners of Jesus Christ had to invent a case against him in order to justify crucifying him. Adolf Hitler had to build a case against the Jews that would not only justify his obsessive hatred but also enlist others in the abuse and extermination of them. These people were compelled to hate their victims in order to abuse, and then blame the victims for deserving the abuse.

In addition, the physical presence of the object of resentment reminds the parent or abuser of their unacceptable, yet denied, feelings toward the victim or child. The victim (or child) is, in fact, a *bona fide* accuser of wrongdoing. The victim/child's very presence states, "You have mistreated me," or "I know that you hate me," or "I could tell the world what you are really like." The victim's presence is a reminder of the victimizer's guilt, so the abusers try to relieve their guilt by ignoring or removing the victim. The victimizers must rid themselves of the accuser in order to appear guiltless, both to themselves and to the community.

Scapegoating or messages to die are not always directed to just the suicidal person, and the family can change their focus from one person to another. In the case of spousal suicide, the surviving spouse may find that he or she is the new target. With the death of one child, another child may become the object of disapproval.

For example, one young woman, whose brother had suicided, was constantly told by her mother, "You're getting to be more and more like your brother. You remind me of him all the time, and you get on my nerves just like he did." As time passed, the young woman began thinking about her own suicide. Eventually, she did it. Maybe that kind of talk sometimes contributes to the fact that suicide seems to "run in families."

Sometimes victimizing comes home to roost. Many years ago, a young child died in the hospital, a victim of severe abuse. The child had been chained to a bed for most of its life, forced to drink its own urine, and fed its own feces. Years later, immediate members of the family were charged with murder. Interestingly enough, other family members were charged as "accessories before the fact," because they knew about the abuse but never reported it. They were judged guilty by association and silence.

Do you know what is the saddest thing of all about rejection, abuse, and family scapegoating? It is actually self-injury. That child or victim is, by birth, a part of his or her parents. When family members reject or hurt that person, they are hurting part of themselves. It's the ultimate case of "We treat others the way we feel about ourselves." Scapegoating and abuse are crazy-making at the least; it can be a game of slow, insidious murder at the most.

The choice of suicide, says Richman, "is never a purely individual matter. Hopelessness ... is intimately related to the decision to kill oneself, and hopelessness is an interpersonal family systems phenomenon. What then of the many suicides who receive the [message] that their self-inflicted death is necessary for the survival of their loved ones?" He asks, "How can they [then] choose life?" How can they avoid becoming their family's sacrificial lamb?

"They can," Richman asserts, "if they [all] recognize that the suicidal urge is the expression of a [family] problem that needs correction. Such a positive use of suicide as a signal can best be accomplished by providing ... a loving attitude so the one in distress knows that he is wanted and accepted. Rather than becoming part of the problem, the family and society can then become part of the solution."[16]

Understanding the situation, forgiving oneself, and a desire to change are the keys to healing an injured dysfunctional family. Abusive families are not necessarily comprised of mean-spirited people who consciously choose to abuse more of their own.

Abusers may be as helpless as victims if their own pain is unrecognized, or too great to respond to a suicidal cry for help from another. They may not see their own actions as abusive but, rather, as the only way they know how to respond to a threat. When abusers' actions arise from their own frustrations and fears, they may attack before they can be hurt more.

Without change through insight or counseling, this habitual abusive response can become a deep inner driving force. Although there may be explanations for abusive actions, an explanation is never a justifiable excuse.

We must never assume that abusing families are that way forever, and we must never underestimate their ability to change. All the strength, determination, and love (yes, love) that goes into maintaining an abusive situation can go into just as energetic a building of a new family system. This happens when families find a way to get rid of the fear and clearly see the benefit of doing so. Then, watch out. That's the joy of counseling for everyone.

This chapter is written to *identify and explain* abuse, victimizing, and scapegoating as it relates to suicide. This is *not to say* that scapegoating is present in all families where suicide occurs. Of course, it is not. Disappointment, rejection, loss, sorrow, and pain are a part of everyone's life. As humans, we can only do our best with what we know at the time, and we still make wrong decisions and mistakes. If we're lucky, we learn from those mistakes. However, it is not thoughtless mistakes that mark an action as abusive, but an *attitude*. It is the predictable, relentless, ruthless consistency of rejecting actions, combined with a certain tone of voice and choice of words, followed by excuses and self-righteous justification, and a lack of concern for the victim's pain—often covered up with a pretense of love—that marks verbal, mental, and emotional abuse.

Unfortunately, we all have the capacity to abuse or victimize others. But the vast majority of families in which suicide or scapegoating occurs feels trapped and need help to become untrapped. That's a different situation from one of premeditated, ruthless cruelty or torture, the sort where the perpetrator feels no guilt or pangs of conscience, but actually experiences delight when slyly planning, or carrying out, a trap or trick upon the object of their vindictiveness. Most family and social scapegoating is reactional and not intentional, although it can *appear* to be to the victim. Life wishes as well as death wishes are present in those who are destructive, even though the death wish may be dominant at the time of abuse.

Identifying the abuse, scapegoating, and double-binding is only the first step. The main problem is to modify destructive relationships. This can be done by sorting out individual fears in order to reduce tension, and then to practice alternatives in family behavior and interaction that lead to further healing.

"Often the attitudes of spouse, relative or friend," assert Robert Litman and Norman Farberow in *The Cry for Help*, "may mean the difference between life or death for persons involved in symbiotic relationships." In addition, a conscious or (especially) unconscious attitude of anger or resentment before a suicide can turn into incredible guilt afterward.

Everyone wants to matter—and everyone deserves to. Realizing that, we can always determine to be more sensitive to another's pain. It may not prevent a suicide, but we may have less reason to accuse ourselves.

We can make terrible mistakes but still come out alive and happy. We may hurt someone terribly through those actions, and although we can't change the past, we can have some positive influence and control over the present and future, provided we understand the past. That is the primary key to forgiving and forgetting.

14

❖

Breaking Free

The source of wounds which destroy our wholeness can be uncovered by exploring our family systems.

JOHN BRADSHAW
Psychologist and Author

Many a scapegoat has lived out much of his/her life hanging on the family cross while hearing and believing the words, "You brought it on yourself." Authorities agree that a child's role in the family is established well before the age of three. The scapegoat can be marked while he or she is still an infant. These early messages are very difficult to overcome, especially when that message has been one of "to die" or "not to be."

But restoration and healing of the spirit is possible. If you want down from that cross badly enough, you may have to find your own way. The first step can be a big one; it means making a decision to change your attitude and your actions, but in the process, your strengths come to the surface. There are a number of additional steps to choose from in your progress.

These can be any combination of the following: developing self-insight and awareness, an understanding of family interaction, joining support groups, improving communication skills, seeking family and/or individual therapy, making a spiritual connection for strength and the ability to forgive, or distancing yourself, if necessary. Just as suicide is multifaceted, healing, recovery, restoration, and so on, depend upon many factors. A good beginning is to understand the basic differences between a functional and dysfunctional family system.

According to John Bradshaw, "functional parents with a strong sense of identity will model maturity and autonomy for children, and will not pass along their own unresolved, unconscious conflicts onto them. The children are not constantly judged and measured by their parents frustrated and anxiety-ridden projections."[1]

This *functional* family system, based on equality, independence, self-discipline, loyalty to each other, and individual freedom to self-expression, does not fall together haphazardly or by happenstance. It develops through communication and conscious decisions of its members to be accountable to themselves and to one another. In any family, children learn to listen to others by the way they themselves are listened to. *Dysfunctional* families are created when the children of other dysfunctional families marry and hand down generations of abusive family behavior, thereby creating codependence.

According to Bradshaw, codependence is a common dysfunctional-family illness in which there is a primary stressor, such as Dad's work addiction, Mom's hysteria, Dad or Mom's physical or verbal violence, a family member's real or imagined illness, divorce, alcoholism, or sexual abuse. "Anyone who becomes controlling in the family to the point of being experienced as a threat by others, initiates the dysfunction," says Bradshaw. "Each member of the family adapts to this stressor in an attempt to control it. Each becomes codependent on the stressor."[2]

He adds, "Co-dependence is at the bottom a spiritual disease because (its) ... core belief ... is that my inner state is dependent upon what is outside of me."[3] People who are caught up in this mode of thinking spend a lot of time and energy making controlling demands on the world and the people around them, regardless of where they are. Richman says, "When most suicidal [or dysfunctional] individuals leave home, they do not leave home; they set up the same maladapted relationships on the outside that existed within."[4]

Many individuals from closed dysfunctional family systems also live in a tiny closed world of their own. Since they cannot see beyond this closed world, they have an exaggerated and unrealistic concept of their place within the whole world, believing that others are as involved with their thoughts and actions as they are. They depend on responses from others for their own self-image and identity. Not all of these people quietly withdraw. Some live a noisy show-and-tell lifestyle, always on stage for a wide-eyed audience. They can be quite amusing or entertaining up to a point.

An example of this is Fred, an independent businessman, who keeps his small staff hopping in attendance to his personal needs, wants, and problems. They mow his lawn and clean his house when business is slow, patiently listen to long tales of woe, provide transportation when he wrecks his car, and clean up broken glass following his temper tantrums. They sympathize when he bad-mouths someone who isn't fooled by his performance, and laugh patronizingly when he makes fun of someone he thinks he has fooled. They apologize to insulted clients for his arrogance and make excuses to clients in order to cover up his drinking problem.

The primary stressor in Fred's family was an alcoholic father who tyrannized and embarrassed the family with mental cruelty, emotional neglect, and uncontrollable rages, while throughout, Fred's mother was the long-suffering victim. Fred's older sister was the family scapegoat, and her child is now being trained for the role of the next generation's scapegoat. Jackie, the child, is constantly berated for "not trying," and for "being lazy."

Jackie is kept in line by Fred's younger sister, whose mode of operation is to rescue Jackie by enrolling Jackie in a series of activities, accompanied by loud proclamations that Jackie "won't stay with it." Of course, Jackie doesn't "stay with it" and can then be chastised for not staying rescued and compared with cousins who *are* achievers. When this younger sister is not setting Jackie up to be rescued, there is still Fred's mother, other siblings, coworkers, and acquaintances to be rescued. Younger sister is pretty busy with managing her family rescue service.

Meanwhile, back at the office, Fred has his own little rescue squad of employees in readiness should a crisis arise. Fred's favorite time for a crisis is early in the day, so he can start drinking before noon. In the lull between crises, employees sit around and talk to Fred about how he can improve his attitude.

Fred listens attentively, agrees with their observations, basks in their undivided attention, and drowns in his own self-importance. An ex-wife, sick of the sycophancy, took Fred's children and left years ago, so Fred has created a new family. He is surrounded by hired assistants, who give advice *to* him and protect clients *from* him, and a secretary, who offers her own form of afterhours comfort and gets paid before going home to hubby— even though Fred's business is floundering.

Neither Fred nor his family have considered the enormous amount of time and effort that goes into perpetuation of the victimizing/rescuer dysfunctional process; nor are they aware of the ridiculous nature of Fred's "Ugh-me-God," mentality. Each time Fred blames someone else for a situation he has created, he is actually giving *that* person *his* power. No wonder he drinks and rants and raves. He makes himself helpless.

Father is no longer able to intimidate Fred and take away his power, so Fred gives it away through unaccountability. Fred's emotional makeup is stuck in early childhood, where it was first traumatized. He has also imitated his father's method of control by "throwing his weight around" and "shooting off his mouth."

Fred could direct his abundant energy and creativeness into successful productivity if he were not still controlled by a pathological terror of not receiving enough emotional affirmation. He could direct his fine intelligence into a determined quest for maturity, honesty, accountability, and self-discipline if he were not compulsively obsessed with alternately adoring himself and victimizing himself.

Fred is living a self-destructive lifestyle that could be termed as subintentional suicide, and is characterized by "hang-ups" such as problem drinking, recklessness, affairs with married women, poor judgment in decisions, an obsessive need for constant attention, incredibly grandiose self-absorption, and misrepresenting the truth. Fred's story illustrates the claim made by Richman and Bradshaw that dysfunctional individuals go beyond their family home to recreate the dysfunctional family system.

In a similar manner, many expendable family members do not directly obey the message to die but continue to live in other dysfunctional and self-destructive ways. They may become ill—starting in early childhood—rather than overtly attempt suicide. Some continue to play the game of always trying to fix things and thereby gain love and approval. Some deny that any form of abuse even exists, always understanding, forgiving, or not noticing. Some separate themselves either emotionally or through physical distance, and some disappear completely.

As stated earlier, there are alternatives that offer more than mere coping with, or surviving, a stressful dysfunctional situation.

Individual therapy or counseling is valuable for helping one to locate and face the causes of dysfunction, for developing skills for dealing with oneself and others, and for achieving self-fulfillment.

Support groups of all kinds are available either as a supplement to, or alternative for, therapy. Support groups are like a new family in which you can learn new and different roles, be accepted, and gain new self-respect. Pam Tanous said of her Ray of Hope support group members, "They have bloomed over the months—like a little flower garden."

Al-Anon, Alateen, and ACOA (Adult Children of Alcoholics) are excellent sources of help when the dysfunctional family or suicidal behavior is complicated by alcohol and/or other substance abuse.

Spiritual counseling can deal with healing of memories, with inner growth, with receiving forgiveness from God, forgiving others, and forgiving oneself.

Churches and synagogues also offer support groups, caring relationships through "extended family" programs, and provide a community that offers involvement and commitment to help change interpersonal social relationships.

Family therapy, which provides healing and growth for all, is invaluable. Some therapists will contact family members directly rather than leaving it to the patient. Sometimes, such a call may bring the entire family, or only a few members, but the therapist should not give up contacting all the family possible. Family therapy can provide ways to break through the rigid roles, deception, and games. Some therapists use a variation of the well known AA "twelve-step program" to help families set up a healthy communication system at home. The common goal in family therapy is to confront those terrifying and unspeakable issues of guilt, condemnation, shame and fear, and move into unconditional acceptance of self and others.

"Eventually, it may be necessary to deal with the guilt," asserts Richman. "The goal of the counselor is to help the family recognize and distinguish between irrational guilt, which is punitive, destructive, blaming and preventive of maturity; and rational guilt, which is healing and leads to ultimate forgiveness, self-acceptance and maturity."[5]

Guilt is a primary issue in effective therapy and healing, according to Richman, and is a primary reason why people refuse therapy. Refusal to confront guilt causes great difficulty for family therapy to be effective—or even occur. The family may proclaim the therapist is "against" them and "for" the victim. Out of pathological fear of exposure, relatives who are the most destructive are also the most clever at avoiding the very people who could help. Their actions mark them as the ones in greatest need and the least likely to be helped.[6]

All abusing family members need treatment, claims Bradshaw. "Even if you were not the one being abused in your family, you still carry the covert secrets of the family system,"[7] and while it's always been known that our families influence us, we're now discovering that the influence is beyond what we had imagined.[8] He continues, "If we do not know our familial history, we are likely to repeat it ... The family is the source of the wars within ourselves and to a large degree, the war with others. Wars are evil.... They embody lying and killing. They seem to have a power that transcends individual choice."[9]

James Lynch, author of *The Broken Heart*, approaches the theme of relationships by illustrating how loneliness and isolation can literally break a person's heart. He cites Dr. Harlow's infant monkeys who were isolated with terry-cloth surrogate mothers, and as a result of the "overwhelming physical and emotional destructiveness of this type of early social deprivation," suffered severe depression. Even after being united with other monkeys, they lived out their lives as loners—isolated—unable to function normally.[10] A child's earliest need is for a warm, loving, accepting parent, in order to mirror an image of affirmation and acceptance of one's self. Without that, disassociation can result.

Disassociation is a *disconnection between an event of victimization or trauma, and the response to the event*. That means a traumatic experience can be so unbearable that victims actually leave their bodies. They don't remember what happened—but they retain the feelings of what happened.

In place of denial, one can choose to confront those early terrors at their source in therapy and resolve them. This requires the kind of insight and self-awareness that banishes codependence. Through confrontation and communication, a person can exorcise the family demon of abuse in order to reconnect through love and understanding. This reconnection is necessary for wholeness and healing to be complete. It takes a great deal of courage, but it develops strength. Someone has said that self-purification will always be a person's greatest weapon.

For some people, the answer to self-affirmation and actualization—in addition to, or instead of, education, counseling, therapy, and support groups—is to make a spiritual connection for strength and guidance. This may be especially valuable when the parent has deliberately withdrawn through actual physical absence or was emotionally detached and unconcerned.

When a parent is physically present but deliberately withdraws love, support, and acceptance from a child, something in that child dies. There is no loneliness like the forsaken loneliness of spiritual abandonment—it is a devastating injury to the blood bond. These messages of denial of a child's "right to be," instilled early in life, produce a starvation of the soul which, in turn, plants the seeds of self-destruction.

As a comparison, consider Jesus's cry of "Why have you forsaken me?" After the Spirit of God had withdrawn, Jesus was left unprotected, open to experience the agony and suffering of the world, without contact with His father. In a similar manner, the child who is emotionally abandoned, without the support of his/her parents, may be in a state of desolation and confusion.

There is, however, tremendous hope here for the person who is looking to religious faith as part of his/her deliverance from abuse. This is the message of the cross—that personal suffering has already been experienced for the believer.

Never underestimate forgiveness as a powerful means of release. Some therapists believe that, for some people, to forgive is more than they can handle right away; that the absence of painful feelings must come first, followed by a lack of desire to dwell on the abuse or forgive the abuser. Then, if the person so desires, forgiveness can begin. I feel it's the other way around. Whichever way you favor, I think true resolution can occur only when both parties seek it. If you *say* you want resolution but are avoiding the *action* required, you are fooling yourself.

Sometimes, the only way to escape abuse is to completely sever ties with the family. But be careful. Old patterns of being a victim can persist. One may continue to trust untrustworthy people and end up being victimized again. If you carry those old love–hate feelings with you, they will spill over into your new life and relationships. Anger and hate are not really the opposite of love, because both feelings still keep us involved. The real opposite of love–hate is indifference: not the "I don't care if you live or die" indifference but the kind which shows in actions and attitude that "I am living a fulfilled life without your approval or disapproval, and want the same for you." Examples of ways to show this are through "detached concern" (as taught in Al-Anon) and tough love.

This is the action taken by Wanda, who tried to break her family's chain of verbal abuse and emotional neglect. Her suggestion for family counseling was met by a whirlwind of resistance and excuses. The family refused to participate, but Wanda continued for herself.

"My brother's objection to therapy," Wanda says, "is that since the past is dead, I should be ashamed to bring it up now. I should forget it. I feel like he's choking me when he says that. How can I go on with the future when I haven't resolved the past?"

Wanda's brother may be using this reference to the past in order to avoid facing the results and responsibility for his own past actions, or inactions, and guilt feelings. It's also a way of punishing Wanda for reminding him of her family's neglect, and a way of hushing her up. In effect, he's saying, "Don't bother us with the can of worms we gave you."

There is no way for her to ignore the past. The past—our history—is the sum total of what we are now. If you had no past, you wouldn't be you—you wouldn't be anyone. That's why people are so disoriented when they lose their memory. Every present moment is an encapsulation of your past and your ancestors' past. If one of them had deviated by one notch (claims Marcel Proust in his assertion of the relevance of the past to the present), your present would be different. Someone once said that the past is not only not dead; it is not even past. Confronting these past events realistically helps us to understand and deal with them constructively.

Wanda's family's refusal to discuss the past is a refusal to consider growth and insight for everyone concerned. Refusal to examine the past can cripple a person's confidence, making him or her afraid to reach out. To deny the past is to deny a valid part of our individuality.

Regardless of Wanda's tactics or the results, her intent was to promote both individual and family healing. Just wanting to reconnect (at the risk of further pain) was a tremendous step for her. However, in doing so, she suffered another loss—the family did not share her desire to forgive and grow. I think that all children, young or adult, want to love their parents, but some parents just make it so difficult.

"I realize," she says, "that I can continue to love my family at the same time I hate their behavior. I can separate the two issues now, and that's a big help to me. I was causing myself a great deal of pain by the way I was perceiving things." That's an important insight about perception because we have the power to decide for ourselves just how miserable we want, or don't want, to be.

Therapy is paying off for Wanda. She realizes that scapegoating makes the persecutor come off as strong and the victim as weak, whereas the opposite may be true. She has discovered she has the strength to separate herself from the abuse. Breaking the habit pattern takes time for both victim and the abuser. Just as scapegoating builds up step by step over time, it takes time—step by step—to overcome it. Those who abuse, and who have been abused, have a tremendous amount of pain and shame to be healed, and tremendous freedom to be experienced if they seek that healing. The freedom is worth it.

15

A Unifying Force

Fear knocked at the door. Faith answered. No one was there.

Old Saying

I also believe that an influencing factor in suicide is lack of a solid moral and ethical foundation in today's society and personal lives. Confusion over misplaced values may have instilled a fear of the unknown, which many people do not know how to confront. Admittedly, many people who do not feel the need for such a foundation are not suicidal. However, most of the suicidal persons I have worked with feel this moral lack deeply and miss or crave these enduring values. I see this (at least, in my experience) as another factor which emerges when survivors try to explain the reasons for suicide.

Ralph Kinney Bennett describes this lack of moral and ethical foundation in his review of Allan Bloom's book, *The Closing of the American Mind*. Bennett says, "In years past ... [our heritage was] rooted in three things—the Bible, the family and the ... American political tradition centered on the Declaration of Independence."[1] Bennett quotes Bloom as stating that "the Bible was the common culture, one that united the simple and the sophisticated, rich and poor, young and old."[2]

That common culture and American tradition provided a background of moral and ethical guidelines and standards which most people, for the most part, could trust and respect. That culture of moral and ethical standards also provided a common bond contributing to stability of individual, home, community, and country.

We are losing that. Morally and ethically, anything goes. What can you believe? Who can you trust? What background do we give young people on which to base and develop character, a code of ethics, and faith in humanity?

"The highest percentage of young people who are suicidal feel unconnected in any significant relationships,"[3] says Rich Van Pelt, pastor, author, teacher, and speaker from Denver, Colorado. He says that while we are improving at suicide intervention, "the fundamental problems still exist."[4]

"We want our children to excel but expect them to do so without the necessary groundwork, without laying a secure foundation,"[5] says Lee Radziwill, in an interview for *McCall's* magazine (1988). She was comparing education and discipline between American and European schools, but her statement about the lack of a secure foundation for education and self-discipline may also be true in the spiritual and moral aspect of character development.

In the rush to be free of sexual and moral confines, in the obsession with career, status, appearance, materialism, and instant gratification, we have replaced America's foundation of moral truths and values with a "me" philosophy, which has created a social selfishness, the kind that can ruin individuals and nations.

Despite a rich plethora of knowledge, skills, and opportunity for all, we have adopted a society characterized by noise, deep involvement with "nothing" relationships, obsession with the body beautiful, no-fault adultery, no-fault divorce, no-fault abuse, no-fault violence, no-fault slander, no-fault selfishness, no-fault sin, no-fault sex, no-fault crime, and no-fault choices.

I believe we throw out the baby with the bath water when we throw out the Bible. And with it, we risk throwing out such values as a sense of honor, truth, self-respect, integrity, morality, and the strength of simple spiritual faith.

It's quite true that belief in God and traditional biblical values are accompanied by guidelines for behavior which demand observance of rules. However, those guidelines and restrictions provide security in knowing what is expected of oneself and others, which is the basis for building trust. With traditional church values, we paid respect to God, to others, and to oneself—in that order.

Nowadays, it is *self* first, *others*, only if convenient for our own gain, and God, not at all. We have lost the kind of security that instills trust. Uncertainty about basics—such as trust—can lead to anxiety, despair, and hopelessness. Just as marriage is not stable without commitment, life is not stable without foundation.

"Some historians say one of the major signs that a culture is on the brink of disaster is the disintegration of the family," claims Van Pelt. "The American family is falling apart all around us. It's no surprise young people are feeling insecure. We need a spiritual awakening to move us back to a biblical, theological value base that sees the family as God's design to provide the security young people need to navigate the turbulent waters of adolescence."[6] I think Van Pelt is talking about inner security which stems from good character.

When security depends upon something outside yourself to make you feel good about yourself inside—such as possessions, achievements, status, flattery, ordering others about, or commanding attention—the result is both a lie and an illusion. Some people constantly seek feedback from others and their environment to get a sense of self-worth and identity. When the environment doesn't supply that, these people can fall apart, because they are only a void inside. Others, rather than analyzing themselves in order to develop insight, will opt to alter tactics—such as blaming someone, or something, else. None of these tactics build or replace strength of character, but rather, may project a false impression of self-assurance which is not actually tied to any sense of direction or foundation.

Nor is it enough to give lip service to honesty and integrity when attempting to impress a child or someone else, but then disregard those values when they don't serve some overwhelming, self-directed purpose. One's lack of inner security is pretty obvious at those times.

Inner security comes from within and develops through the recognition and acceptance of one's abilities and limitations. *Inner strength* is based on a solid code of ethics and conscience, from which one is willing to operate without dishonorable compromise. *Inner peace* (for me) stems from communion with, and reverence for, a supreme God. The sum of this security in people is refined and reflected by traits of good manners, integrity, and sincerity, as well as respect, tolerance, and esteem for others. I believe this lack of spiritual foundation and inner strength has generated a fear of life itself, which may contribute to self-destructive behavior.

Fear is, perhaps, the most powerfully energizing force within us when used in a positive way, but when compounded by guilt and shame, it is also a basic motivating factor behind much destructive behavior. Fear causes us to lie, distort or withhold the truth, be aggressive or evasive, to attack or run away. Fear is behind denial, deception, jealousy, greed, condemnation, stealing, murder, rape, and intimidation. Fear of disapproval motivates us to achieve or fail. Fear of something or another makes us angry, anxious, guilty, defensive, shy, secretive, put on an act, cover up, or be the clown. We reject some people through fear and accept others through fear.

We fear the guilt of being found out, the shame of not measuring up. We are afraid of not being accepted, of not being wanted— of not being. We fear being alone or lonely, and we fear pain. Some of us live because we fear dying, and some of us die because we fear living. Fear can be aggressively or passively at work within us, a demon on our back or a whisper in our ear.

How do we conquer destructive fear? Some will say the family must instill inner security from early childhood through affirmation, approval, and parental modeling. Others will say that life experiences will develop inner peace and security. But whether we grow from the family support system or personal experience, or both, we must still have a base of strength to counteract all those fears.

"The answer to individual fear is a living glorified Lord; the answer to any collective fear is a corporate faith in a living God," says a prominent religious leader. While that has meaning for me,

I realize that Judeo-Christian principles are not the answer acknowledged by all. Someone from another background, or another philosophy, may look to a different base on which to build his or her set of principles. But whatever our differences in belief, if we are to confront and conquer the specter of fear that destroys the joy of life—and the will to live—we must have that ethical and morally truthful spiritual center as a unifying force.

IV

Appendixes

Survivor's Bill of Rights

I have the right to be free of guilt.

I have the right not to feel responsible for the suicide death.

I have the right to express my feelings and emotions, even if they do not seem acceptable, as long as they do not interfere with the rights of others.

I have the right to have my questions answered honestly by authorities and family members.

I have the right not to be deceived because others feel they can spare me further grief.

I have the right to maintain a sense of hopefulness.

I have the right to peace and dignity.

I have the right to positive feelings about one I lost through suicide, regardless of events prior to or at the time of the untimely death.

I have the right to retain my individuality and not be judged because of the suicide death.

I have the right to seek counseling and support groups to enable me to explore my feelings honestly to further the acceptance process.

I have the right to reach acceptance.

I have the right to a new beginning. I have the right to be.

In memory of Paul Trider. Also, thank you to Jann Gingold, M.S., Dr. Elisabeth Kübler-Ross, and Rev. Henry Milan.

16

❖

Postvention/Grief
Resource Guide

Booklets and Pamphlets

Adult Children of Alcoholics, P.O. Box 14075, Chicago, IL 60614.

After Suicide: A Unique Grief Process, by Eleanora "Betsy" Ross (her husband's suicide), Ray of Hope, Box 2323, Iowa City, IA 52244.

Bearing the Special Grief of Suicide, by Arnaldo Pangrazzi, One Caring Place, Abbey Press, St. Meinrad, IN 47577.

Child Survivors of Suicide: A Guidebook for Those Who Care for Them, United Mental Health Services of New Jersey, AAS, 4201 Connecticut Avenue, N.W., Washington, D.C. 20008.

Cowbells and Courage, by Patrick W. Page, Centering Corporation, 1531 North Saddle Creek Road, Omaha, NE 68104.

Dancing With the Skeleton, by Kirsten Derrek, Centering Corporation, 1531 North Saddle Creek Road, Omaha, NE 68104.

Feelings After Birth: Postpartum Adjustment (brochure), P.O. Box 1282, Morrisville, PA 19067.

Grief After Suicide, Mental Health Association in Waukesha County, Inc., 2220 Silvernail Road, Pewaukee, WI 53072.

Healing a Father's Grief, by William H. Schatz, Medic Publishing Company, P.O. Box 89, Redmond, WA 98073.

Hurting Yourself, Centering Corporation, 1531 North Saddle Creek Road, Omaha, NE 68104.

Mourning After Suicide, by Lois Bloom (her son's suicide), Pilgrim Press, 132 West 31st Street, New York, NY 10001.

Sad Ain't Forever, by Patrick W. Page, Centering Corporation, 1531 North Saddle Creek Road, Omaha, NE 68104.

Sibling Grief, by Marcia Scheerago, Medic Publishing Company, P.O. Box 89, Redmond, WA 98073.

S.O.S. Coming Together is a Beginning (also many other booklets), Suicide Prevention Center, Main P.O. Box 1393, Dayton, OH 45401.

Suicide of a Child, Centering Corporation, 1531 North Saddle Creek Road, Omaha, NE 68104.

Suicide: A Pastor's Ministry Reference. Contains "Suicide: Hearing the Call for Help" and "Suicide: Someone I Love Has Died," Shepherd Staff Publications, Division of Logor Art Productions, Inc., 6160 Carmen Avenue East, Inver Grove Heights, MN 55015.

Suicide: An Unpardonable Sin? and *When the Seagulls Don't Come*, by Reverend Wasena F. Wright Jr., Annandale United Methodist Church, 6935 Columbia Pike, Annandale, VA 22003.

Suicide: Questions and Answers, by Adina Wrobleski, Afterwords Publishing, Minneapolis, MN 55407.

Suicide: The Danger Signals, by Adina Wrobleski, Afterwords Publishing, Minneapolis, MN 55407.

Suicide: Your Child Has Died, by Adina Wrobleski, Afterwords Publishing, Minneapolis, MN 55407.

This Is Surviving, by Sondra Sexton-Jones (her husband's suicide), Centering Corporation, 1531 North Saddle Creek Road, Omaha, NE 68104.

When Reason Fails, by Bruce Conley, Human Services Press, P.O. Box 243, Springfield, IL 62705.

Why Women Kill Themselves, Suicide Prevention Group, PA, Millburn, NJ.

Books

About Mourning: Support and Guidance for the Bereaved, by Savine G. Weizman and Phyllis Kamm, Human Sciences Press. New York.

Adult Children of Abusive Parents, by Stephen Farmer. Lowell House: Los Angeles, CA.

Adolescent Suicide: Assessment and Intervention, by Alan Berman. American Psychological Association; Washington D.C.

Adults Who Lost Their Parents by Suicide Before Their Time, by Mary Stemming and Maureen Stemming. Temple University Press: Philadelphia.

After a Suicide: Young People Speak Up, by Susan Kuklin. Putnam: New York.

After Suicide, by John H. Hewett. Westminster Press: Philadelphia.

After Suicide: A Ray of Hope, by Eleanora "Betsy" Ross. Lynn Publications: Iowa City, IA.

After the Death of a Child, by Ann Finkbenner. Free Press: New York.

Aftershock, by Andrew Slaby. Random House: New York.

Alcoholics Anonymous Big Book (basic text; the story of Bill T. and other members), 3rd edition, 1976, World Services: New York.

And Then There Was One: Our Journey from Death to Rebirth, by Margo Williams. Pooka Publishing: Sacramento, CA.

The Algebra of Suicide, by Irving Berent. Human Sciences Press, New York.

The Bell Jar, by Sylvia Plath. Harper & Row: New York.

Between Survival and Suicide, edited by Benjamin Wolman. Gardner Press: Lake Worth, Fl..

Beyond Codependency: And Getting Better All the Time, by Melody Beattie. Harper & Row: New York.

The Broken Heart: The Medical Consequences of Loneliness, by James J. Lynch. Basic Books: New York.

Breaking the Silence, by Mariette Hartley (her father's suicide). Putnam: New York.

Breaking the Silence: A Guide to Help Children with Complicated Grief, by Linda Goodman. Taylor and Francis: London, England.

By Her Own Hand: Memories of a Suicide's Daughter, by Signe Hammer (her mother's suicide). Soho Press: New York.

Caring Enough to Confront, by David Augsburger. Herald Press: Scottdale, PA.

Caring Enough to Forgive, by David Augsburger. Herald Press: Scottdale, PA.

Clergy Response to Suicidal Persons and Their Family Members, edited by D. C. Clark. Exploration Press: Chicago.

Children Who Don't Want to Live: Understanding and Treating the Suicidal Child, by Israel Orback. Jossey-Bass Publishers: San Francisco.

Clergy Response to Suicidal Persons and Their Family Members, edited by D. C. Clark. Exploration Press: New York.

Clues to Suicide, by Edwin S. Shneidman and Norman L. Farberow. McGraw-Hill: New York.

Coping—A Survival Manual for Women Alone, by Martha Yates. Prentice-Hall: Englewood Cliffs, NJ.

Coping with Separation and Loss as a Young Adult, by Louis E. LeGrand. Charles C Thomas: Springfield, IL.

The Courage to Be, by Paul Tillich. Yale University Press: New Haven, CT.

The Courage to Live, by Ari Kiev. Thomas Crowell: New York.

Crisis Intervention and Suicide Prevention: Working with Children and Adolescents, by Gary A. and Letha I. Crow. Charles C Thomas: Springfield, IL.

The Cry for Help, by Norman Farberow and Edwin Shneidman, McGraw-Hill: New York.

Dead Reckoning, by David Treadway, HarperCollins: Scranton, PA.

Dead Serious (a book for teenagers about suicide), by J. M. Leder. Avon: New York.

Dear Momma, Please Don't Die, by Marilee Horton. Thomas Nelson: Nashville, TN.

Don't Take My Grief Away from Me, by Douglas Manning. Harper-Collins: San Francisco, CA.

The Encyclopedia of Suicide: The First Comprehensive A to Z Reference of Suicidology, by Glen Evans and Norman Farberow. Facts on File, Inc.: New York.

The Enigma of Suicide, by George Howe Colt. Summit Books: Arlington, TX.

The Family Circle Guide to Self-Help, by Glen Evans. Ballantine Books, Random House: New York.

Family Therapy for Suicidal People, by Joseph Richman. Springer: New York.

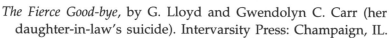

The Fierce Good-bye, by G. Lloyd and Gwendolyn C. Carr (her daughter-in-law's suicide). Intervarsity Press: Champaign, IL.

Final Celebrations: A Guide for Personal and Family Funeral Planning, by Kathleen Flagg. Pathfinder Publications: Ventura, CA.

The Gift of Hope, by Robert Veninga. Little, Brown: Boston.

The Gift Of Inner Healing, by Ruth Carter Stapleton. Word Books: Waco, TX.

Grief as a Family Process, by Ester Shapiro. Guilford: New York.

Grief Counseling and Grief Therapy: A Handbook for the Mental Health Practitioner, by F. William Worden. Springer: New York.

Grief Magnified: Voicing the Pain of a Suicide, by Gail Kittleson. G & R Publishing: Waverly, IA.

Grief Counseling and Sudden Death, by Polly Doyle. Charles C Thomas: Springfield, IL.

A Grief Observed, by C. S. Lewis. Seabury Press: New York.

Griefquest: Reflections for Men Coping with Loss, by Robert Miller, Abbey Press: Saint Meinrad, IN.

Grief Relief, by Victor M. Parachin. CPB Press: St. Louis, MO.

Healing After the Suicide of a Loved One, by Ann Smolin and John Guinan. Simon & Schuster: New York.

Healing a Father's Grief, by W. Schatz. Medic Publishing: Redmond, WA.

Healing for Damaged Emotions, by David A. Seamands. Victor Books: Wheaton, IL.

Healing of Memories, by David A. Seamands. Victor Books: Wheaton, IL.

Helping a Child Understand Death, by Linda Jane Vogel. Fortress Press: Philadelphia.

Helping People Through Grief, by Delores Kuenning. Bethany House: Minneapolis, MN.

High Risk: Children Without a Conscience, by Ken Magid and Carole McKelvey. Bantam: New York.

How It Feels When a Parent Dies, by Jill Krementz. Alfred A. Knopf: New York.

How to Survive the Loss of a Parent, by Lois F. Akner and Catherine Whitney, William Morrow: New York.

The Inability to Mourn, by Alexander and Margarete Mitscherlich. Grove Press: New York.

Jewish Reflections on Death, edited by Jack Reimer. Schocken Books: New York.

The Jewish Way in Death and Mourning, by Maurice Lamm. Jonathan David: New York.

A Labor of Love: How to Write a Eulogy, by Garey Schaffer. GMS Publishing: San Diego, CA.

Leaning Into the Wind: Journal of a Woman Whose Husband Committed Suicide, by Betty Bryant. Fortress Press: Philadelphia.

Learning to Say Good-bye: When a Parent Dies, by Eda Leshan. Macmillan: New York.

Left Alive: After a Suicide Death in the Family, by Linda Rosenfeld and Marilynne Prupas. Charles C Thomas: Springfield, IL.

Life after Grief, by Jack Clark (his wife's suicide). Personal Pathways Press: Marietta, GA.

Life after Suicide, by Terence Barrett. Aftermath Research: Fargo, ND.

Loneliness: The World's Number One Killer, by Ralph Wilkerson. Melodyland Publishers: Anaheim, CA.

I Wish I Were a Lovely Meadow: When a Parent Commits Suicide. Dougy Center, Portland, OR. (a compilation of children's own writing about a suicided parent—ages 9–15).

The Many Faces of Grief, by Edgar N. Jackson. Abingdon Press: Nashville, TN.

The Many Faces of Suicide, by Norman Farberow. McGraw-Hill: New York.

May I Hate God?, by Pierre Wolff. Paulist Press: Wilmington, DE.

Men and Grief, by Carol Stauslaker. New Harbinger: Oakland, CA.

Mental Health Through Will-Training, by Abraham A. Low (founder of Recovery, Inc.). Willett: Glencoe, IL.

A Message of Hope, by Pat Harness-Overly (her son's suicide), Centering Corporation, 1531 North Saddle Creek Road, Omaha, NE 68104.

Moral Justification of Suicide, by Jerry Jacobs. Charles C Thomas: Springfield, IL.

The Mourning After, by Stanley P. Cornlis. R & E Publishing: San Jose, CA.

My Son, My Son, by Iris Bolton (her son's suicide). Bolton Press: Atlanta, GA.

No One Saw My Pain: Why Teens Kill Themselves, by Andrew Slaby and Lili Frank Garfinkle. W. W. Norton: New York.

No Time to Say Good-bye, by Carla Fine (her husband's suicide). Doubleday: New York.

On Becoming a Counselor, by Eugene Kennedy. Seabury: New York.

On Death and Dying, by Elisabeth Kübler-Ross, Macmillan: New York.

On Suicide: Greater Writers on the Ultimate Question, edited by John Miller. Chronicle Books: San Francisco.

Out of the Nightmare: Recovery From Depression and Suicidal Pain, by David Conroy. New Liberty Press: New York.

A Personal Guide to Living with Loss, by Elaine Vail. John Wiley: New York.

The Power to Prevent Suicide, by Nelson and Galas. Free Spirit Publications, Minneapolis, MN.

Preventing Elderly Suicide, by Joseph Richman. Springer: New York.

Sad But OK: My Daddy Died Today, by B. Juneau. Blue Dolphin Press: Nevada City, CA.

The Savage God: A Study of Suicide, by A. Alvarez. Bantam: New York.

Self-Help Organizations and Professional Practice, by Thomas J. Powell. NASW Publications & Sales: Silver Spring, MD.

Sermons on Suicide, edited by James T. Clemens. Westminister/John Knox Press: Louisville, KY.

Shade of the Raintree: The Life and Death of Ross Rockridge, Jr., by Larry Lockridge (his father's suicide). Viking Press: New York.

She Never Said Goodbye (his wife's suicide), by Robert Dykstra. Harold Shaw: Wheaton, IL.

Silent Grief: Living in the Wake of Suicide, by Christopher Lukas and Henry M. Seiden. Scribner: New York.

So Long at the Fair (for adolescents and teens), by Hadley Irwin. Margaret K. McElderry Books: New York.

A Special Scar: Experiences of People Bereaved by Suicide, by Alison Weitkheimer. Routledge: London, England.

Stronger Than Death: When Suicide Touches Your Life, by Sue Chance (her son's suicide). W. W. Norton: New York.

Suicide, by Norman Linzer. Human Sciences Press: New York.

Suicide After Sixty: The Final Alternative, by Marv Miller. Springer: New York.

Suicide: A Killer is Stalking the Land, by David Wilkerson. Fleming H. Revell: Old Tappan, NJ.

Suicide: A Study in Suicidology, by Emile Durkheim. Free Press: Glencoe, AL.

Suicide Clusters, by Loren Coleman. Faber & Faber: Winchester, MA.

Suicide and Grief, by Howard Stone. Fortress Press: Philadelphia.

Suicide: Guidance for Grades 1-8, by Anita Russell and Karen Rayter. Peguis: Winnipeg, AL, Canada.

Suicide and Its Aftermath, by Edward Dunne, John McIntosh, and Karen Dunne-Maxin. Norton: New York.

Suicide in Later Life, edited by N. Osgood. Lexington Books, New York.

Suicide in America, edited by Herbert Hendon. Norton: New York.

Suicide in Canada, edited by Anton Leenaars. University of Toronto Press: Toronto, Canada.

Suicide: Opposing Viewpoints (college and high school supplementary text), edited by Chris Hancock. Greenhaven Press: San Diego, CA.

Suicide Over the Life Cycle. American Psychiatric Association Press: Washington DC.

Suicide: Prevention, Intervention, and Postvention, by Earl A. Grollman. Beacon Press: Boston.

Suicide: Survivors, by Adina Wrobleski. Afterwords Publishing: Minneapolis, MN.

Suicide Survivors Handbook, by Trudy Carlson. Centering Corporation, 1531 North Saddle Creek Road, Omaha, NE 68104.

The Suicide Syndrome: Origins, Manifestations and Alleviation of Human Self-Destructiveness, by Larry Morton Gernsbacher. Human Sciences Press: New York.

Suicide: The Philosophical Issues, edited by M. Pabst Batin and David Mayo. St. Martin's Press: New York.

Suicide: Why?, by Adina Wrobleski. Afterwords Publishing: Minneapolis, MN.

Suicidology: Essays in Honor of Edwin Shneidman, edited by A. Leenaars. Jason Aronson: Dunmore, PA.

Sun Shower, by Karen Kenyon (her husband's suicide). Richard Marek: New York.

Surviving Your Crises: Reviving Your Dreams, by Donald E. Watson. Mills & Sanderson: Bedford, MA.

Survivors: After a Suicide What Can We Do?, by Bill Steel and Mary Leonhardi. Ann Arbor Publishers: Naples, FL.

Survivors of Suicide, by Albert C. Cain. Charles C Thomas: Springfield, IL.

Survivors of Suicide, by Rita Robinson. Newcastle: Hollywood, CA.

Talking to Children about Death, by Earl Grollman. Beacon Press: Boston.

Telling Yourself the Truth, by William Backus and Marie Chapian. Bethany House: Minneapolis, MN.

Too Young to Die: Youth and Suicide, by Francine Klogsburn, Pocket Books, New York.

Unconditional Love and Forgiveness, by Edith Stauffer. Triangle Press: Ojai, CA.

Understanding Suicide, by William R. Coleman. David C. Cook: Elgin, IL.

Unlocking the Secrets of Your Childhood Memories, by Dr. Kevin Leman and Randy Carlson. Thomas Nelson: Nashville, TN.

What Shall We Tell the Kids?, by Bennett Olshaker. Dell: New York.

What You Should Know about Suicide, by Bill Blackburn. Word Inc.: Waco, TX.

When You're Angry with God, by Pat McCloskey. Paulist Press: Mahay, NY.

The Widower, by Jane Burgers and Willard Kohn. Beacon Press: Boston.

The Widow's Guide to Life, by Ida Fisher and Bryon Lane. Prentice-Hall: Englewood Cliffs, NJ.

When Bad Things Happen to Good People, by Harold Kushner. Schochen Books, New York.

When Someone Asks for Help: A Practical Guide for Counseling, by Everett Worthington Jr. Intervarsity Press: Downers Grove, IL.

Who Needs God?, by Harold Kushner. Pocket Books; New York.

Why Knock Rock?, by Dan and Steve Peters, with Cher Merrill. Bethany House: Minneapolis, MN.
Why Suicide?, by Eric Marcus. HarperCollins: San Francisco, CA.
Why We Hurt and Who Can Heal, by John C. Cooper. Word Inc.: Waco, TX.
Words I Never Thought to Speak: Stories in the Wake of Suicide, by Victoria Alexander. Lexington Press: Lexington, MA.
You and Your Grief, by Edgar N. Jackson. Hawthorn Books: New York.

Catalogs and Distributors

The Bureau for Drug Abuse, Violence and Recovery, P.O. Box 9, Calhoun, KY   (800) 962-6662
Centering Corporation, 1532 North Saddle Creek Road, Omaha, NE 68104   (402) 553-1200
Compassion Books, Rainbow Connection 477 Hannah Branch Road, Burnsville, NE 28714   (704) 675-9670
Center for Books on Aging, Seref Press, 1331 H. Street NW, Washington DC 20005   (202) 737-4650
Childswork/Childsplay (for teachers and therapists) P.O. Box 61586, King of Prussia, PA 19406   (800) 962-1141
Hazelden Publishers and Education (alcoholism, addiction, self-help, spiritual, and recovery), P.O. Box 176, Center City, MN 15012 (800) 328-9000
Human Sciences Press, Inc., 72 Fifth Ave., New York, NY 10011   (212) 243-6000
Human Services Press, P.O. Box 2423, Springfield, IL 62705   (217) 787-7227
Learning Publications, Inc., P.O. Box 1338, Holmes Beach, FL 34218   (800) 222-1525
Learning Resource Center, National Funeral Directors Association, 11121 West Oklahoma Avenue, Milwaukee, WI 53227   (800) 228-6332
Media Publishing Company, P.O. Box 89, Redmond, WA 98073   (206) 881-2883

Norton Professional Books, c/o National Book Company, Keystone Industrial Park, Scranton, PA 18512 (800) 233-4830

Resources—Grief/Suicide, John Miller. Office of Evangelization-Catechesis, 777 Valley Road, Clifton, NY 07013 (201) 777-8818

Springer Publishing Company, 536 Broadway, New York, NY 10012 (212) 431-4370

SIEC: Suicide Information and Education Centre, Suite 201, 723 Fourteenth Street, N.W., Calgary, Alberta, Canada T2N 2A4 (403) 283-3031

Wellness Reproductions, Inc., 23945 Mercantile Road, Suite K6, Beachwood, OH 44122 (800) 283-3031

Directories

American Self-Help Clearing House, St. Clares-Riverside Medical Center, 25 Pocono Road, Denville, NJ 07834 (201) 625-7101

Suicide Prevention and Survivors of Suicide Resources, American Association of Suicidology, Suite 310, 4201 Connecticut Ave. NW, Washington DC 20008 (202) 237-2280

Bereavement and Hospice Support Netline, URL: http://www.ubolt. edu/www/bereavement. Sponsors: Hospice Foundation and University of Baltimore, Baltimore, MD (410) 837-5310

Death and Dying from A to Z, Croner Publications, 211-05 Jamaica Avenue, Queens Village, NY 11428 (718) 464-0866

Directory of National Self-Help/Mutual Aid Resources, AHA Services, Inc., P.O. Box 99376, Chicago, IL 60693 1-800-AHA-2626

Directory of Survivor of Suicide Support Groups: United States and Canada, American Association of Suicidology, 4201 Connecticut Avenue N.W., Suite 310, Washington, DC, 20008 (202) 237-2280

Encyclopedia of Associations, Gale Research, 835 Penobscot Building, Detroit, MI 482126 (313) 961-2242

National Directory of Bereavement Support Groups and Services, ADM Publishing, P.O. Box 751155, Forest Hills, NY 11375 (718) 657-1277

National Directory of Children's Grief Services, Dougy Center for Grieving Children, P.O. Box 86852, Portland, OR 97268 (503) 775-5683

National Mental Health Consumers' Self-Help Clearing House, 1211 Chestnut Street, Suite 1000, Philadelphia, PA 10907 (800) 533-4539

Responding to Grief: A Complete Resource Guide, by Rev. Richard Gilbert, The Spirit of Health, 114 Washington Avenue, Point Richmond, CA 94801 (888) 224-7685

Survivors of Suicide Bibliography. John McIntosh, 2707 Huntington Place, Mishawaka, IN 46544

Journals, Magazines, and Manuals

Adolescence and Depression, Dorothy Kinsey, National Institute for Mental Health, 5600 Fishers Lane, Rockville, MN 20857 (301) 468-2600

Bereavement, Bereavement Publishing, Inc., Andrea Gambill, 8133 Telegraph Drive, Colorado Springs, CO 80920 (719) 282-1948

Bereavement Support Groups: Leadership Manual, Alice S. Demi, Grief Education Institute, P.O. Box 623, Englewood, CO 80151 (303) 177-9234

Children and Suicide: Training Manual, Suicide Prevention Center, Inc., P.O. Box 1393, Dayton, OH 45406 (513) 223-9096

Crisis: The Journal of Crisis Intervention and Suicide Prevention, Holgrete and Huber Publishing, 1725 W. Harrison St., Chicago, IL 60612. (312)942-2177

Grief Counseling for Survivors of Suicide and Sudden Death Victims: A Training Manual of Concepts and Materials, Polly Doyle, Charles C Thomas Publications, 301-327 East Lawrence Avenue, Springfield, IL 62708 (217) 789-8980

The Living Alternative Handbook: A Model for Guiding Adolescents in Coping with Depression and Suicide, Polly Joan, Suicide Prevention and Crisis Service of Tompkins County, P.O. Box 313, Ithaca, NY 14850 (607) 272-1616

Omega: Journal of Death and Dying, Department of Communications at Arizona State University, Tempe, AZ 85287 (800) 638-7819

Suicide and Life-Threatening Behavior, Human Sciences Press, New York.

Thanatos, Florida Funeral Directors Services, P.O. Box 6009, Tallahassee, FL 32314   (904) 224-1969

Newsletters

Caring Concepts: A Coffee-Break Newsletter for Caring Persons, Centering Corporation, 1531 North Saddle Creek Road, Omaha, NE 68104   (402) 553-1200

Compassionate Friends, Inc., P.O. Box 3696, Oak Brook, IL 60522 (708) 990-0010

The Forum Newsletter, Association for Death Education and Counseling (ADEC), 638 Prospect Avenue, Hartford, CT 06105   (203) 232-4825

Friends for Survival, Inc., P.O. Box 214463, Sacramento, CA 95821 (916) 392-0664

An Outreach Program for Survivors of Suicide Loss. Crisis: The Journal of Suicide Prevention, edited by David Clark and Ad Kerkhof. Hogrefe & Huber

Helping Hands: Self-Help Network of Kansas, Wichita State University, 1845 Fairmount, Wichita, KS 67260   (800) 445-0116

Lifesavers, American Suicide Foundation, 1045 Park Avenue, New York, NY 10028   (212) 410-1111

Newslink, American Association of Suicidology, 4201 Connecticut Avenue N.W., Suite 310, Washington, DC, 20008   (202) 237-2280

Obelisk, Loving Outreach to Survivors of Suicide Loss, Catholic Charities, 126 North Des Plaines, Chicago, IL 60661   (312) 655-7283

Sharing & Healing, %Al and Linda Vigil, 11335-162 Affinity Court, San Diego, CA 92131   (619) 271-6889

SIEC Current Awareness Bulletin, #201, 1615 Tenth Avenue, S.W., Calgary, AB, Canada, T3C 0J7   (403) 245-3900

Surviving Suicide, American Association of Suicidology, 4201 Connecticut Avenue N.W., Suite 310, Washington, DC 20008   (202) 237-2280

Voices, Newsletter of SA\VE, P.O. Box 24507, Minneapolis, MN 55424 (612) 946-7998
Wings, Roots and Wings, Ltd., P.O. Box 1051, Wausau, WI 54401 (715) 845-3424

Organizations

Al-Anon Family Groups Headquarters, Inc. (includes Alateen), P.O. Box 862, Middletown Station, New York, NY 10018 (800) 356-9996

Alcoholics Anonymous (AA), World Services, Inc., 475 Riverside Drive, 11th Floor, New York, NY 10115 (212) 870-3400

American Association of Retired Persons, Widowed Persons' Service (WPS), 601 E Street N.W., Washington, DC 20049 (202) 356-5219

American Association of Suicidology (AAS), 4201 Connecticut Avenue N.W., Suite 310, Washington, DC 20008 (202) 237-2280

Association for Death Education and Counseling (ADEC), 638 Prospect Avenue, Hartford, CT 06105 (203) 586-7503

American Suicide Foundation, 1405 Park Avenue, New York, NY 10028 (212) 410-1111

Center for Inner Growth and Wholeness, JoAnn Mecca, P.O. Box 9185, Wethersfield, CT 06109 (203) 563-3035

Concerns of Police Survivors, Inc. (COPS), P.O. Box 3199, Camdenton, MO 65020 (573) 346-4911

Compassionate Friends (chapters), P.O. Box 1347, Oak Brook, IL 60521 (312) 323-5010

The Dougy Center (ages 3-19), 3909 S.E. 52nd, Portland, OR 97286

Friends for Survival, Inc., P.O. Box 214463, Sacramento, CA 95821 (916) 392-0664

Grief Education Institute, P.O. Box 623, Englewood, CO 80151 (303) 777-9234

Heartbeat (chapters), 2015 Devon Street, Colorado Springs, CO 80909 (719) 596-2575

International Association for Suicide Prevention (IASP), 1725 W. Harrison Street, Chicago, IL 60612 (312) 942-7208

Link Counseling Center, 348 Mt. Vernon Highway, N.E., Atlanta, GA 30328 (404) 256-9797

National Hospice Association (NHA), 1901 North Moore Street, Arlington, VA 22209 (703) 243-5900

National Institute of Mental Health (statistical information), 5600 Fishers Lane, Rockville, MD 20857 (301) 443-4513

Ray of Hope, inc., (chapters), P.O. Box 2323, Iowa City, IA 52244 (319) 337-9890

Safe Place, The Samaritans (chapters), P.O. Box 1259, Madison Square Station, New York, NY 10159 (212) 673-3000

Seasons: Suicide Bereavement (chapters), 6805 Fairfax Road, Apt. 123, Bethesda, MD 20814 (301) 951-3665

Suicide Awareness\Voices of Education (SA\VE), P.O. Box 24507, Minneapolis, MN 55424 (612) 946-7998

The Suicide Education Institute of Boston, 437 Newtonville Avenue, Newton, ME 02160 (617) 332-5165

Suicide Prevention Center, Inc., P.O. Box 1393, Dayton, OH 45401 (513) 297-9096

Suicide Prevention Advocacy Network (SPAN), 5034 Odins Way, Marietta, GA 30068 (770) 998-88199

The Word Pastoral Care Center, 114 Washington Avenue, Point Richmond, CA 94801 (510) 236-2075

Theos Foundation, Inc. (chapters), 306 Penn Hills Mall, Pittsburgh, PA 15235 (412) 243-4299

Youth Suicide National Center, 1825 Eye Street N.W., Suite 400, Washington DC 20006 (202) 429-2016

Videos, Films, Workbooks, Camps, Other

AIMS Multimedia (many videos regarding substance abuse), 9710 De Soto Avenue, Chatsworth, CA 91311 (800) 367-2467

Amanda the Panda (summer camp for children 6–16), 1000 73rd Street, Suite 12, Des Moines, IA 50311 (515) 223-4847

Cherished Memories Memory Album, the Grieving Well Center, Inc., P.O. Box 622256 (407) 895-9285

Children Only Die When We Forget Them, Pat Schwiebert, Compassionate Friends, P.O. Box 12553, Portland, OR 97212 (503) 284-7426

Helping Children Heal from Loss: A Keepsake Book of Special Memories, by Laurie Van-Si and Lynn Powers. Portland State University, Continuing Education Press, P.O. Box 1394, Portland, OR.

Journey of Hope (video helping children to cope with death), John Morgan, King's College, 255 Epworth Avenue, London, ON, Canada, N6A 2M3 (519) 432-7946

On the Edge (a film about teenage suicide), Young Alberta Filmmakers, Suite 1602, 8830 85th Street Edmonton, Alberta, Canada T6C 3C3 (403) 469-0922

S.O.S.—Runaways and Teen Suicides: Coded Cries for Help, University of Southern Maine, 96 Falmouth Street, Portland, ME 04105 (207) 780-4141

Survivors, (video) Bill Steel and Mary Leonhardi, Ann Arbor Publishers, P.O. Box 7249, Naples, FL 33941

Survivorship After Suicide (video), Ray of Hope, inc., P.O. Box 2323, Iowa City, IA 52244 (319) 337-9890

Teenage Suicide: An Approach to Prevention (video), LexCon Productions, 2720 Sunset Boulevard, West Columbia, SC 29169 (803) 791-2094

Support Group Guidelines, AAS Suite 310, 4201 Connecticut Avenue SW, Washington, DC 20008 (202) 237-2280

The Ultimate Rejection (video), James Craig. Wright State University, Dayton, OH Suicide Prevention Center, Inc., P.O. Box 1393, Dayton, OH 45406 (513) 223-9096

Willowgreen Productions (numerous videos on grief, loss, and healing), P.O. Box 25180, Ft. Wayne, IN 46825 (219) 424-7916

Notes

Chapter 3. After-Suicide Grief

1. *Diagnostic and Statistical Manual of Mental Disorders*, Third Edition, 1980, pp. 236–238.
2. Albert C. Cain, "Survivors of Suicide: Current Findings and Future Directions," in *Proceedings: Sixth International Conference for Suicide Prevention*, Robert E. Litman, Ed., Ann Arbor, MI: Edwards Brothers, 1972, pp. 194–196.
3. Ann Kaiser Stearns, *Living through Personal Crisis*. Chicago, IL: Thomas Moore Press, 1984, p. 82.
4. Cain, p. 195.
5. Ibid, pp. 195–196.
6. Ibid, p. 195.
7. Ibid., p. 194.
8. David Crenshaw, "Reluctant Grievers: Children of Multiple Loss and Trauma," *The Forum*, July/August 1992, p. 6.
9. Edwin Shneidman, "Foreword" from *Survivors of Suicide*, edited by Albert C. Cain. Springfield, IL: Charles C Thomas, 1976, p. x.

Chapter 8. About the Children

1. Edwin Shneidman, "Foreword," in *Survivors of Suicide*, edited by Albert C. Cain. Springfield, IL: Charles C Thomas, 1972, p. ix.
2. Albert C. Cain and Irene Fast, "Children's Disturbed Reactions to Parent Suicide," in *Survivors of Suicide*, edited by Albert C. Cain. Springfield, IL: Charles C Thomas, 1972, pp. 93–120.
3. John H. Hewett, *After Suicide*. Philadelphia: Westminster Press, 1980, p. 68.

4. Glen Davidson, *Death: What Do You Say to a Child?*, Springfield, IL: OGR Service Corporation, 1979, pp. 10–11.
5. Ibid.
6. Hewett, p. 69.

Chapter 9.   About God

1. *NIV Study Bible*, Judges 16:30, I Samuel 31:4, II Samuel 17:23, I Kings 16:18, Matthew 27:5.
2. Walther Zimmerli, *Old Testament Theology in Outline*, Atlanta, GA: John Knox Press, 1979, p. 134.

Chapter 10.   In the Aftermath

1. Bruce H. Conley, Lfd., "The Funeral as 'First Aid' for the Suicide Survivor," p. 1.
2. William T. Anderson, quote from letter of October 1987.
3. *Coroner's Handbook on the Function and Operations of the Office of the Coroner*. Springfield, IL: Illinois Department of Public Health, 1980.
4. Ibid.

Chapter 12.   Reflections about Suicide

1. A. Alvarez, *The Savage God: A Study of Suicide*. New York: Bantam, 1971, pp. 91–92.
2. William Styron, *Darkness Visible*. New York: Random House, 1990, p. 62.
3. Ibid., p. 79.
4. Ibid., p. 77.
5. Alvarez, p. 74.
6. Ibid., p. 127.
7. Ibid., p. 52.
8. Joseph Richman, *Family Therapy for Suicidal People*. New York: Springer, 1984, p. 189.

Chapter 13.   Deadly Messages

1. Joseph Sabbath, "The Suicidal Adolescent: The Expendable Child," *Journal of American Academy of Child Psychiatry*, 8(2) 1969, p. 273.

2. Joseph Sabbath, "The Role of Parents in Adolescent Suicidal Behavior," *Paedopsychiatrica*, 38, 7, p. 211.
3. Joseph Richman, *Family Therapy for Suicidal People*. New York: Springer, 1984, p. 167.
4. Ibid.
5. Ibid.
6. Ibid., p. 168.
7. Ibid.
8. Ibid.
9. Ibid., pp. 164–166.
10. John Bradshaw, *Bradshaw On: The Family*. Deerfield Beach, FL: Health Communications, Inc., 1988, p. 70.
11. Ibid., p. 72.
12. Richman, pp. 145–146.
13. Ibid., p. 167.
14. Ibid., p. 130.
15. Ibid., pp. 131–133.
16. Ibid., p. 189.

Chapter 14. Breaking Free

1. John Bradshaw, *Bradshaw On: The Family*. Deerfield Beach, FL: Health Communications, 1988, p. 48.
2. Ibid., p. 164.
3. Ibid., p. 233.
4. Joseph Richman, *Family Therapy for Suicidal People*. New York: Springer, 1984, p. 135.
5. Ibid., p. 172.
6. Ibid., p. 129.
7. Bradshaw, p. 127.
8. Ibid., p. 1.
9. Ibid., p. x.
10. James J. Lynch, *The Broken Heart*. New York: Basic Books, 1977, pp. 178–179.

Chapter 15. A Unifying Force

1. Ralph Kinney Bennett, *An Editorial Review of* The Closing of the American Mind *by Alan Bloom*, New York: Simon & Schuster; and *Reader's Digest*, October 1987, p. 83.
2. Ibid., p. 83.

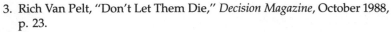

3. Rich Van Pelt, "Don't Let Them Die," *Decision Magazine*, October 1988, p. 23.
4. Ibid., p. 23.
5. Lee Radziwill, "What We Can Learn From European Women," *McCall's Magazine*, October 1988, p. 180.
6. Van Pelt, p. 23.

References

Aquinas, Thomas. *Summa Theologica*. Westminster, MD: Christian Classics, 1991.

Alvarez, A. *The Savage God: A Study of Suicide*. New York: Bantam, 1971.

Archibald, LaRita. "Toward Healing After My Son's Suicide," *Friends for Survival Newsletter* (1997), 15(5):6–7.

Augenbaum, Bernice, & Charles Neuringer. "Helping Survivors with the Impact of Suicide." In *Survivors of Suicide*, by Albert Cain. Springfield, IL: Charles C. Thomas, 1972.

Augustine, *The City of God*. New York: Viking Press, 1984.

Augsburger, David. *Caring Enough to Forgive*. Scottdale, PA: Herald Press, 1981.

Backus, William and Marie Chapian. *Telling Yourself the Truth*. Minneapolis, MN: Bethany House, 1985.

Barker, Kenneth (Gen. Ed.). *New International Version Study Bible*. Grand Rapids, MI: Zondervan Bible Publishers, 1985.

Batchelor, Julie. *Superstitious? Here's Why!* New York: Scholastic Books, 1969.

Beattie, Melody. *Beyond Codependency*. New York: Harper & Row, 1989.

Berne, Eric. *Games People Play*. New York: Random House, 1964.

Bradshaw, John. *Bradshaw On: The Family*. Deerfield Beach, FL: Health Communications, Inc., 1988.

Buechner, Frederick. *Telling Secrets*. San Francisco, CA: HarperCollins, 1992.

Cain, Albert C. "Survivors of Suicide: Current Findings and Future Directions," from *Proceedings: Sixth International Conference for Suicide Prevention*, Robert E. Litman (Ed.). Ann Arbor, MI: Edwards Brothers, 1972.

Cain, Albert C. *Survivors of Suicide*. Springfield, IL: Charles C Thomas, 1972.

Conley, Bruce, Lfd. "The Funeral As 'First Aid' for the Suicide Survivor," presented at the 15th Annual Meeting of the American Association of Suicidology, New York, 1982.

Coroner's Handbook on the Function and Operations of the Office of the Coroner. Springfield, IL: Illinois Department of Public Health, 1980.

Crenshaw, David. *Bereavement: Counseling the Grieving Throughout the Life Cycle.* New York: Continuum, 1991.

Davidson, Glen. *Death: What Do You Say to a Child?* Springfield, IL: OGR Service Corporation, 1979.

Diagnostic and Statistical Manual of Mental Disorders, Third Edition. Washington, D.C.: American Psychiatric Association. Division of Public Affairs, 1980.

Doyle, Polly. *Grief Counseling and Sudden Death.* Springfield, IL: Charles C Thomas, 1980.

Durkheim, Emile. *Suicide*, trans J. A. Spaulding and G. Simpson. New York: Free Press, 1951.

Dustow, Sue. "Suicide Causes Grief Chain Reaction." *Canadian Funeral News*, Calgary, Alberta, Canada, March 1988.

Farberow, Norman, and Edward Shneidman, *The Cry for Help.* New York: McGraw-Hill, 1965.

Farmer, Steven. *Adult Children of Abusive Parents.* Los Angeles, CA: Lowell House, 1989.

Gazda, George M. *Group Counseling: A Developmental Approach.* Boston, MA: Allyn & Bacon, 1975.

Grollman, Earl. *Suicide: Prevention, Intervention and Postvention.* Boston: Beacon Press, 1972.

Hewett, John H. *After Suicide.* Philadelphia: Westminster Press, 1980.

Hill, Douglas. *Magic and Superstition.* London: Hamlyn Publishing Group, 1968.

Hill, M. N. Suicidal Behavior in Adolescents and Its Relationship to the Lack of Parental Empathy. *Dissertation Abstracts International, 36*, p. 472.

Jacobs, J., and Teicher, J. D. "Broken Homes and Social Isolation in Attempted Suicides of Adolescents." *International Journal of Social Psychiatry, 13*:138–149.

Johnson, Wanda. *The Care of the Suicide Survivor: A Model for Funeral Home Personnel.* Dayton, OH: Suicide Prevention Center, 1982.

Kiev, Ari. *The Courage to Live.* New York: Thomas Y. Crowell, 1979.

Klagsbrun, Francine. *Too Young to Die.* Boston: Houghton Mifflin, 1976.

Krementz, Jill. *How It Feels When a Parent Dies.* New York: Knopf, 1981.

Lewis, C. S. *A Grief Observed.* New York: Avon Books, 1957.

Lukas, Christopher and Henry M. Seiden. *Silent Grief: Living in the Wake of Suicide.* New York: Scribner, 1987.

Lynch, James J. *The Broken Heart.* New York: Basic Books, 1977.

Magid, Ken and Carole A. McKelvey. *High Risk: Children Without a Conscience.* New York: Bantam, 1987.

Maris, Ronald. Why 30,000 Americans Will Commit Suicide This Year. *U. S. News and World Report*, 1984, pp. 48–49.

Marsh, Thomas. *The Coroner: A Working Relationship with EMTs. Emergency Newsletter*, 1982.

Marshall, Catherine. *To Live Again*. New York: Avon Books, 1957.

Mastroianni, Michael. When a Student Cries for Help. *Teachers in Focus*, November 1995, pp. 5–8.

Mirnith, Frank, and Paul Meier. *Happiness Is a Choice*. Adas, MI: Baker Book House, 1978.

Peck, M. Scott, *People of the Lie*. New York: Simon & Schuster, 1983.

Plath, Sylvia. *The Bell Jar*. New York: Harper & Row, 1971.

Pope John Paul II. *Catechism of the Catholic Church*. Rome: Vatican Press, 1996.

Proust, Marcel. *Remembrance of Things Past*. New York: Random House, 1934.

Ray of Hope Files and Support Group Meetings. Iowa City, IA: Ray of Hope, inc., 1978–1989.

Richman, Joseph. *Family Therapy for Suicidal People*. New York: Springer, 1984.

Richman, Joseph, and M. A. Rosenbaum, "A Clinical Study of the Role of Hostility and Death Wishes by the Family and Society in Suicide Attempts." *Israeli Annals of Psychiatry and Related Disciplines*, 1970, pp. 128–131.

Richman, Joseph. "Symbiosis, Empathy, Suicidal Behavior, and the Family." *Suicide and Life-Threatening Behavior*, 1978, Vol. 8, pp. 139–149.

Sabbath, Joseph."The Suicidal Adolescent: The Expendable Child." *Journal of American Academy of Child Psychiatry*, 1969.

Saint Augustine. *The City of God*. London: Oxford University Press, 1963.

Schuyler, Dean. "Counseling Suicide Survivors: Issues and Answers." *Omega*, 4(4):313–321, 1973.

Suicide and Life-Threatening Behavior (1981), 2:349–359.

Schmitt, Abraham. *The Art of Listening with Love*. Nashville, TN: Abingdon, 1982.

Seamands, David A. *Healing of Memories*. Wheaton, IL: Victor Books, 1985.

Shneidman, Edwin S. "Postvention: The Care of the Bereaved." *Suicide and Life-Threatening Behavior* (1981), 2(4):349—359.

Shneidman, Edwin, and Norman Farberow. *Clues to Suicide*. New York: McGraw-Hill, 1957.

Soloman, Mark. "The Bereaved and the Stigma of Suicide." *Omega*, 13(4), 1982.

Stapleton, Ruth C. *The Gift of Inner Healing*. Waco, TX: Word Inc., 1976.

Stephens, Boyd G. *Forensic Medicine and the First Responder*. Van Nuys, CA: Emergency Medical Services, 1987.

Styron, William. *Darkness Visible*. New York: Random House, 1990.

Survivorship after Suicide (video), Iowa City, IA: Ray of Hope, inc., 1983.

Tillich, Paul. *The Courage to Be*. New Haven, CT: Yale University Press, 1952.

U.S. Department of Health and Human Services. *Alcohol, Drug Abuse and Mental Health Newsletter*. Washington, D.C.: Government Printing Office, 1984.

Vail, Elaine. *A Personal Guide to Living with Loss*. New York: Wiley, 1982.

Van Pelt, Rich. "Don't Let Them Die." *Decision*, October 1988.

Vining, Ed. "The Funeral Director as a Caregiver," *Forum Newsletter*, 7(7), 1984.

Vogel, E. F., and N. W. Bell. "The Emotionally Disturbed Child as the Family Scapegoat." In *A Modern Introduction to the Family* (pp. 412–414). New York: Free Press, 1960.

Worden, W. J. *Grief Counseling and Grief Therapy*. New York: Springer 1982.

Wright, Traci. Options for Youth Survivors After Suicide, *Surviving Suicide* (newsletter), *8*(3):1–4.

Wrobleski, Adina. "The Suicide Survivor's Grief Group." *Afterwords* (newsletter), Spring, 1982.

Zimmerli, Walther. *Old Testament Theology in Outline*, Atlanta, GA: John Knox Press, 1979.

About Ray of Hope

Ray of Hope, inc., a national self-help organization, whose ministry provides service, education, and consultation in the areas of suicide postvention, loss, and grief, was founded in 1977 by Eleanora "Betsy" Ross after the suicide of her husband. Ray of Hope holds workshops for survivors and interested groups, helps establish Ray of Hope chapters and/or independent support groups, and offers private counseling.

Support group meetings are open to survivors (family, friends, or helpers) who are grieving over a loss by suicide. Meetings are held in a relaxed, accepting atmosphere and provide people the opportunity to share with others who have had similar experiences.

Emphasis is placed on anonymity and privacy. Professionals from education, medicine, counseling, and so on may be invited as speakers or discussion leaders. We do not provide medical or psychiatric treatment, or material assistance. We are not a therapy group for suicidal persons. We are not a religious organization, nor are we allied with any sect or denomination. However, members may share their religious and spiritual views.

Individual counseling and support group organization consultation by telephone is provided by prearrangement and prepayment. Phone (319) 337-9890.

Mission Statement

1. To view suicide as a social, health, and spiritual problem which can be treated.
2. To provide comfort, education, and support for bereaved individuals, their families, and friends.
3. To bring together the bereaved with other survivors and helpers, so that through sharing of experiences and growth, they may gain insights into behavior patterns and relationships.

We believe that sharing what we have learned with someone else in need completes our own healing. By turning the grief process into a growth experience, we can find meaning in a senseless tragedy and hope for our future.

Funding

Ray of Hope, inc. is a not-for-profit 501(c)(3) organization. Our volunteers receive no salary or financial compensation. We respond through phone counseling, packets of printed information, and personal contact with everyone who calls or writes us. Tax-deductible contributions are gratefully appreciated and used to cover publications, distribution, and all other program costs. Please remember the Ray of Hope ministry by honoring your loved one with funeral memorials, love gifts on anniversaries and special times, and in your will. Thank you so much for sharing in this caring outreach to suicide survivors.

Send donations to Ray of Hope, inc., P.O. Box 2323, Iowa City, IA 52244.

Ray of Hope Chapters

Iowa City, IA	(319) 337-9890	Nova Scotia, Canada	(902) 597-3611
Bloomsbury, NJ	(908) 479-4070	Parsons, KS	(316) 421-3254
Brooklyn, NY	(718) 738-9271	Rockford, IL	(815) 962-0782
Lincoln, NE	(402) 476-9668	Rock Island, IL	(319) 337-9890
Norfolk, NE	(402) 379-2460	Centralia, IL	(618) 532-5512

In∂ex